# No Compelling Reason

WILLIAM BOUDREAU

Brule Publishing
Minneapolis, MN

ALSO BY WILLIAM BOUDREAU

*A Green Fisherman Never Caught A Brown Trout*

*Recipes for Clean Water,*
*A Homeowner's Stormwater Survival Guide*

*Stained Glass Houses (play)*

*No Compelling Reason*



Printed by Book Printing Revolution
Minneapolis, MN, USA
www.bookprintingrevolution.com

ISBN: 978-0-9631176-2-5

nocompellingreason@gmail.com

*Cover Design: Jeff Walkup*

# 1

# *Great Expectations*

From his tiny office on the second floor, Dr. Harold Nicholson captained Mattapan Hospital for Chronic Diseases as it plunged through the billows of the nearby North Atlantic. As the ranking officer aboard the smallish vessel, Nicholson was responsible for much more than the 'cargo' of subjects and crew of researchers. His was the broader stewardship of Medicine, Science and yes, Harvard itself.

Yet the facilities he sought so valiantly to maintain faced the irresistible assault of a vast cold and somber sea, a living entity of complete malediction to the human species. Whatever he might do to preserve this frigate of ennobling research, a 3,000-mile fetch of implacable hostility menaced his efforts.

Nicholson reasoned that the founders of the community (and its large hospital and sanitarium) must have arrived on a sunny day, and having been blinded by a stab of white light, mistook our local star for an equally rare appearance of the deity. Having the 'ok' from the terrible one Himself, they colonized what is essentially a low rock pile jutting pugnaciously into an immense violent weather system. In building on the site, with its exposed shallow bay, they tied their fate to the frigid, miles-deep god, Atlantic, who lured the locals to their doom with a delicious bounty of foods while he hid, pouncing and killing thousands in icy embrace.

When he wasn't swallowing them whole into an endless gut

crawling with the nightliest of creatures, he gnawed on them brazenly as they dashed their way through the vapor-filled streets. And when they finally escaped to the safety of their homes, he stalked them with an arsenal of tools, tinkering to destroy the last thin wafer of refuge the 'Townies' shared.

His great claws stripped windows of glazing, crumbling the sashes into gray ash. A whisper from his hoary lips and joints corroded, terminals turned blue, connections rotted, grilles wilted and antennae no longer responded. Periodically, as if testing, he cast his hand over the land and aluminum siding vanished, concrete evaporated and wood snapped as if it were string.

When, as a motivational device, the Hospital invested in custom canvas window awnings with a traditional Scottish pattern, the colors faded within days. In a month they had stretched to nearly twice their original size, and tears began to appear. After 10 weeks, Nicholson declared the effort a $15,000 loss, and had the tattered canvas taken down. But the lengthy aluminum tubes that supported the canvas had fused to the building, adding a derelict, skeletal quality to the Hospital's appearance.

Still, the institution clung to life, buoyed by a bargain struck on the promise of a final surrender of human agony. Alone, at the apex of our communal fear, stands the great event of Death, the measure of all else. Except for the Flight of Capital, Pain poses the only other serious test to human vanity. Chronic, throbbing pain reduces life to an unhappy, teeth-grinding tour of mortality. War against this enemy of the people has universal approval.

Ever since one Scribonius Largus, a Roman physician, applied the *torpedo ray*, a fish that stuns its prey with pulses from its muscle contractions, to the foreheads of his patients, discovering that electrical current could relieve headaches, a breakthrough against Pain has become a quest for the proper voltage.

In the 1800's Western science 'discovered' a potent plant—the opium poppy—an alkaloid of grayish green leaves and 4,000 years of use as an Oriental painkiller. Called 'opioids,' these related ***narcotics*** (inducing sleep or drowsiness) represented a humane escalation in the campaign against suffering. Of Opium, Morphine (from *Morpheus,* god of dreams), Heroin, Laudanum (opium mixed with alcohol), and Codeine, *Morphine* is the preferred drug for relief from severe pain.

Narcotics are unique in that while they are technically "depressants" impacting the central nervous system, i.e., the brain, their chief effect is on the limbic system and the thalamus—those areas involved in pain. Unfortunately, morphine and heroin in particular are highly addictive, both physiologically and psychologically. They so successfully mimic the body's own painkillers (endorphins), morphine introduced to treat post-operative pain, results in the body producing less natural endorphins, until a dependency to morphine occurs.

During the years when World War I armies were operating at peak efficiency, Mattapan creeped with multiple amputees, their cries for dear friends—their own missing arms and legs—a challenge to Progress. Stiff morphine doses might hasten the cure; unlimited availability would, perhaps, moderate the endless shrieks of nerves cut from familiar pathways.

And then there were those who only thought they died on the battlefield: the victims of 'combat fatigue' or 'shell shock.' These "hysterical neuroses" reveal no entry wound except in the mind of the afflicted where they dash up and down the control board: *Phobia,* Anxiety, **Fear**—PANIC! Their pain is certainly real to them; they deserve a cure for their suffering.

During the War To End All Wars and its aftermath, morphine-based analgesics pushed to the front where the enemy swarmed: amputation, menstrual cramps, teething, diarrhea, consumption (tuberculosis), sleep disturbances, etc. Until outlawed in 1942, America was a candy store of narcotics with medical use the commonest route to addiction. Unless treated, narcotic addiction may result in death by overdose or a marginalized street existence.

Alas, when withdrawn, the sweet, golden warmth of morphine inspired passionate, hallucinogenic longing. The instant feel good high of morphine, and its manipulation of the body's own pain suppressors, created a new class of drug side effects: addiction.

Today, it is removed before the onset of cravings. And when it is the patient marks the exact moment when this endorphin engine disappears from the brain by waving a large red flag. (Doctors and nurses caught stealing morphine from hospital pharmacies have no idea that the drug logs they kept as medical practitioners, could reveal them as medical addicts.)

As a response to the increasing evidence against promiscuous morphine use, two other pain reducing techniques, Electro-Convulsive Therapy (ECT) 1933, and Psychosurgery, (1938) were introduced. Both involved radical intrusion into patient futures by either inducing brain seizures in order to release opiate-like endorphins, or by surgically attacking the prefrontal cortex, or thinking part, of the brain itself.

ECT patients were administered repeated *grand mal* seizures by a machine perfected in a hog slaughtering house. Skin peeled and burned, bones snapped and years of personal archives disappeared in a bright blue arc. Soon, a litany of catastrophic side effects attached itself to ECT: nerve cell degeneration, acute memory deficit and pronounced confusion.

Psychosurgery meanwhile, carved up 100,000 brains in 20 years until a grim post-operative picture began to emerge. Lobotomized patients demonstrated unnatural quiescence, an indifference to their surroundings and an unwillingness to leave established routines. It was observed that lobotomized patients appeared to be 'vegetables,' not a 'whole person.' In response to this tragedy, most psychologists are skeptical of treatment options which require the destruction of brain tissue, preferring behavioral or pharmaceutical intervention.

While morphine remains the standard of surgical pain management, synthetic morphine derivatives (Librium, 1960; Valium, 1963) are our leading antidepressants—a batch of new drugs to tame symptoms of mental illness. Antidepressant, antianxiety, antipsychotic drugs have been labeled ***psychotropic*** (***psycho***—mind; ***tropic***—having an altering effect), because they impact one's psychological makeup.

Antipsychotic compounds: Chlorpromazine (Thorazine); Haloperidol (Haldon); Thioridazine (Mellaril); etc. are used to treat severe mental disorder marked by pronounced deterioration of both thinking processes and social functioning, with extreme delusions and hallucinations.

Antianxiety compounds: Chlordiazepoxide (Librium); Diazepam (Valium); Meprobamate (Miltown); are used in non-psychotic cases of moderate 'tenseness' and anxiety. These 'minor tranquilizers' are used daily by 20% of US adult population to reduce stress and aid sleep. Specialized receptors in the central nervous system for benzodiazepines (Valium, Librium), relieve anxiety by inhibiting brain activity.

Antidepressant compounds (1950's): Amitriptyline (Elavil); Imipramine (Presamine); Phenelzine (Nardil); are used primarily with severe depression. When enduring negative moods are debilitating, or turn suicidal, the therapist must intervene. The pattern of neural excitement produced by antidepressant drugs elevates mood and increases psycho-motor performance.

Antimania compounds: Lithium (lithium carbonate) aka Lithane, known to alleviate symptoms in 'manic' episodes of bipolar disorder. Unfortunately, side effects may include tremors, swelling, and reduced sexual motivation /performance.

These natural and synthetic compounds comprise the most frequently prescribed treatment drugs in medicine. But their effects on the brain, the euphoria, the numbness, the 'buzz,' have caused them to be included on another list of frequently-ingested drugs: ***psychoactive*** drugs.

Psychoactive drugs have been used for many centuries by most cultures both in a medical and a spiritual context. Psychoactive drugs produce a change in normal consciousness, particularly in regard to perception and mood. Some psychoactive drugs are legal and socially accepted: caffeine (coffee plant), nicotine (tobacco plant), and alcohol (grain). A large portion of *recreational* drug use, however, is deemed illegal.

In addition to *narcotics,* and *'depressants'* i.e., (antianxiety compounds), psychoactive drugs include *stimulants* and *hallucinogens.*

Stimulants press the central nervous system to release neurotransmitters which produce a focused, on-edge, ready-to-go hyperalertness. The two principal stimulants are cocaine and amphetamine. The stimulant high can be psychologically addictive: a feeling of well-being, reduced sensitivity to pain, and a sense of increased power. But there is no evidence of a physical addiction.

Amphetamines such as Dexedrine, Benzedrine, etc., are synthetic, derived from a shopping list of dangerous substances from ether to battery acid. Amphetamine, or 'speed,' is used by truckers to stay awake, and dieters to suppress appetite. It's been known to quell depression in clinical doses. However, prolonged use, or a 'trip' lasting several days, ends in a 'crash,' of sleep, depression and scattered thinking, or amphetamine psychosis. Chronic abuse leads to physical degeneration, brain damage and possible death due to cardiovascular failure.

Cocaine use may result in mood swings and damage to the nasal mucus linings since the drug is often inhaled. The high is shorter than with amphetamine, and generally considered less draining, though cocaine abuse offers the same threat of physical collapse as amphetamine.

'Crack,' a purified version of cocaine, and 'freebasing,' a procedure that mixes ether with cocaine to hurry the drug to the brain to increase the power and intensity of the rush, are even more likely to lead to addiction and physical and mental problems.

Hallucinogens, the last major category of psychoactive drugs, severely distort the perception of reality with vivid, 'psychedelic' hallucinations. Hallucinogens are truly mind-altering as they dilute the neurotransmitter, serotonin, which normalizes our sensory information. LSD (lysergic acid diethylamide), peyote (peyote cactus), PCP or Phencyclidine (veterinary anesthetic, or 'angel dust'), and, to a lesser extent, marijuana (cannabis sativa plant), are the most notable hallucinogens to date.

These drugs produce euphoria, though not in all cases, and not at all times during the experience. Generally, the 'trip' distorts time, explodes into vivid hues, shifts shapes, 'sees' sound, hears colors—and that's just the first 10 minutes. As a group, the hallucinogens are the least likely of psychoactive drugs to demonstrate physical or psychological addiction, with the exception of a 'high' risk of psychological addiction for PCP.

LSD found widespread, though mostly experimental use, from the 1940s to the 1960s. LSD, or 'acid,' is a powerful, unpredictable drug and should command respect. For several hours, the LSD trip takes place in a phenomenally different world from that we all know and complain about. Unlike a motion picture, you cannot get up and leave a trip when the action gets heavy. What you are seeing is taking place right at home, because you've chosen to go trippin' in a foreign country some say is spiritual, all would admit is unparalleled. Beware those plastic-looking people.

Peyote (mescaline) is taken from peyote cactus in the southwestern United States and northern Mexico. The drug is used as a spiritual guide to the inner self by numerous native tribes. While certainly hallucinogenic, it is said to be less intense and more predictable than LSD.

PCP appeared in the 1950s as a surgical anesthesia, but disorientation and hallucinogenic side effects ended a promising medical career, although still used for horses. PCP trippers may experience panic or a feeling of unlimited power which makes them dismissive of others. Long-term use damages the brain, causing depression, memory loss, and (rarely) death.

Marijuana (hemp) is by far the most popular hallucinogen. Pot, grass, weed—marijuana comes from the plant *Cannabis sativa,* a native of Asia. The psychoactive ingredient is THC, or tetrahydrocannabinol. Effects of the drug, and reaction to it, depend on its THC content. Marijuana produces altered states but they are not nearly as intense as other hallucinogens. Typically, visual hallucinations are not present. The marijuana high includes feelings of calmness, increased sensory awareness, changes in space and time, and the munchies—increased appetite especially for sweets. First-time use, or unusually high doses of THC, may result in temporary thought disturbances and/or rapid emotional changes, including paranoia and panic.

Marijuana is one of the most researched drugs in the history of pharmacology. Still, federal law enforcement classifies marijuana as a 'narcotic,' though to the scientific community, marijuana is not a narcotic, but an hallucinogen. It was made an illicit drug in the U.S. in 1937.

There have been three major medical reviews of *cannabis sativa* since 1885. Nicholson's would be the first to use civilian subjects, coached by a team of individual luminaries within the bosom of the country's premier academic and research institution. Nicholson paused to explore the possibilities:

The current study would be the most comprehensive ever with a range of research covering motivational, physiological, psychological, medical, social and emotional data. The 'Nicholson Project,' he joked, would set the standard for human pharmacological study. The Journals would be after him for profiles; numerous businesses too, would press him to advance their cause. Undoubtedly, Harvard would come forward with an even more prestigious post—a Presidential audience in the White House for presentation of the Report was not out of the question. Europe will take notice; he could well be knighted for his contributions to…

"D-d-r-r-r-i-n-n-g, d-d-d-r-r-i-n-n-g!" Wha! Who knows I'm here? Nobody has this number? "Oh, hello Karen. Un-huh, un-huh well, if you have to, but don't you think you oughta get a second opinion before you shell out fifteen hundred bucks on a new clutch? (Another clutch: Why d'ya need five-on-the-floor in the city? For the dunes. The dunes? You've been to the dunes once in 20 years.) Ok, ok, but if you want me to pay for it, you'll have to wait for the 15th. Because. Look, I can't talk now. Ok, later. Yeah, me too. Bye."

For many researchers, federal laws make it nearly impossible to design experiments, involving illegal drugs, which don't drown in red tape. Fortunately, old school ties opened a channel to the Department of Health, Education and Welfare, which grew a quality marijuana product for testing.

The biggest worry facing Nicholson—5′ 11″, thin, wiry, with fashionable daubs of silver at his temples—was that infernal human penchant for exaggeration, concealment, fictionalizing and just plain fraud. Many components of the new data scheme were self-reporting, the kind of subjective questions, "How are you feeling?" that a few bad apples could skew the results just to serve the cause of mischief. A half-dozen times he must have reminded staff not to befriend the subject humans. Such liaisons were unprofessional and could damage the study. 'They are not to be trusted. I say this not to condemn them, but to prepare you.' Pure and simple: humans made poor research subjects.

No, not because they constituted independent, unpredictable free spirits. On the contrary, people as subjects tend to be meek, followers rather than leaders, and predictable in behavior. That was the problem: in an institutional setting, human subjects regress, becoming lazy and conspiratorial, rather than energetic and democratic. Real guinea pigs will fight to the death over food and sex; put humans together and they'll find a way to cheat the government.

And these subjects were repeated drug users! The profile was frayed: chronic tobacco, marijuana and alcohol use; minimal respect for authority; high degree of alienation. They had their own agenda all right. Yet this particular group possessed above average intelligence, ambition and empathy. Still, experience demonstrates that primate subjects will inveigle to break experimental protocols. The rich tapestry of emotions and participant demographics required the utmost caution to insure results were honest and objective. If there was to be any movement at all in society's approach to marijuana, it had to come from this particular experiment, this year, with this group of subjects and from these results.

For Congress to make changes in the existing drug laws and criminal codes, it required a clear, unequivocal mandate from society as a whole, and that would only come about if legislators could point to a clear, unequivocal message from scientific research. And that depended on methodological certainty. And staff discipline. And a hundred other delicate levers that rested in his hands.

It would be up to him, Dr. Harold Chatham Nicholson, to manage this beast, to perform the alchemy which separates the dross of incompetence from the gold of academic legend. Make no mistake; this was to be a wondrous, dangerous undertaking.

Somehow, he must extract the absolute truth, the exact impact of a drug that alters perception even as it is being perceived. A chemical that beguiles the brain, whispering 'Stop! Enough with the normal routine already. Let's get wild!' A substance strong enough to squeeze the mind into passages blocked millions of years ago by an anonymous building superintendent.

And doing this in what is basically a criminal setting, with severe restrictions on personal freedom, and a population of bright young lawbreakers. Stretching their tolerance with an elaborate testing schedule they will grow to hate; in a time of national turmoil and doubt, with the future of the human race hanging in the balance.

# 2

# *Day One*

It was 10:30 a.m. in the cafeteria of Mattapan Hospital for Chronic Diseases, July 8, 1972. The subjects had begun trickling in after 9 only to find themselves waylaid by a phalanx of paperwork in the form of histories, disclaimers, releases, and explanations. By 10:30 they'd been identified, weighed, measured and released back to the corral.

That allowed John Wayne Hammer, aka 'The Hammer,' to scope out the ceiling tiles with the special optics of G Force, his one-man army, unlocking its distant corners with a hidden switch. Somewhere under that glob of paint, huh?, lay evidence of surveillance by TD, Top Dog, the super-secret spy agency that collected comprehensive data on Unsuspecting Citizens. There had to be something, maybe only a simple listening device, but it just made sense strategically, to do information gathering on your opponent.

Now, if it was a microphone, it would get the best pick up if it were planted right... right... here. Shit, he'd parked exactly in the middle of the table, directly below TD's surveillance mic! 'Far frick'n out,' he thought, lifting himself from the bench and anchoring his arms to the sides of the table. Drawing back his leg, he delivered a series of short, furious kicks to the table's middle supports that would give them something to think about.

"Hey!"

Wayne looked up from his exertions; the others seated at

the table regarded him warily. "Couldn't help but notice you kicking the crap out of the table," said Jake Early, sweeping a strand of sandy-colored hair from his eye.

"Oh, sorry," Wayne jockeyed, "foot fell asleep."

"Ya sure?" Jake shot back, "I woulda thought it was dead." Jake's long hair straddled his head like a tent, curtaining his face in such a way as to highlight his even, white teeth. "Now, where was I?" asked Jake.

"I believe you were telling us what you would do for the little folk once you took power..." answered Galen Bergman, probing a cold cluster of styrofoam eggs with his fork. He surreptitiously pealed away his ridiculous name tag while squinting through wire-rimmed glasses at flakes of dead skin on his shirt. Goddamn seborrhea.

"Right, smart ass!" cackled Early through soft, red lips.

"In fact," broke in Ira Stern, bristly brown filaments sprouting from the openings in his clothing, "you were clueing us in on the profits to be made in bootleg marijuana." Ira's broad forehead and restless deep set eyes fused into an intense, guileless stare so uncomfortable Jake was forced to move only to find Ira staring at the spot he'd left.

"Yeah, right, if you're deal'n," said Jake unsteadily.

"Jake!" shouted a tall youth also framed in lengthy, oily hair, as he too, fell victim to the gray enamel walls.

"Sutter! You sonofabitch!" exclaimed Jake, looking up.

The new arrival embraced Jake. "I can't believe it. I thought you were gone back to Santa Fe?!"

"No way you gonna keep Jake the Snake outta no *mary-ee-wha-na* experiment. No way! Light up the kif, torch the leaf; simmer the tea, smoke the doobie; bong the bhang; don't let the weed go to seed, mah'n; Serb the herb!" he shouted gaily.

'Oh great,' sighed Bergman, feeling a stab of opposition. With narrow sleeping cells and low ceilings, home for the next 30 days came complete with a coupla hippies joined at the lip. "Do you two know each other?" he asked.

"Naw," Jake scoffed, "we just met at the interview is all."

"Yeah," Bergman responded, "well, didn't they tell you at the interview that there'd be no pot for five days?"

"Whaa—what? No reefer?! Wha' the 'ell you talkn' about?" protested Sutter.

"Five full days, SOL man," Bergman replied. "It's a shame. No pot; what are we to do?"

Galen wasn't happy to discover the two hippies, Jake Early and Sutter McClellan, were pals. He hated hippies.

Meanwhile, the Wayne guy was under the table crawling along ant-like on his hands and knees in search of something.

"Are you ok, man? 'Cause you look kinda wasted—" answered Jake. He turned to Sutter and whispered, "The dude's a downer, man, a dry drunk. They shoulda screened out juicers and only played with heads."

"Yeah, right," laughed McClellan. "Fuck'n juicers, head-cases, man."

"Oh, man, I need some dope!" Jake insisted.

"No smoke," broke in Ira "need to establish baseline data..."

"Hunh?" Jake grunted. "Who are you?"

"Ira Stern—'Shep.'"

"Well, Ira—" Jake intoned, "what about this Vaseline crap?"

"Baseline," Ira corrected.

"They want to test you sober," Bergman interrupted, "since it's apt to be brief."

Jake sniffed. "I was asking the dude over here and you hafta jump in like this fart that won't go away."

Bergman pictured the ad: Wanted: male subjects for 30-day paid marijuana study. All replies confidential. "I knew a guy who had that, smelled a fart all the time, turns out a piece of shit was lodged in his nose, hard to say how it got there..."

Shep put his head back and brayed.

"Well," broke in Wayne, "they're gettn' their money's worth with you, that's for sure. A cupla elephants. You know," he continued quietly, motioning Bergman and Early closer, "they're listening to everything we say..." he pointed upward, "everything."

Bergman blinked. "Do you think they'll hear me," he asked, his voice rising, "if I threaten to kill every paranoid fanatic I can find!"

"Hey, jus' try'n to help you out," Wayne explained, his eyes searching for that new piece of equipment employed by the enemy. "You pop off like that, you'll attract attention. That would be bad for The Cause."

At that moment another man hulked into the room pulling at a frayed terrycloth robe. "Yeah man, it's cool," he boomed in the voice of an ancient forest. "We're gonna have a coupla days off here, and then we goin' enjoy Mr. Muggles, some fi-i-ne Mississippi-grown reefer."

"And who the hell are you?" quizzed Jake.

"Thaddeus Montgomery Ward, 'Sweet as cream on blueberry pie; but fuck with me an' you gonna die!'" He produced a calling card. "See?" he said, pointing to the etched declaration "Actor" under his photo, "that indy-kates I um a spe-chul person." Thaddeus paused to let it sink in.

"How come they can just lock up the weed and we can't do anything about it?" a lithe, wiry French-Italian named Tony

Duquesne yelled. "I mean, it's a plant, right? How dare they declare it illegal! It doesn't make any sense. It's un-nat-ural." He wore a suit, an older model, with wide leather lapels, a silver marijuana leaf pin on one; the other bearing a simple button, "DYLAN."

"Right on! Instead of illegal, it should be mandatory to grow pot," Bergman laughed.

"Three years for possessing less than an ounce, hard time for non-tokers!" hollered Jimbo Reese, across whose wide white T-shirt was written: **'If You Can Read This, You're Smarter Than The Clay Creek Board of Supervisors.'** Under marbled eyes, large forearms, mighty hams gaped from the straps of his overalls.

"Jail for *failure* to do weed," laughed Chris Conner, "I like that." Chris's intricate whorl of white hair glowed against skin the color of chewed gum.

"Make pot the new money," suggested Ron Green, his collegiate shirt and slacks accenting a solid build. "Say, 20 Homegrown for a dozen eggs."

"A dozen *organic* eggs," put in Bergman.

"With two roaches change," added Jake.

"I believe hemp, raised for rope, was once this nation's number one cash crop," Shep sniffed. "Of course, there aren't many clipper ships these days..."

"You could grow your own bank, man!" riffed Ron Green.

"I'm afraid talk of a First National Bank of Weedola isn't going to endear you to the powers that be," cautioned Bergman.

Of course, Top Dog would hardly let you grow money, thought Wayne.

"Why don't they just get outuv the way, let us decide what is good for us?" fumed Sutter.

"You? What's good for you?" Thaddeus squeezed the tattered fringes of his robe in massive fingers, "hippies march'n up the street been awfully lucky nobody drive 'n down in a big ol' tank."

"We ain't ask'n for a fight," said Jake, "all we want is to be able to smoke a joint in peace without gett'n hassled."

"Well, you ain't smok'n nothin' but the pole for the resta the week, right Berge?" Bergman nodded.

"How in the hell do you know so much?" quizzed Ron.

"I taken the opportunity to arrive last night," replied Thad, bowing slightly, "along with Berge here. We been debriefed."

"Yeah," challenged Sutter, "by whom?"

"By them."

"Who's 'them'?"

"Those guys over there," said Thaddeus, pointing to the cohort of scrubbed professionals milling about the entrance to the cafeteria, "they're the guys in the little white coats," he laughed.

"Gentlemen! May I have your attention, please?" Dr. Nicholson cleared his throat. "The experiment is about to begin." Nicholson studied his notes for this first, crucial orientation. In hours the clinical lab would be pouring in raw data. Searching his sharply-angled penmanship for the key word or phrase that could make or break the experiment, he was keenly aware 'Primate Interaction' studies were a notorious career graveyard.

"Your consideration, please!" he said with a firm smile. "I know what you want gentleman, you want to start earning your —your mary-jew-wanna..."

"Yeah, alright!" hollered Sutter.

"Whoa...what's this stuff about 'earn'n' man?" said Jake coolly.

Dr. Nicholson's nose itched; a clear fluid dripped onto his

lip. "Well, gentleman," he ventured, "we can't give you mary—"

"Why not?" shouted Jake.

"Yeah, why not?" nodded Sutter. "You get it free don'chu?"

Nicholson pondered: "Hhmmm...no, no, gentleman, you must earn it."

"Oh yeah," said Thaddeus. "You some kind a *dealer,*" he put the word on the floor along with the dirt, "make us pay for wha' you get'n free?"

"This experiment is not being undertaken for your benefit alone," replied Nicholson. "It just so happens that a critical component—" It was time to reveal the centerpiece of this enterprise: the Intrapersonal Motivational Profile… "of your attendance here has to do with how much, how m-u-c-h ah, *labor* you'd be willing to supply for, ah, really, good, ah, mary...mary... Oh, here's Mr. Wick now, he can supply you with more details. I just want to remind you please, enjoy your, ah, stay..." Nicholson retreated hastily, stung by the swagger, the *familiarity.*

"I'm Jonathan Wick, Lab Supervisor; welcome to the National Commission on Marihuana and Drug Abuse's Boston Free-Access Study hosted by Harvard Medical School," panted Wick. "Our purpose here is to assess the drug marijuana, i.e., *cannabis sativa,* from many perspectives so as to inform the debate over its future role in society."

Wick, bald, sincere, round, with a starchy complexion, stared at his 10 subjects. "Dr. Nicholson has selected the highest quality experimental marijuana ever—4.5% THC—three times street potency."

"Yahoo!" the subjects yelled in a single voice, "yahoo!"

Bergman noticed Shep was now at his elbow, rocking gently. "Can you beat this?" he smiled, "a frick'n marijuana experiment. It's better than sex!"

"How would you know?" giggled Sutter.

"We will be trading marijuana with you," continued Wick, "for your cooperation on a battery of daily tests. Because we need to establish a template for each of you, that's a kinda medical profile, there will be five days without the drug at the beginning and end of the study."

"Hey, that's a rip, man," Sutter called out.

"Believe me, the wait will be worth it."

"Have you tried it?" Jake asked, "have you copped a buzz, man, with our dope?"

Another member of Nicholson's staff, a distinctive blade of white through his hair, advanced. In his left hand swung a piece of stainless steel the size of a golf ball. He tugged on his beard for silence.

"Hey, shut up!" Jake hollered to the group.

"Thank you, I'm Jim Bedikker—Badger." "Yo!" cried Jake. "Hey, believe me, the stuff is dynamite, even if it ain't free."

"So, just how do we earn it?" asked Ron.

"I'm glad you asked me that friend," said the Badger, his face suddenly becoming sharper, bluer, "you can earn an unlimited amount of weed, ah, cannabis, with this—"

"What's that?" asked Chris.

"This," said Badger, "is an I-M-P, or Imp."

"I repeat the question," ventured Chris to general laughter.

"Hunh?" Badger replied.

"What do you have in your hand?" asked Green, carefully pronouncing each word.

"It's an Imp. It's an acronym, dodos."

"We know it's an acronym for crying out loud," broke in Shep, "the question is: What does it stand for? Hunh? Is it, Inexplicable Mysterious Package?"

"Infernal Metal Prick?" offered Ron.

"Intimate Mounting Position?" joked Jake.

Chris braced for the embarrassment, "It's My Penis?"

"It's My Pussy," wheezed Sutter.

"Gentlemen, gentlemen," Bergman gasped, "can we raise the level of conversation?"

"Hey!" Badger interceded, "Geez, whatta buncha animals. I was getting to the Imp thing. It's a, itza," he moved to confer with Wick. "It's an 'Inventory of Maximum Performance,'" he said at last.

"I'm mostly pleased if my performance in a majority of points imitates minimum possible," Ira gamed.

"No, no, no," the Badge rejoined, "This here gizmo on the top of the Imp here is a, is a plunger, which, if, if, ah..."

"Plunged," offered Chris.

"Right," drawled Badger, smiling despite himself, "you beat the crap out of it." He had their complete attention. "...And it will record points for each hit, until these rollers here, register 9,999. Then it will turn over to 0000." He stopped to push back his heavy mane with its mesmerizing streak of hair thick and white as vanilla taffy. "Before it turns over, you've got to get it credited and counted by one of us—the staff."

"In order to get a jo—a 'marijuana cigarette—' you need 6,000 hits on the plunger. But you're not limited to 6,000 points. You may collect as many as you like on any day." Satisfied, he began handing out the palm-sized instruments.

"Remember," repeated Wick, "your points are the medium of exchange during the course of this experiment!"

"I know what it is now," said Jake, picking up the device and idly punching at it. He poked Sutter. "It's an Important

Mother Piece of shit."

"In addition, subject participants will be paid $2 a day for every day they fully comply with the schedule of tests," Badger went on dryly. "The hospital will supply all personal and medical needs, meals, and once it gets organized—entertainment.

"But," Badger paused, "this must be a closed experiment."

"Meaning what?" asked Thaddeus.

"No leaving the ward. No phone calls either in or out."

"What?!" screamed Jake. "You never said anything about this! I've got a business to run. A damned good one too." He towered over the smaller Badger.

"And I've got a girl out there. Killer sex, man," Sutter joined in.

"Hell, no way this goin' down," Wayne scowled. With a snap of his wrist, he sent the 'Imp' skittering across the floor. Infrared sensors and voice bugs the size of a moth be damned.

Badger's gaze followed the gadget. "Points from the Imp will be the medium of exchange for the duration..." The Imp hit the wall and spun wildly. "6,000 points equals one, ah, marijuana cigarette consumed during the experiment, or $1 redeemed after it," he repeated.

"Oh!?" interjected Jake. "You mean, if I do, say, 60,000 clicks a day, I make 10 bucks. I could smoke one or two joints and still make $8 a day—8 times 30?"

"20," Shep corrected.

"Oh yea, 20," Jake conceded. "Let's see, that's $160."

"When the gig's over?"

Badger nodded.

"Far out!"

"Now," Badger tore on, "you will be called individually for a series of physical measurements that will provide heart, lung and respiratory system data. This is normal, do not resist. Your pod is ready to replace you should you thwart the hopes of the Master. You there, bean-brain," he said to Wayne, "pick that up."

Before leaving for his cell, Wayne retrieved the IMP. He glanced idly at the numbers that filled the window: 1,387!?

* * * *

Jake and Sutter walked together, "Hey, man, you're tak'n it pretty good, no weed an' all," ventured Sutter.

"Yeah, well, it bums me some, but it ain't like I don't have me own resources," Jake answered slyly. He lifted a backpack from his shoulder and rummaged through it producing a foil packet the size of a cookie.

"You sonofabitch!" said Sutter admiringly.

## 3

## *Another Day Before Paradise*

Thad approached the Badger, "That phone bit's ok for these other guys," he whispered, "but I'm an actor. Auditions, call backs. Opportunity, see? You aren't telling me I can't make calls!" Thad had spent hours on the topic, working in his head and among the other subjects. With part optimism, part well-laid plan, part persistence and much BS, Thad knew he would prevail.

"The rules are for everybody, that's why they're called er, ah, rules," replied Badger.

"But I ain't 'everybody,'" insisted Thad. "Don't you be call'n me 'everybody,'" he said, assuming a boyish pout, "cuz I ain't. I'm Thaddeus 'Gorilla King' Ward and I tell you which rules I obey!" he spoke with a twinkle in his eye. "You, former white slaver, are under my power!" his deep baritone stirred Badger's hair, his gold tooth and the confluence of pink and brown skin about the corners of his oratory, entranced.

Badger wavered, "Oh, crap," he murmured, motioning over another grad student whom he introduced as Dave Minter.

Thaddeus inflated himself to maximum stature. Minter's fiery red mustache twitched like a woodpecker as the pair conferred. "Now, as the Badge said, we can't change the rules, they come from higher up."

Thad sucked in his breath. "A phone is not an option for an actor," he boomed. "I have to be available," his voice dropping to a murmur. "We're talkin' career parts, hmmmm? and voice-overs, hunh?" Arms extended and knees flexed, he launched into soliloquy: "'That if I then had waken after long sleep, Will make me sleep again; and then in dreaming, The clouds methought would open and show riches ready to drop upon me; that, when I waked I cried to dream again...'"

"Shakespeare?" asked Minter, impressed.

"The Tempest, Act I, Scene 2," Thaddeus shot back.

"Let me point out that you will not be leaving this ward," said Minter.

"All the more reason my good fellow, to sue-ply ady-quit com-muni-ca-shun. I expect to have a phone in my roooom," urged Thaddeus.

"Look," entreated Minter, "it's like this, we want you to stay on the reservation. There's some great pot com'n, huge THC."

"Is that right? Mendacino Gold? Maui Wowie? Thai-1-On?"

"Better. Off the Richter scale."

"Mmmmm... My Richter goes pretty high..."

"You have to abide by the rules," said Minter softly, adding, "you may have noticed a payphone in the hall just outside the ward. Any recollection that I was the one who told you will disappear with the first joint," he smiled, snapping his fingers.

"Hey, you're alright, man," Thad offered, his large brown hand encircling Minter's like a caramel roll absorbing a pat of butter.

* * * *

B-ward was the central stake in the clinic's 'E'-shaped layout. A-ward lay parallel and north, while C-ward spread south.

B-ward's 10 ribs—identical sleeping cells on either side of a wide corridor—were equipped with steel frame beds and a sealed foam mattress. Each subject-participant was assigned his own room. All the rooms had doors but none of the doors had locks.

Below the subject's rooms, were meeting rooms for Group Interaction (with a single 10-foot folding table), examinations, and staff.

The day room was unique, spacious and cool, with grouted floors and patio viewing of the courtyard. A ping pong table and a television drew randomly on the dozen straight-backed wooden chairs, while fluorescents glared from their cages on the ceiling.

D-ward, the long north/south spine of the building, housing the kitchen, laundry and nursing units, sagged under the weight of its connections.

Ira eased himself into the brittle sunshine poised on the steel staircase, drawn there by the bouquet of seaweed chowder from down the street. He concentrated on the IMP. Trained as an accountant he wanted to know exactly how long it would take to arrive at 9,999.

Of course, with his IQ, he should have gone on and obtained a Ph.D. in Math, or earned millions with his own consulting firm. But accounting was a good, solid wall to hide behind, however gray in the public mind. 'What's so wrong with that I ask you?' his mother invariably squared off in defense of his choice.

Clicking away steadily, he sought a rhythm. The task offered none of the thrill of taming the chaos of numbers with brilliant, complex formulas. The progression emerging from the IMP was linear, no flash of transforming measurement. Numbers became players when they are added to the statistical priesthood of income, spending, household formation, migration, population, death, sex and race. Accountants were bloody anchors of advanced Capitalism. Without accountants, Capitalism would fray into a thousand ridiculous schemes got up for Heaven on Earth.

Starting slowly with his right thumb, he warmed to the machine's surging gears: 9, 39, 99, 179, 399, 799.... The IMP spoke in an audible 'clunk' as it added each new decimal place: 9–10, 99–100, 999–1,000... Ira slid into a thumb-pressing trance before numbness slowed his pace: 2,073.

He switched to his left and continued punching, figuring a daily total of 72,000 points, or just over seven circuits of the cylinders, would net $10 and two joints. He could live with that. But his left hand sacrificed the smooth performance of the right, and the muscles soon tightened. He went again to the right hand and punched until temporary paralysis: 4,718.

Ira checked his watch. Half a circuit required 33 minutes...72,000 points meant nearly eight hours continuous effort...eight hours... Of course! 'An eight-hour workday,' he said to himself, swatting at a sharp pain in his neck. The clicker represented the normal 40-hour work week. The question the experiment asked: would someone stoned on marijuana work as hard as a sober person? Well, let's make'm work for pot and tally how much they earn! Divide by the workday and you have an index of marijuana's value...

Raising his gaze from the IMP, Ira saw wavering on the rail of A ward's upper balcony, a flock of flightless, featherless creatures flapping in the direction of the sea. Sharing this barracks by the bay, where they felt the ocean's sting but never saw its chatoyant beauty, was a spectral collection of souls who had succeeded in falling apart. Robed and pj'ed, theirs the grimmest of victories, seized at the cost of the succulent portion of life.

'Shell-shocked,' said Badger dismissively, when asked about the figurines in muslin gowns who gathered outdoors when the winds died and the sun crept out. It was a term of interest to Ira as the promising career of his uncle was destroyed by 'combat fatigue.' He recalled the definition: "any acute, hysterical neuroses originating in trauma suffered under fire in modern warfare." 'Hysterical neurosis'? thought Ira; they looked stoned to me.

* * * *

"Christopher Conner?"

Called into the yellow tiled examining room with creamy turquoise trim, Chris was brusquely steered through a robust vital signs routine: height/weight, blood pressure, temp, eye/ear exam, blood sample (ouch!)—everything was checked but the 'exits,' he ruefully noted.

"How often do we have to do these?" Chris asked. He could think of nothing else to say but felt it important that he at least try to make small talk.

"Every day," replied Badger gruffly.

"Every day?" Chris winced.

Badger grabbed Chris by the elbows, maneuvering him before a transparent plastic five-gallon bucket. "You're lucky we don't throw you down the well."

A thin disk floated on six inches of faintly greenish fluid. Piercing the center of the disk, a plastic yardstick rose to eye-level where it formed the words, 'Vital-O-Meter.' Snaking its way from the side of the drum into Badger's hand was a length of 1" tubing. Badger ripped the sanitary packaging from a paper skirt and slapped it on the end of the tube. He thrust it at Chris, "Blow!"

Chris blew until his head throbbed. "How'd I do?" he wheezed.

"Hmmpt," Badger mumbled, pushing him out the door. Chris got two paces, "Hey, slack-brain," Badger yelled, "take your clicker!"

Punch-step, punch-step, punch; Chris lurched down the hall. Maybe because the pot wasn't available yet, there wasn't this, this scandalous camaraderie, or whatever you call it, that he expected. Everyone was pretty much staying to themselves. Shep and Thaddeus had staked out the dayroom, dominating with matters that sounded significant but meant little to him: "The day room is exactly 40 feet by 60 feet," insisted Shep, "2,400 square feet or 240 square feet per person, less than half the standard called for by the Geneva Convention for treatment of POWs!"

"Well, you're not a prisoner of conscience," Thad shot back, "you're a lazy Jew."

"At least I'm not a usurious Jew! Whereas you could pass for a shiftless Negro..."

"A shiftless Negro!?"

"You're an actor for chrissakes—a parasite."

"And you're a repressed, cold-hearted, underachieving, bean counter!" waged Thad.

Shep paused, giving time for a smile to creep across his face. "Well, that didn't take long, did it?" said Shep and the two of them laughed.

Sutter and Jake spent a lot of time in Jake's room listening to records... Galen read a lot; Wayne seemed to have lost something, and Ron Green lifted weights.

A movement from the far end of the ward caught his eye. Someone was waving frantically at him. Chris sensed abandonment and broke into a run.

'Group' was underway, the shades drawn against a mid-summer heat wave, when it seemed the sun was no longer above the earth but below it, like a cooking fire. Fresh from the bright corridor, the darkness in the room blinded Chris temporarily. Hearing Minter's voice, he weaved toward it, settling into the first available chair. Chris could not be certain his eyes were even open. He stretched his eyelids just to be sure, hallucinating an unearthly green face smiling through the gloom. He'd expected to see only a gray wall but there definitely was a mask of some sort no more than a foot away.

His eyes did their thing adapting to the reduced light, subtly altering the ghostly portrait to look very much like... Jake!? A prickly heat about his neck exploded in laughter. What was goin' on? He looked away from Jake's face only to encounter eight others...

Oh, God! The reverse chair trick, the cheesiest prank in the book! And he'd fallen for it. "Shit!" he surrendered, slumping into his chair. "This is what the nun's used to call a boner."

Dr. Nicholson sighed, "This is the first test of the day," he intoned, "all tests will be less than 45 minutes, with the exception of the Maudsley House Inventory. The testing day will begin precisely at 9 o'clock each morning." He paused to search for that one word which would tranquilize these monkeys who were already showing symptoms of confinement.

"Say, what's up Doc?" Jake interrupted.

"Yes? Question?" said Nicholson, trying to smile.

"Wha' d'ya got there; some kinda mind bender?" asked Sutter.

"This?" responded Nicholson. There was much to do—meetings with fellow faculty, learned scholars, local and state politicians—all eager for a personal briefing about the 'hot' project, and suggesting, even demanding, to be kept 'up to date'. A lot of people who ignored him when he sought the rights to the U.S. trials, suddenly wanted on the bus. "It's just a slide projector."

"Hold on professor," said Jake, scratching his head, "you're goin' too fast."

"Ahh," the doctor sighed, the seconds pealing away like the sonorous echoes of a distant bell. "I will, ah, quiet gentlemen, please! Thank you. I will project a number sequence on the wall, there," he said, pointing. The numbers "249" appeared on the wall upside down. Nicholson fidgeted helplessly with the remote until rescued by Badge.

"I will start with three numbers and gradually increase to nine," he continued, "then I will..." He pushed the remote without result. "I thought it was ready?" he asked impatiently.

"It's ready," responded Badger.

"Good," said Nicholson after a successful test. "Now, as I project the sequence on the wall, you are to write them down."

"On what?" Tony burst out.

"Oh, no," moaned Nicholson, seeing they didn't have pad and pencil.

"Right here," Minter entered waving a sheaf of pencils. Nicholson motioned him closer and handed him the remote, whispering something in his ear.

"Get the lights," Minter directed, "Here we go..." 249 again appeared on the wall, right side up. Followed by 5137, 12739, 367284, 1653082, 57098342.

"Wait, wait, wait," Jake intervened.

Minter stopped the projector. "You've got a problem?" he asked.

Jake rose and turned to face the other subjects. "Problem?" he repeated. "Yes, I have a problem. You're going too goddamn fast is my problem!"

"Right on!" the room erupted.

"The slides are set at a rate of one per second. This is sufficient time to memorize the sequence, or to write it. However, it is *insufficient* time to do both," said Shep. "The problem is not one of mind, but of muscular coordination," he concluded.

"And poor lighting," added Jimbo.

"Too much oxygen, not enough THC," claimed Sutter.

"Marginal educational quality in our public schools," added Bergman.

"Dark family secrets," said Chris, wide-eyed.

"No gym class," said Jimbo.

"What? Oh, that is bent," observed Tony.

"Actually, it is a mind problem," put in Wayne, "the mind that set the timer." Wayne could see Army Psy-Ops all over this number. In all probability, if he could ace this, we might just be talking Special Forces.

"Well, y-e-s," answered Shep dismissively, "if you look at it that way..."

"Guys—" convened Minter, "has it occurred to you that the purpose of this test might not have anything to do with lifting all boats?"

"Some of us are supposed to fail?" Ron mused.

"Exactly," answered Badger. "Yu'se supposed to try to the best of your individual abilities. Savvy?"

"The company admits the interval is arbitrary," explained Minter. "Who completes the sequences, or whether anyone does, isn't the point. What's important is that the test is 'reliable.' That is, it's administered the same way every time, in every setting. Now, let's give it another try, for the Gipper."

9162 was soon followed by 29675, 326847, 3692817, 15390826, and 260791483.

"Now," Minter paused, "we'll be writing the number sequences in reverse order. The number 814," he said as it appeared on the wall, "will be written 4-1-8; 1728 will be written 8-2-7-1. Any questions? Ok, let's begin."

When 916 appeared, Chris wrote 619; 5724 became 4275, written 5-7-2-4; 45928 changed to 82954, with 4 entered first, 5 second, 9 next etc., written right-to-left ; 603951 substituted for 159306; 7518924 for 4298157; 15920768 for 86702951; and 592714836 as 638417295. The trick was to simply jot down the numbers right to left, with 6 written first, followed by 3 to its left, 8 again left, then 4 and so on, each number falling left of its predecessors. That way he could remember the numbers as they appeared instead of actually transposing them left to right.

Trying to concentrate, he nevertheless felt the pressure of Badger's predatory stare. Chris froze like a resting fly. Badger stalked Chris his eyes narrowing. Grabbing his sleeve; however gently, he looked him in the eye, "Wait a minute, wait just a minute. Aahhh...we seem to have a misunderstanding here," he cautioned. "It seems that some of you are just writing the numbers backward. And, well, the idea is to, ah, memorize the groupings in reverse. So 729541 is written 1-4-5-9-2-7, not 7-2-9-5-4-1 written right to left. That's what we mean when we say 'memory' test, not gimmick test. Jesus Christ! Now let's try it again."

"Hey!" Tony Duquesne shouted, "where'd that kindly doctor go?"

"Yeah, the one with the warm bedpan manner?" put in Sutter.

"Wait, wait. You mean this guy isn't the only dimwit in here?" Badger gasped, letting go of Chris's sleeve.

"Did you all do this? Show of hands," ordered Minter. "Hmmm," he mumbled as the hands went up. "Ok, we can't use these numbers. I'll make sure you get paid for today's test and we'll start fresh tomorrow."

At the back of the room, Nicholson was furious. Not at Minter or Beddiker. They were doing their best; these problems should be aired right away, before they have a chance to take on weight and challenge the results. That wasn't the problem. The problem was the respondents. They simply couldn't be trusted to take on the project's goals as their own!

Nicholson rubbed his eye sockets until brilliant red flares danced. The physical and psychological effects of marijuana were already well reported in previous research:

**Physical** 1) slight but noticeable elevation of pulse rate and blood pressure; 2) dilation of the pupils, sluggish reaction to light; 3) dryness of the mouth and throat cavities; 4) minor visual distortion of proximity, distance and color; 5) episodes of shorter, faster breathing; 6) tremors of the tongue and extremities; 7) injection of blood into conjunctiva, or membrane of the inner eyelid; 8) no significant changes in basal (resting) metabolic rates, blood chemistry, liver and kidney function, or electrocardiograph studies - i.e., no direct action on the organs themselves; 9) generally, there is no physiological dependence and only slight tolerance with most smokers able to discontinue the habit without difficulty.

**Psychological** 1) significant cerebral excitation transmitted through the autonomic nervous system; 2) apprehension and anxiety; 3) euphoria, i.e., sense of well-being, contentment, cheerfulness and gaiety; 4) loquaciousness; 5) lowering of inhibitions;

6) increased hunger and thirst; 7) feeling of being 'high'; 8) uncontrollable bursts of laughter; 9) increase in alpha wave brain relaxation leading to drowsiness, languor, a pleasant feeling of fatigue.

These conclusions, from the LaGuardia Committee on Marijuana, 1944, had not been seriously challenged. But he, Nicholson, hoped to do just that. Dr. Harold Nicholson was going to put his mark upon History.

Nervously, he checked his Patek Phillippe. Marijuana had been under the microscope many times since its recreational use was noticed in this hemisphere nearly 150 years ago. *Cannabis sativa L.*, is one of several members of the hemp family, a sturdy plant whose lengthy fibers, twisted into rope or flattened into canvas (the word itself, is derived from *cannabis*) captured the oceans' breath for sailing ships; and hammered into cloth, separated the wriggling masses into colorful individuality. When it wasn't working on the docks or in the fields, the drug's medicinal and spiritual qualities accorded it religious status in several cultures.

Marijuana is a 'mild' drug, without profound side effects or loss of motor control. But is it also the 'gateway' drug, the portal to crueler and more devastating drug use? Nicholson didn't know; his job was to capture the psychoactive mechanism, the means to unraveling the drug's euphoric effect: what was taking place in the smoker's brain, what clever sparks leapt from dendrite to dendrite, speeding across newly-wired synapses?

Objective data could only go so far; after heart/lung, EKGs, memory and motor tests, he still lacked a handle on pot use. Some experiments suggested an endorphin effect, a delicate stroking of the brain's pleasure receptors. This 'euphoria,' offered real possibilities. If he could map the changes made by

THC, then he might induce the same effect without the drug... It didn't seem likely that recreational drug use would ever be encouraged: some drug use appeared to break down the barrier to more drug use.

Nicholson knew 'Mary Jane' was no pushover. 'It's a subtle drug,' a fellow researcher warned, 'that despite tens of millions of regular users has not been traced to a single death. By contrast,' the man pointed out, 'hundreds of researchers had disappeared' after a brush with cannabis, the 'least harmful' of recreational drugs. So much could go wrong on the path to 'duplicable results' the Holy Grail of true science, one had to be very careful...

* * * *

As Chris turned to hand in his answer pad, he saw Jake comparing his answers to Sutter's. Chris watched as Jake made a couple of erasures. Suddenly, Jake lifted his head and looked directly at Chris. It was an animal look, cold and indifferent. Discovered, Chris felt jolted.

Shep yawned.

"How'd you do?" Chris quickly asked him.

"Hunh? Oh, you mean on the numbers-memory thing? Yeah, well I aced it. Child's play."

"No kidd'n'? How?" Chris pleaded.

"Next test," Badger announced, "is the last test—for today. By each of your chairs," Badger read without inflection, "there is a button-response device connected by wire."

"Say, what do you call this puppy, anyway?"

"'Scuse me?"

"Name?"

"Name is the Time Estimation Test. No more questions.

Look," he stressed, "this test asks you to fix a given period of time in memory on your own, with no help whatsoever and absolutely no watches!

"I will give you a target, say 50 seconds, and then I will say 'Start!' and you will push the button and keep it pushed until you feel the target has been reached. You will then release the trigger and not touch it until given a new command. There will be eight targets each session, ranging from 8 to 190 seconds. You will receive a nickel for each correct response within 10%." Badger paused, "Any questions? Good, then we will proceed. Remember, Big Brother is watching! Ok, the first one—30 seconds. Start now!"

Chris concentrated, 'one-Mississippi, two-Mississippi, three-Mississippi'—guessing a steady repetition—'six-Mississippi, seven-Mississippi, eight-Mississippi'—was his best shot at—'twelve-Mississippi, thirteen-Mississippi'—the target. After several intervals however, 'a hundred thirty Mississippi, a hundred thirty-one Mississippi...' he found it hard to focus. 'A hundred fifty-fifty-fifty-what? When Badger ordered a six-minute interval ('You must remain quiet!'), Chris searched for an inconspicuous spot to throw in the towel.

'Hey, I'm sweating,' he thought, his thumb squeezing the plunger desperately. 'Geez, I've forgotten the target!' But his attention was diverted by the swift, determined movement of Badger and Minter as they converged on the back row of desks. The two of them fell upon Thaddeus who seized up with laughter. Thrashing and gurgling until out of breath, Thad was stripped of his wristwatch, now a trophy Badger held aloft.

"For Chrissakes," laughed Minter, "are we going to have to bring in the Army, or what?"

"Well, I didn't think you could see me," gagged Thaddeus,

stretching out on the floor to tame the wildfire in his lungs.

"God, this is going to be a madhouse when you yahoos are stoned," Badger predicted.

Jake stealthily removed his own watch and slipped it into his pocket.

"That was the last one," Badger said flatly, "of that test. We got one more test to go."

"Hey man, you said that was the last one!" objected Ron.

"I lied," he flatlined. "Now, line up here for the Shooting Gallery." He grabbed Chris who was at the front of the room and steered him to a video arcade game. Armed with an M-16, Chris found himself transformed into a U.S. sniper aiming to destroy the tanks and foot soldiers of his enemy.

"Remember," Minter called out loudly, "the better your performance, the more points you win. The more points you win, the more money you get!"

Chris noted that his adversary, fated to run the same slow-moving gauntlet before the advanced firepower of the U.S. Army, lacked weapons and any obvious kinship to the Anglo-American race. He pulled the trigger. Flapp! It sounded like he was firing into mud, or a bag of tissue and blood. Flapp! Flapp! He felt just enough excitement to put him on edge. He squeezed the trigger the way he thought he should. The human targets crumpled in a storm of molten lead. He kept blasting until the 'flapp, flapp' was just an echo. He was out of ammo.

"Tough luck, grunt," said Badger.

"Hunh?"

"Your score, bonehead, is 870, less than 10% hits. No bonus under 5,000 points. Cheer up, GI. You're just not a born killer."

"870?" scoffed Jake. "Shit, you wouldn't last a minute in Vietnam."

"Vietnam!?" Chris cried out. "Me?"

"Well," said Sutter, pointing at the machine's garish artwork, "look who you been shooting: black pajamas, straw hat—The Cong, man. You been shooting at VC, dig? Blam, blam, blam—Vietnamization."

"Yeah," nodded Jake, "if Nixon can eliminate the Cong, he's comin' after us dopers, man. Better practice your marksmanship, dude." With that, Jake and Sutter stuck their fists in the air and began to chant, "Ho, Ho, Ho Chi Minh; the NLF is gonna win! Ho, Ho."

# 4

# *The Importance of Being Wayne*

1387?! This could be the kind of experiment where the substance—pot—was already being administered via the air exchange, or the food. Wayne's judgment had just been hit by large ordinance from Top Dog. He could have sworn the number on the IMP was in the 60–70 point range when he happened to scramble its transmissions. Now it was nearly 1,400. He began to press the plunger furiously in the expectation that he could affect the rate with astronomical returns. Wayne knew the IMP was doing more than advertised. If he could break the code, he could own a fabulous piece of spyware.

He pressed as fast as his thumb, screaming in pain, could depress the plunger, stopping only when temporary paralysis forced his hand: 1561. No breakthrough, no 'open sesame.' He tried again punching the trigger lightly—a measured blow: 1467. Losing points?! Another punch: 1439. Once more: 2184!! Wheww! Another punch: 1758. Awhh! Again: 1719. Another: 2367! Wayne calibrated each jab at the plunger. Repeated hits produced a pattern: number sequences ending in '9' went up when struck; all other sequences went down. In addition, he learned that the more '9s' the better. In no time he leaped from 2599 to 4375, ran to 4379 and leaped again to 4493, ran to 4399 and leaped (!) to 6813, punched—whoops!—to 6756, ran to 6759 leaping to 6816, 6819 to 6873, 6899 to 7656, 7659 to 7682, 7699 to 9057, 9059 to 9088, 9099 to 9684, 9689 to 9760, 9769 to 9910, 9919 to 9968! Suddenly he was so short of breath he felt he was going to faint. He opened his mouth and exhaled.

Wayne paused before the run-up to 9,999.

He'd broken the code. Top Dog was vulnerable after all. Ruthless, well-paid, unchallenged to this point, they took their supremacy for granted. He showed um! Three days (72 hours ) and he owned the IMP. It was probably a goddamned record, Wayne rejoiced. But... He hated to think it, but, you know, what if... I mean, it had been awfully easy. Wayne ingested Intelligence Reports and Soldier of Fortune magazines like second-hand smoke. He saw signs of a 'boomerang,' a mission rigged to look like failure in order to conceal a malevolent purpose that not even the most experienced analysts could figure out.

While it might seem farfetched, there were certain 'indications' that Top Dog wanted him to discover the IMP code. Perhaps they'd singled him out for advanced placement? He knew there were elite schools where a select few, the future leaders, learned, well, *everything*. Maybe they were evaluating him as a team player? But which team? With whom should he share this powerful secret? His instincts told him to sit on it for awhile, until the background noise, the 'chatter,' became clear. He went to his room and gently laid the Imp down on the table next to his bed. When the others had established a schedule, he'd slip in. In the meantime, a couple of napkins he'd taken from the dining room covered up the fact that the IMP was pregnant.

* * * *

Tony heard that yesterday they had taken an IQ test. Of course the staff didn't call it that, but someone recognized it, well, anyway. Shep supposedly scored a pre-pot 177—at the high end of 'genius'—placing him in the company of Beethoven,

Shakespeare and Batman.

"You don't look that surprised?" commented Tony, after sifting the darkness to find Ira in front of the tv.

"What?" said Shep reflexively. "Geez, you gotta watch this, it's 'Gunsmoke,' the best goddamned show on the tube."

"I thought you weren't supposed to know your IQ?" puzzled Duquesne.

"Are you kidding? Have a 180 IQ and not know about it?" he-he'd Ira.

"Yeah, I guess," Tony mumbled. "Say, where'd you go to school?"

"City University of New York. I never really graduated, but I've been taking courses there for years. They don't charge me, I think I have 900 credits."

"And my old school?" put in Jake, "That would be 'Screw U.' Ok, quit playing with your clickers and get your butts down to Group!"

When the group was complete, Badger closed the door. "Today you will be asked to come to some agreement on matters you may disagree with. Don't complain! You can't change any of it. Do your best. Did I say, 'don't complain?'" Badger snarled.

"Do you think he's serious?" asked Sutter.

"Could be," Jake responded, 'it's on sale this week, only $1.39 a pound."

"Remember, each of these 'Ways of Life,' require a personal statement of whether you like it 'very little' or 'a lot,' as well as a group opinion. The group decision has to be unanimous."

"OOOooooo," whined Jimbo, "we gonna have this horse poop every day?"

"Hey, you signed on to do a little work every day. You're

not going to have this horse poop everyday, but you will have some horse poop every day. It's in the contract. Work—horse poop—every day! Now read it and shut up!" yelled Badger.

**Ways to Live #3:**

**A. This way of life makes central the sympathetic concern for others.**

**B. Seeking satisfaction for oneself and not the group, is to be avoided.**

**C. Sexual enthusiasm, intellectual aggressiveness and personal ambition will only lead to dissatisfaction for these things hinder the sympathetic love among persons which alone gives significance to life.**

**D. If we are aggressive we block our receptivity to the personal forces upon which we are dependent for genuine personal growth.**

**E. In order to preserve cultural values, change should occur within society only after careful research and consideration.**

**F. The comfort and joys of home and the family are a man's greatest treasures.**

Thaddeus stood before the group. "Let's view the 'sitchy-a-shun': we could debate some of this stuff for quite a while, I mean this sentence about sexual enthusiasm. Ha, ha, ha. It's filled with horse poop.

"And this deal about change, lotsa unanswered questions if you get my meaning, but I could live with it just to save time. 'Time,' said the Bard..."

"I can't believe we're actually supposed to argue this, this sophistry," growled Shep. "They sure aren't shooting very high."

"Ok, professor, we know what you think. Anybody else

wanna comment before we move on?" Thaddeus demanded.

"I give it two hemorrhoids," said Jake.

"Yeah, no beat, blah lyrics, definitely a chick tune," added Sutter.

"Then it's unanimous, we like Way of Life #3 a whole helluva lot."

"Wait," said Bergman, "for the sake of saving time, we're going to tank on this sentimental picture of society? Where would all us pot smokers wind up under this outfit?"

"He's right," agreed Shep, "under this regime, we'd be in the cattle-car business, building and filling."

"Hey, man! You agreed to get this done quickly. We got three more to go," Thad pleaded.

"What's wrong with 'sympathetic concern,' or 'group satisfaction?'" put in Jimbo. "Don't we want 'personal growth' and 'cultural values'?"

"Right," added Chris. "Sounds like good Christian values to me."

"Initially, yes," argued Shep, "but then it takes a dangerous turn toward orthodoxy, pacifism and infringement of individual freedom."

"Halleluiah, brother," said Bergman.

"Is life so dear or peace so sweet as to be purchased at the price of chains and slavery?!" cried Thaddeus. "Forbid it almighty God, I know not what course others may take, but as for me, give me Liberty."

"Oh, for Chrissakes!" exploded Jake in frustration, "You assholes! This is a waste of goddamned time. Ok, ok, it's a piece of shit way to live, alright? Let's go on."

"I mean, just because a statistical majority says war is A-ok, that doesn't make it moral. The world needs heroes," offered

Bergman.

"Shut up," said Sutter.

Badger wound among them handing each an 'Open Evaluation' form. Jimbo began reading, his voice becoming audible as his indignation rose: "Fill in the names of the others participating...and...your...evaluation...of them, using the numerical code at left to make your ratings... 1 'least applicable'; 4 'most applicable.'

| Name | | |
|---|---|---|
| | Shows Courtesy | 1 2 3 4 |
| | Listens to Others | 1 2 3 4 |
| | Agreeable | 1 2 3 4 |
| | Makes Constructive Contributions | 1 2 3 4 |
| | Demonstrates Shallow Thinking | 1 2 3 4 |
| | Openly Antagonistic | 1 2 3 4 |
| | Inconsiderate | 1 2 3 4 |
| | Doesn't Listen | 1 2 3 4 |

"So you want us to squeal on each other?" said Tony.

Minter and Badger exchanged glances. "Yeah, that's about it," they admitted. "Though you do get bonus points," Minter said sheepishly.

"Bonuses, hunh? And we can put down anything we want?"

"Your honest answers are requested."

"Well, here's my honest answer," said Thad, "take a hike. I'm giving everybody here highest marks. You other guys can do what you want."

"Can he do that?" Badger whispered.

"Maybe we should have said 'quiet' honesty'?" agreed Minter.

* * * *

Tony awoke sweating. His limbs were heavy but his mind was alert. He braced for sunlight stabbing into his eyes but got instead a commotion ringing in his ears. It must have been around 7. Early birds, not used to regular chow, attacking the food cart probably. The noise grew however, beyond what could be expected from sugar deficit. Convinced it wouldn't stop he got up to investigate.

He found Jake and Sutter banging the food covers together like cymbals. "Jeez," he complained, "what's with all the noise?"

"You tell us," Sutter challenged, pointing at the breakfast kettle filled with oily, melting grains. Tony peered in. "Oooo," he cooed. "Waiter, there's a ghoul in my gruel." He was joined at the kettle by Shep.

"What the hell is that?" asked Jake.

"Well," said Shep, "some would see it as a miracle of life, animated protein. Myself, I think it's a disgusting maggot."

"A fuck'n goddamned maggot in the fuck'n goddamned oatmeal," moaned Jake. "Hey, what the hell are you doing?" he challenged Shep who'd begun trolling in the hot, buttery cereal.

"Whaddya think? I'm hungry."

"Just don't eat the, the—"

"The ward mascot."

"Yeah, whatever. Don't destroy the evidence."

Shep continued to probe with his spoon, "Seems there'll be plenty to go around."

Chris stared at his half-eaten bowl. "Are we eating the same stuff?" he asked out loud.

Wayne had been working recon at the point. Lot of coming and going out there. Faces he didn't recognize. He'd been nearby when Jake outed the maggots. Jake finished his bowl when Sutter, five minutes behind him, asked, "What's this?'

Wayne had come up in close support. He planned an intercept. As soon as—there!—he'd spotted Wick passing the double doors.

Stealthily, Wayne opened the doors, drew close and snagged Wick by the coat. Wayne motioned 'Quiet,' and proceeded to pull Wick back to the kettle, repeatedly barking, 'Urgent business.' Wick remained calm, as if dealing with para-military psychotics before coffee was relatively routine. He did manage to ask Wayne, 'How did you get in here?' before delivery to Jake.

"What are you going to do about this?" fumed Jake, holding a spoonful of maggots inches from Wick's face.

"Me? What am I going to do about it? I'm not going to do anything, I've already had my breakfast," Wick retorted.

"Hey, this is no laughing matter buddy," Jake shot back.

"Of course it isn't," conceded Wick. "And we won't treat it as such, either. How many of you may have eaten one of these creatures?"

"I think I might have," said Chris. "I'm not really sure how many."

"Well, just to be on the safe side, I'm sending you to the infirmary immediately." He pushed Chris down the hall toward the twin doors. "They'll take care of it," he shouted. "Anybody else?" offered Wick, returning to group. "No? No one?"

"Hey," asked Jake, "what are you going to do with him?"

"Pump his stomach, of course," answered Wick.

"Listen," Jake said testily, "I wanna talk to the frick'n cook!"

Wick stiffened, "I don't think that's a good idea."

"Wha' do you mean?" asked Jake.

"Well," said Wick, "the fact is we're not very popular here. Remember this is suburbia. Not big on long hair and drugs. We can't go around offending people. We'll deal with this through channels; I promise meals will improve."

"What's the beef, Doc. Are they pissed off because we smoke dope, or is it our dope smoking that off pisses them?"

"That's a good question, one I promise to answer after you've answered one of mine. Actually, not one but several, several hundred actually," he said tactfully. Wick then handed out what he called the 'Maudsley Hospital (London) Drug Dependency Survey.' "There are 566 simple True/False questions. I will read them. You will answer on the Survey. They go quickly. Ten a minute if there are no interruptions," he cautioned.

He charged over a murmur of dissent, "Do you think persons are following you? Do you know who is plotting against you? Have you had contact with extraterrestrial beings? Do you hear strange voices? Do you believe in the devil? Do you have trouble remembering names? Do you enjoy reading newspaper stories about violence? Do weird things happen to you? Have you ever wanted to murder someone for the excitement of it? Do you hate your mother? Father? Have you experienced black and tarry bowel movements?"

"Excuse me, Doc," said Jake, "I'm hav'n one now."

"Quiet, please," Wick commanded.

"An extraterrestrial friend of mine, is telling me to off you," countered Jake.

"Hey," Bergman whispered to Shep, "somethun's fishy."

"The test?" said Shep.

"Yeah."

"It's really the MMPI—Minnesota Multiphasic Personality Inventory. 1950s determinant of sanity."

"Isn't it illegal to give that thing?"

"Without identifying it as a psychological force test, i.e., sane or insane..."

"Well?"

"Not everywhere, apparently."

Again, Wick tore into the questions: "Do you feel you know more than those around you? Have you had sexual desires you were ashamed of? Do you occasionally have to conceal your true thoughts from others? Do you hear voices?"

"There's that voice again telling me to kill," broke in Jake.

"Just answer it," urged Wick. "Now, have you ever dressed yourself in women's clothing, especially bra and panties?"

"Oh, God," pleaded Tony, "don't make me answer that one!"

An hour later when the test was complete, Bergman approached Wick, but Jake had already planted himself in front of the desk. "Ok, Doc, what are the answers?" Jake asked just as Bergman made his own inquiry: "Isn't that the MMPI?"

Wick smiled. "I don't believe that test is administered except in cases of suspected mental illness..."

"So you're saying marijuana produces mental illness?" queried Bergman.

"Not at all, looking for mental dysfunction isn't the same as labeling all pot smokers as addled," Wick answered affably. "The question is: 'What has one to do with the other?'"

"Phew! Doc, you got a live fastball, there. Could you give me the instant replay?" panted Jake.

"Well, if a drug is accused of affecting one psychologically for the worse, we want to know if there was any predisposition, any existing mental problems, before the drug was present?"

"Yo!?" laughed Shep.

"To tell the truth," said Wick slowly, "we haven't yet found any profound behavioral changes due exclusively to marijuana smoking. Pot, by itself, does not make you a dangerous anarchist. Though you may tend to hang out with those who are.

"And that's the major problem: the fact that so many mark their passage with a contempt for society is a dangerous development... It's not only repeated retreat to euphoria, but the establishment of a generation built around lawbreaking."

"Why don't they just legalize the shit, man?" asked Jimbo.

"Not in our lifetimes. It's been pretty well demonized."

"Hey," shouted Green, "they brought Nixon back."

# 5

# *Anticipation*

"Today is the day before the day after the day before," mused Jake, "tomorrow is the day."

"I can feel the weed down there, it's talking to me," responded Sutter.

"Yeah, well it's tell'n me I'm out," answered Jake. "You wouldn't have any would you, man? C'mon, don't hold out on me or I'll kill ya!"

"Oh, Jesus, man," Sutter gasped. "Hey, seriously man, do you remember the first time we got stoned together?"

"We were what—20-year-old virgins—and a one-ounce bag cost $10?" Jake reminisced.

"Yeah, we smoked the whole damned bag," laughed Sutter, recalling the sweetened slice of pot as a warm, nutty bread. "You regressed somethun' weird, man," he accused Jake. "First, you couldn't talk."

"I was a rock, man, rocks aren't supposed to talk." Jake marveled at the recollection. Rocks are smart. Not being able to speak leaves you plenty of time to think. No way he could get that stoned today.

"Then you barked like a dog, man, and ran around on all fours.

"I was trying to add excitement to your life."

"Man, you licked my face!"

"Sure, pin it on man's best friend," retorted Jake. "But

whacked as I was, I felt damn good."

"You invented your own goddamned language: 'Ooga-booga, flu ethyl shit,'" recalled Sutter.

"The world needs a new language, one I can understand."

"But you sounded like a pig, man," mocked Sutter.

"You hafta remember I started out as a rock. Dig it; I evolved."

"'Evolved' to baby talk, man..." Sutter giggled. "From 'woof, woof' to 'goo-goo, da-da.'"

"Wait a second, pal," interrupted Jake, "seems to me some-body was body rocking, claimed they were in a damned earth-quake!"

"Oh, god!" groaned Sutter, warming to the unique event. "Dig it. I was the earthquake..."

"Yes, and next, Mr. Earthquake is talking to a tree."

"Oh, wow, man," sighed McClellan, lost in the particular emotion born that day. Boy, they'd gone through someth'n! He and Jake had started at 10 a.m. bound for Eagle Peak. It was early July and they'd planned on getting to the tree line by 3 p.m. Two hours to hit the Peak at 8,900 feet and three to return, down hill being so much faster. That day, the Peak wore a scarf of puffy clouds that cooled the endless rock piles from red to gray as they passed overhead.

They were 19 and on their first solo vacation. Smoking crude joints heavily coated with saliva, they'd managed to get permanently altered. Events of that day were so skillfully painted in his memory that the brushstrokes appeared freshly woven in a single glorious moment of creativity.

For hours they plodded uphill until, exhausted, they gained an exquisite view of the valley below draped in a mantle of piney green. When they weren't laughing, or exploring their new mind, they were sharing rivers of sizzling magical energy.

"We're like blood brothers," Sutter declared.

"Naw, man," Jake corrected, "better than that. We're THC brothers!"

"Hey Brotha!" Jake shouted to Chris then drifting past their door. Chris leaned in. "It's Thursday the 12th and you had juice and scrambled eggs for breakfast," Jake shouted.

'A code!' Chris guessed, joining the current in the center of the hallway. Suddenly, Badger sprang from cover and swam toward him. "You!" he demanded, "come here."

"Don't be nervous," said Nicholson evenly.

"I'm not nervous," Chris said, staking out a patch of Nicholson's face to concentrate upon.

"Good," Nicholson replied, lifting his eyes to meet Chris's. "Very, very good."

Chris hung on, establishing co-ordinates on a swatch of Nicholson's cheek marked by redness and swelling, but lacking, fortunately, scaly white skin or some ugly hair follicle gone ape.

"This is a short conference simply to see how you're getting along, ok?" Chris guessed first-degree burns. "So," said Nicholson, "how're you getting along in here?"

"Just what kinduva doctor are you?" Chris asked. A tanning lamp, most likely.

"Oh, I'm sorry," said Nicholson, "I thought I'd told you. I'm a psychiatrist."

"Are you here to help us?"

Nicholson fought back a sneeze. "W-eee-ll, not directly. You see, I'm a research psychiatrist, not a clinical psychiatrist. A clinical psychiatrist works with symptomatic illness, you know, problems so, well, 'complete' they're brought to the attention of a clinician. Anyway, how are we? How are you getting along?"

"Pretty good, I guess."

"No problems fitting into group?"

"No," Chris answered—too busy even to get to the beach; Chris would love to be that busy—"no problems at all."

"Good. Good," Nicholson observed, "just a few more questions." He appeared to shrink when he suddenly shot forward, "Can you tell me what day it is?"

"Thursday, the 12th," Chris said automatically.

"Un-huh, un-huh. And what did you have for breakfast?"

"Let's see—I think it was scrambled eggs," Chris reflected.

"Hhmmm..." Nicholson calculated. "Says here you slept through breakfast?"

"Well, I, ah, just wasn't hungry."

"Then how did you know what was served; did someone coach you?"

"I-I-I—" Chris hedged.

"We're almost done," Nicholson apologized. "Now, can you tell me if you've had any, ah, sexy dreams?"

"Hunh?" Chris procrastinated.

"You know, dreams of women?"

"Oh," Chris laughed, "sure, women, lots of 'um." Chris grew alarmed his visual attachment to Nicholson's jaw might be noticed. Psychiatrists probably had a name for it, 'chingaper,' or something.

"What about wet dreams?" Nicholson prodded, "have you masturbated?" Chris lost his grip on Nicholson's proboscis. "Ok, that's all," said Nicholson. "See you tomorrow. Next! Ah, a Mr. Thaddeus Ward, please." Chris exalted, convinced that he had avoided a trap.

Thaddeus strode into the small room and immediately came to a halt, "Je-ez..." he stammered, "there's a woman in here!" He knew it was a woman. Something had changed, some little angle of life shifted enriching every possibility.

"Hi!" he greeted her dark brown curls and small, muscular frame. "You can call me Thad," he said, extending his hand. "I'm... Oh!" she blanched, turning her head. Thaddeus questioned the space where her hand had been. He noticed his robe hung open. "Ooops," he grinned, rewrapping himself. "Sorry, miss, ah, if only someone would fetch me a drawstring!

"Badger!" Thaddeus bellowed.

"Excuse me, Miss, may I ask your name?" Thaddeus pleaded in velvet.

"Melody." She spoke over her shoulder as she drew blood from Chris. He seemed paler than usual, Thad thought, maybe it was the lighting?

"Well?" he asked Melody.

"Well what?"

"Well, now that you've had a preview..."

"Awh, that's disgusting!" Melody cried out. She grabbed the blood samples and made for the door.

"What about my blood, don't you want my blood too? Do I sense discrimination here?" cried Thaddeus.

"I'll come back for your blood when it's returned to your head."

"Gosh damn, Wilt, we're goin' see her again."

"Now, Mr. Ward," questioned Nicholson, "are you feeling sexy?"

Thaddeus smiled, "Doc, I'm feeling sexy, nexy and plexy."

"Excellent," concluded Nicholson, "excellent."

Nicholson wasn't especially eager to wipe noses on the ward; Karen had insisted upon it, as means of "staying with the current." He was opposed to fraternization, but Karen was right, it was important to see firsthand what had been brought up in the nets. He normally tended to the academic side anyway, though he didn't term it a 'weakness' as Karen thought, but a necessary refinement in the pursuit of originality.

Lately, he'd been reviewing the numerous marijuana studies in an attempt to sift free those variables that could knock it out of the park! And he knew it might come down to an accidental discovery, a prospect both exciting and fearful.

For example, the relationships between the *cannabis* plant and its close relative, the hops plant, were remarkable: both produce at maturity a thick, powdery resin from their flower tops that becomes a chief ingredient in the two most wide-spread psycho-active drugs of our time: beer and pot. And like hops, which can be fermented to produce different levels of kick, *cannabis* can be cultivated to yield degrees of potency.

The plant *cannabis sativa* is known as Indian Hemp because of its Asian origins. Renowned for its numerous uses (some say 50,000 applications), *cannabvis sativa* has launched many a murderous battle to secure its favor. Much of this conflict can be traced to the fibrous male plant, source of hemp rope, a vital commodity in the Napoleonic era of large wind-driven war ships; and of hemp seed, a virtual cornucopia of natural elixirs sufficient for all ailments from post-partum depression to the energy crisis.

Until replaced by synthetic fibers and oils which mimicked their properties, hemp and hemp seed were valuable agricultural products in paints, dynamite, paper, soap, food, etc. Hemp's legitimate commercial applications disappeared the same year—1937—that its psychoactive dimension was targeted.

It's from the feminine side of *cannabis sativa,* that we reap the varied thought-altering concoctions reflecting cultivation undertaken for a usage now disparaged in the West. The flowers of the female plant, nurtured for millennia in the East, pursue a complex agenda, fighting off fatigue, battling depression, and reaching for a higher understanding, a deeper integration into the life of the mind.

The degree of the encounter is determined by traditional economics: *Bhang,* the cheap spread, is much like our marijuana in that it is merely the cut tops of uncultivated female plants. *Ganja,* a more sophisticated offering, uses a specially cultivated seed and select harvesting to produce a higher grade smoking mixture; again using the female plant tops. *Charas* (hashish) is the pure resin extracted from the female tops of the ganja plants. Ganja and hashish step beyond the lowly street dweller, marijuana, toward more exquisite intoxication.

Hashish is said to be an intense, internal conversation as the self relates holistically with the rest of creation: One sees a tree, feels empathy toward it and ends by 'becoming' the tree... As a poet put it, 'while smoking hashish you may feel yourself evaporating until your pipe is smoking you...'

But hashish hallucinations are not true hallucinations. The mind may perceive strange things, or things behaving strangely, but these things are in fact, real. Hashish may distort, but it cannot create.

* * * *

Another crazy dream for Shep, a frothy collage of people strutting across his personal space at such a tender interface he was smacked by smelly waves of coffee, tobacco, grapefruit, and peanut butter-like aromas pouring off their slow-brewing guts.

Even now he was pelted by a scolding rain of invective so hostile his hand rose to shield... What? Something grabbed his arm. "Get up!" yelled a ghastly apparition. "Pick your lazy ass out of that damn fart sack and join Group!" Shep rubbed his eyes, fighting the warm glue of sleep. "Out, now!" Badger grabbed the bed covers and threatened to dump him on the floor. "If you wouldn't stay up watching frick'n all-night television—"

"My dear Mr. Badger, please call me Mole," begged Shep.

"Oh, bullshit."

"Where's Toad, and Rat, dear Rattie? I thought ours was a rare friendship..."

"Bullshit squared," said Badger. "Please. Ah, god!" he reeled as the naked Shep, hairy as a raccoon, tumbled from anchor. "Oh, Jesus!" Badger sniffed, "have you showered since you got here?"

"I must say I resent your coming in here every morning humming the same tune. My shortcomings are evident to even the most casual observer. But endless carping only seals me off. I need affirmation."

"Bul-l-l shit. Hey - what's after squared?" asked Badger.

"Cubed," Shep replied.

"Bul-l-l shit - cubed!" shouted Badge. "Now get your stubborn, conceited ass to Group before they get on my case for bein' too goddamned leen-yunt."

"Group," yawned Shep, stretching in all directions, "lacks salt."

"Shut up!" said Badger, handing him the latest analytic paradigm:

1) If we choose D and they choose D, both lose $.50

2) If we choose D and they choose C, we win $.50;

3) If we choose C and they choose D, we lose $.50'

4) If we choose C and they choose C, both win $.50

"Dig it," Jake explained, "we take D on the first round so they know we can't be messed with."

"You got 20 responses there Bro," put in Thaddeus, "how stupid do you think they are?"

"I don't know, they've got Bird dog over there," said Jake.

"Ya got no choice," sneered Shep. "It's a force-test."

"Hunh?"

"You have to take number 4 because it expresses the least conflict and the greatest good. Any other choice and you're branded as unbalanced," scoffed Shep.

"Unbalanced?" questioned Wayne, sticking out his tongue, "or just plain crazy?"

They watched as Wayne lifted his tangerine-colored chair and advanced on the dais where Wick sat scribbling.

"Should we stop him?" Jimbo ventured.

"Screw me if he ain't," laughed Jake.

Wick failed to detect the threat until the chair's shadow loomed across his desk. "What's that?" Wayne shouted, quickly storing the chair under one arm while reaching with the other for the sheet Wick protected.

"Can't show it to you—rules," Wick protested, after a desperate lunge from Wayne fell just short of wrestling the paper from his grasp.

"Can't huh? Well, what if I throw this goddamned furniture against the goddamned wall?" Grabbing the chair's slender aluminum legs, Wayne did a 360 and let go. Phantom currents piloted the chair over Shep's head and into the stone wall behind him. The legs of the chair struck first, gathering the load before springing outward toward Group. Jimbo stood up, hurling his own chair to intercept and the two pieces locked angrily, twisting and scraping across the concrete floor.

Wick quivered slightly. "Hey, if it means that much to you," he offered. "It's called 'Bales's Social Interaction Scale.'"

Wayne read the columns of numbers, mostly '1s' and '2s', then he saw their names. "What the hell is this for?" he snorted.

"The better to grade you with, Mr. Smoker," Wick replied villainously.

"Ah, what is this shit?" yelled Jake, "why the Gestapo tactics?" He pointed to the coded figures which tailed the subject's names. "This is shit!"

"It's an alienation yardstick," said Shep. He held the paper to the light and cocked his glasses: "A) shows solidarity; gives help and reward; B) agrees, understands, concurs and replies," he read, "C) gives evaluation and analysis; expresses feeling and wishes; D) gives orientation and information; repeats, clarifies and confirms...' Ok, that's #1 son. Here's the evil twin: A) disagrees; shows passive rejection; withholds help; B) shows tension and asks for help; withdraws out of field; C) shows antagonism; deflating others and asserting self; D) Well, D doesn't get any better," he quit, exhausted.

"Who are you guys?!" Jimbo hollered. "Why are you doing this?" His tone was hard to misinterpret, like headlights on a dark street.

"Basic psychology," Wick explained. "Population of unemployed, draft age, daily drug users... Can't tell 'um apart without a scorecard," he smiled.

"I don't want this crap written down and saved somewhere," Jake challenged.

"Little paranoid are we?" countered Wick.

"Say, I'm not so sure I want a record of this with my name on it either," agreed Jimbo.

"You guys are making history," said Minter. "You're getting every test there is, even the old discredited ones. I know it's a rock for you, but hey, this may be the study that paves the way to legalization."

"Get real!" ordered Jimbo.

"Get a doctor!" shouted Shep, "I just stabbed myself."

"With your own fingernails," sighed Minter, "more anomalous behavior."

"Assmoleous what?" sputtered Jake.

"Oh, jeez," laughed Minter, "'anomalous behavior.' You know, when you act out an exclusively personal motive threatening group cohesion. Unusual behavior like 'throwing objects,' 'self-inflicted injuries...'" He pointed to Thaddeus looming large and square in his blue terry-cloth flag: "'inappropriate attire.'"

"There you go again man, dissecting us," put in Jake.

"You agreed to a certain amount of testing and surveillance or you wouldn't be here. Now, am I right in asking for a sincere effort?" Minter argued.

"I don't know man, I'm not reacting well to captivity..." Jimbo conceded.

"Gett'n that pot tomorrow just might save our sorry ass," suggested Jake.

"But you're go'n to take our names off these reports, right?" pushed Ira.

"Oh, sure, no problem," promised Minter with a wink.

"But Mr. Hammer will not receive his daily $2 for compliance," Wick announced quietly.

Wayne sat nearby staring emptily at the floor. Ok, they knew he knew. He'd laid down the gauntlet. It's the only way to cut through all the b.s., all the posturing. As of this moment, there would be a dialogue, a real dialogue. He let them know he was ready.

# 6

## *What's Your Tea Time?*

Bergman played in a meadow by the sea with a young woman, her long, yellow-streaked hair floating above her like wings. The field where they frolicked lay at a great height; far below waves wrinkled the horizon with shards of green glass. Galen chased after her but couldn't get a glimpse of her face. While he felt an immense pleasure to be with her, he was frustrated that he had no idea—well, an idea, but only an idea—what she looked like. However they leaped and turned, she adroitly kept her face from his. Curiosity became compulsion: he had to see her. He stalked now with conscious intent, using every bit of male advantage to close the gap between them so as to finally gaze upon her face!

Suddenly, just as he reached for her, the grass gave way to a distant silver crescent toward which the faceless, golden-haired woman plummeted. As he clung, gasping, to the edge of a cliff, his eyes followed the slowly-dissolving figure down, down, down... Instinctively coiling for impact, Bergman opened his eyes to find his hands clenched on his pillow. Noise poured down on him from the rec room. "Why, those sonofabitch'n potheads!" he cried, bolting out of bed, "starting without me!" He thought they had a deal. They'd all take that first puff together! A crazy idea seized him.

The game room ricocheted with their giggles as Thaddeus and Chris played table tennis. For Thaddeus, life smoothed into simple shapes and smaller sizes when stoned. There was something likeable and familiar about pot. He could walk as a child in a sugar bowl of clean streets and broad parks with trees to hide behind and steep hills to roll down. It was not his childhood, nor that of anyone he knew. Yet in those subtle pot insights that are more feeling than thought, more flash than substance, he saw that that didn't matter. What mattered was holding on to the inner fantasy, the path of happiness, never allowing it to be washed away by the ordinary flotsam that swirls at our feet.

Chris on the other hand, felt uneasy. He wasn't normally a big pot smoker and had gotten bad vibes on trips where the weed was pretty hairy. Right now, his mind was moving at a speed—and in directions—whew! Everywhere things were bouncing around like excited electrons. It was hard to focus, difficult to pin down.

Trying again to serve the small white ball glowing, growing, alive in his hand, it slipped and went skittering across the table. Hands turned into paddles as Thad, watching him from across the net, cracked up. When Chris tried to pick up the ball with his paddle hands, it darted about determined to escape.

Chris was down on his knees trying to follow the incessant pop-pop-pop of the pressurized orb as it caromed noisily over the terrazzo floors. Chris heard a chain saw: pop, erererereraahh, pop-pop, erererereraheraaahhh... He grabbed at the ball but it scooted toward Thad. It was Thad's ball after all. Chris could feel the pain in the floors as he knelt on the tiles trying to recall what he was looking for. He squeezed under a chair and found himself staring at a pair of polished leather shoes. What in the?

"So, how are you boys doing? Any sexy dreams? Do you all like hot dogs? Remember, no playing with your wieners!"

Standing before him was Bergman in a blue suit, cranberry shirt and yellow tie. Under his arm was a clipboard and from his extended hand, a tape recorder microphone stared. The table-tennis ball, so white and visible, had skillfully disappeared.

"Are you doing ok, are you making friends? Excellent, ex-cell-ent!" Bergman mimicked.

"Who are you?" Chris asked feebly.

"Me?" replied Bergman, "I'm a researcher, it's my job to record your first reactions..."

"Shit!" thought Chris, one powerful joint away from the dock. Of course, it made sense. How better to get real insider info than by planting a spy? And if one spy was sent in why not another to watch the first. They could all be spies. Maybe Chris too, was supposed to be spying but the paperwork hadn't gotten to him? Sometimes messages get lost; maybe they were getting impatient for overdue reports. He hadn't taken notes nor paid much attention. And, yes, he was really stoned, almost to immobility. That had to be part of any report. He shivered.

"Chris, Chris!?" Thad entreated. "Are you ok, man?!" Adding Chris's low pulse-rate to his dead hotel clerk stare, Thad guessed he'd shut down completely. "Man!" he cried, helping Chris to a chair. He wiped a drop of drool from Chris's chin.

Thaddeus fell backward in his own mind, crashing into a pile of empty boxes. He struggled to hold his balance amid the disarray. "Why the hell you do this?" he asked Bergman.

"I can't believe it, man. He swallowed it!" cried Berge, staring at Chris shocked as a new tree stump.

"Isn't that what you wanted?" said Thaddeus disgustedly. "Now get your ass outta here!"

Bergman turned to go, "Say, you guys were stoned, right?"

"Yeah," Thaddeus seethed, "we were. Git! And take off

that ridiculous suit!"

Bergman paused before Chris's crumpled figure. "Listen, I'm sorry. I meant it as a joke..." he snorted. "No biggie, huh? I had no idea you were gonna—an all."

Chris struggled to reduce the load to manageable size. So now this spy was saying he wasn't really a spy, just found humor in telling people he was? That meant he was either a very dumb spy who couldn't keep his identity secret, or he was a master spy who pretended to be a spy so no one would question him when he did spy things.

The dumb or very smart spy ran off at this point. Strong hands helped Chris to his feet. Someone was slamming away at the doorbell. He would have to answer it. "Yes?" Chris mumbled.

"You ok, boy?"

"Berg-man, Berg-man," Chris blurted. "Is he a spy?"

"Berge?" laughed Thaddeus, "they don't let jerks become spies, is my take."

"If he was a spy, he'd want me to think he wasn't. So he says, 'forget it, I was just kidding.'" Chris talked rapidly, the words tumbling out with the rapid staccato of a bouncing ping-pong ball.

"Hold on," Thad urged, "nothin' to worry about." He paused, "How ya feelin'?"

"Too much weed," Chris said emphatically. "Too strong. One a day from now on."

"Yeah."

"I thought I was the only one on real grass, you guys were faking it," said Chris, eerily animated.

"Really?" replied Thaddeus. "Damn near swallowed it myself, I mean that goddamned Berge was dressed like that s.o.b.

Nicholson, is that a coincidence or what!? Powerful shit, that dope for sure."

"Man, I was terrified!" Chris admitted. "I thought once I lit up, you guys were gonna pull a gun and bust me. I was certain of it. I just felt weird, you know, like when you were ditched as a kid. Not that you're bad guys or anything, but, well," Chris felt the urge to go on investigating what happened until his own reactions could be traced.

"Yeah, yeah," Thaddeus agreed, staring at the clicker in his large hands as if it were a diamond. "Geez, I don't know whether I'm more horny than hungry, hungrier than horny."

* * * *

Badger descended on the 'wreck room' determined to gather his giddy charges for testing. "Bergman, Bergman!" he shouted. "Where in the hell is that bastard?"

"Hey," called Sutter, "what's your hurry? Sit a spell and watch your mind."

"Can't," Badger exclaimed, "we got an OD."

"Huh?" Jake interjected.

"Bergman didn't get the call somehow," Badge explained, turning off the tv and pushing the smokers ahead of him as if he were a broom.

"Oh, yeah," coughed Jake. "I was supposed to get him up. So Berge OD'd. Well, maybe there's a God after all. I just never liked the guy."

When Bergman showed up for Group, Badge checked his watch: Ouch! There were just too many tests for these potheads. "Perhaps we may begin?" he broke in, throwing the first digits on the wall.

"Hey, wait a second!" yelled Tony.

Badger stopped the projector. "Yes?" he said impatiently.

"There's an empty chair, someone's missing. The pale dude," Tony observed.

"Forget it," Badger sniffed. "He's a scratch."

"Is he okay?" Tony persisted.

"Oh yeah," Badge answered. "OD'd is all."

"OD'd? You mean from too much pot?" asked Jimbo.

"Yeah, that's right, too much of a good thing," Badger snickered. "He's ok now, he's resting."

"I didn't think it was possible." Oh, wait. Jimbo recalled a time when, on a hike with friends, they happened upon a group of *cairns,* stones mounded to serve as landmarks. They were so wasted they set about rearranging and combining the rocks until they had obliterated all trace of the original placements. It was only hours later, when some cheesed-off rancher caught up with them, that they discovered they'd dismantled the border between public hiking and a private hunting preserve.

"Depends on the individual," Badger said coldly, "dosage varies. Some people, on a first trip or not used to heavy THC, get too hung up in the whole deal."

"What's an actual OD?" asked Ira.

Badger pursed his lips in thought. "Oh, a typical pot overdose might consist of paranoia, catatonic trance, depression, babbling—did I mention paranoia?"

"But it can't kill ya?" Jimbo wondered.

Beddiker lowered his olive-colored eyelids sending his brows into a scramble. "Hell, anything can kill ya. But it ain't likely you could die flat out from pot; there are only so many pot receptors in the brain."

"What if you smoked several pounds at a time?" Jimbo speculated.

"Wow, that would be somethin'!" exclaimed Sutter.

"That's not physically possible," Ira countered.

"You don't get it," Badger remonstrated, "a dose is a dose. Once you've reached the threshold level of pot intoxication, you're stoned. You can't get any higher. Excess THC isn't stored, it's flushed, quickly. More smokin' ain't worth the tokin'."

"But you can smoke to get back to the threshold when you lose it?" Ira inquired.

"Sure," Badger agreed. "You can get stoned several times a day, you can practically stay stoned, but you can't pile on the fuel to escape earth gravity."

"Ya wanna bet?" smirked Jake.

"So I don't have to worry about dying just because I smoke pot?" asked Jimbo, concerned.

"Oh yeah," Badge digressed, "you always gotta worry about dying. But pot ain't gonna kill you unless you smoke it while searching for a propane leak."

"Hey, Badge, will Chris still get his $2?" asked Tony.

"Yeah, it's a done deal, wasn't his fault," answered Badger.

"Ooooooo-ooo...Badge," Jake wailed, "I'm not feeling so hot, maybe I better... Hey, wouldja mean, it wasn't his fault? What happened?"

"Don't worry 'bout it wouldja? We're 20 minutes behind already, nuth'n serious...now, let's go," urged Badger.

"973!" shouted Jake as Badger restarted the machine.

"Aw, c'mon..." moaned Badger. He tried again.

"8461!" called Sutter.

"You know, you're supposed to do this quietly," pleaded Badger. He squeezed the remote.

"52984," Thaddeus whispered.

"This is a frigg'n zoo and it's only the first frigg'n hour. I'm gonna be a friggi'n mess. Now, shut up you goddamned pot heads so we can get this frigg'n thing over with!"

"We want to hear what happened to Chris," Jake said frankly.

"Yeah," asked Sutter, "what's the story, man?"

"He OD'd, ok? Berge will tell you what happened."

"Booger!?" barked Jake.

Badger scanned the group. "Berge!" he commanded.

Bergman sighed involuntarily. "Well," he danced.

"C'mon!"

"Ok, ok," Bergman paused, wishing to be just as honest as he needed to be, "you know, I was pissed that no one got me up to do the pot thing together like we ah, all promised, so I bent his mind some; Chris, that is. I didn't mean any harm but-t-t, well, I think he was borderline to begin with."

"What the hell is that supposed to mean?" asked Jake. "What in the hell did you do to him?"

"Acting impulsively of course, I pretended to be one of the staff, you know, a scientist instead of one of you clowns."

"'Us clowns?'" said Jake heatedly. "Is that why you're writin' shit down all the time?"

"Those are letters, it has nothing to do with you," said Bergman. "The reference is not meant to offend..."

"Yeah? Well, I'm offended. I think you got a lotta fuckin' nerve to jack somebody's head around like that," said Jake angrily.

"I'm sorry, I'm not happy about what I did. I apologized to Chris..."

"You did?"

"Yeah. It was a joke gone bad. Shit happens."

"Yeah, you would know."

"I'm pretty sorry about the whole thing, really."

"So you're one of us?" sneered Jake.

Bergman nodded.

"That's the worst fuck'n news I've had all day," Jake declared.

"Crap. I knew this would happen," Badger revealed, "this shit's too powerful for your little minds. An overdose was inevitable with this much THC. This is the best pot science can supply. We got one OD already. Now, you wanna go bonkers too? Calm down. Give yourself time to get used to it, Jeez."

Badger shook his head at Minter as he arrived. "Frisky, huh?" asked Minter.

"You gotta git a hit 'a this shit," whispered Badger in passing.

Minter looked over group, trying to shape things so they wouldn't get bored. After the Numbers Test, he outlined today's Moral Ways circumstances: In a moment of weakness, you sold a friend some marijuana which you knew to be worthless. It wasn't a large transaction but you could use the money to finance a trip to Washington, D. C. in order to attend a peace rally. What would you do if the friend smoked the dope, then called wanting his money back because it was no good?

"Answer the following questions:

1. Return the money? a) would; b) would not; 2. Justify your response (chose one): a) friend has a definite right to money; b) friend has some right; c) friend has no right to refund."

"This is a scream," Shep enthused. "Am I ripped, or what!"

"Yeah," groaned Jimbo, "I haven't been this stoned since ah, since ah, since ah..."

"Sinsemilla," Ron interjected.

"Wow, that's a long time," laughed Tony.

* * * *

Two hours after ingesting the drug a lassitude took over B-ward allowing Minter to make notes: "Thaddeus appears isolated, non-communicative; Bergman upset, refusing to smoke until Chris, who remains absent, rejoins Group; Sutter continues a kind of body-rocking, while laughing to himself; Jake pounds the clicker methodically, he is in a world of his own; Ira appears in a trance, except for incessant itching; Ron draws elaborate sci-fi designs; Wayne sits on the edge of Group, shaking his head; Tony cannot sit still, he's driving people crazy with his abrupt motions; Jimbo requests something to read."

* * * *

"I'd give him," Thaddeus drawled.

"You'd give him what?" asked Minter after a lengthy silence.

"Hunh?" wondered Thaddeus, "Oh, yeah... I'd give him... Shit."

"You'd give him shit?" asked Jake.

"That's one thing he probably doesn't need," Shep laughed.

"Stop!" screamed Thad, "you're... I—" he gagged, wracked by mirthy tremors.

"I'd give him, " Jimbo began.

"More shit," broke in Tony.

"Stop it," gasped Thaddeus, "you're kill'n me, I can't breathe!" Swinging his large arms, Thaddeus struggled for air, his body spazzing in helpless laughter.

"You know, I didn't think it was all that funny," said Minter soberly.

Thaddeus shook until his words rattled, "It-'s-s-s not what-t they said-d, it-'s-s how they said-d-d it."

* * * *

Tony noticed that Minter was following him. Whenever Tony traveled from the day room, to the hall, the hall to his room, Minter wasn't long out of sight. Everyone was a little paranoid with this heavy of pot, and, of course, there'd been that deal earlier... But the feeling of being gumshoed began to wear on Tony. He laid a snare. This time, when Minter caught up with him, Tony sprang up into his face: "Haaahhaa!" he shouted.

Minter staggered backwards. "Wha in the hell?!" Minter called out.

"Hey, you were followin' me, man," Tony explained.

"Yes, yes I have," Minter acknowledged, "as I tried to tell you, as long as you've got a joint I have to follow, record how much you smoke, and then recover what's left so it can be measured, *que pasa*?

Tony began to see. "Ok, man, I'm sorry. Here, you can have the joint," Tony offered. He fumbled through his pockets at least twice before turning to Minter. "Hey man, I'm really sorry, but I don't know what I did with it?" he apologized.

Minter took a step toward Tony and grabbed his wrist, turning his palm upright. "It's in your hand, bozo," he smiled.

Tony looked at the glowing ember-tipped joint, marveling. He saw a hundred campfires. "Why do you think it was trying to hide?" he asked.

"There should be a merit badge for putting up with you characters," Minter confided. Tony stared at him.

"You look like somebody," Tony said sincerely.

"If I do, it's because I am," Minter nodded.

"No, no, I really mean it," Tony insisted.

"I'm sure you do," Minter smiled.

"You really do look like someone old, but famous. That's it, you look like Buffalo Bill," Tony alleged.

"Who, oh, excuse me, whom?" joked Minter.

"Not Buffalo Bill. Custer, George Armstrong Custer, the Battle of the Little Big Horn," said Tony triumphantly.

"No, not me, never been to the Little Big Horn, though they tell me it's nice. Never been scalped either, though I gotta figure that to be less nice." Minter stroked his shoulder-length hair.

"You look just like him, you really do," Tony persisted.

"I think he'd be about 132 years old right now, if he survived his own massacre, evidence of which suggests otherwise," Minter retorted.

"Hey, man, you're Custer," Duquesne declared.

"You've seen him, a friend of yours?" quizzed Minter/Custer.

"You need to get stoned," said Tony, forcing the tiny remnant of the pot cigarette into a tube.

"I think I'll wait for the book, if you don't mind,"said Minter/Custer. Beside him, Tony gagged.

# 7

## *Anomalies*

Since his return—'I was never really gone,' Chris insisted—he saw things differently. He felt people were counting on him to be more assertive, more 'into it.' But it seemed like such a joke after smoking this way out weed—and these damned games! This one threatened to overwhelm the 'green' time (stoned), with the 'mean' time (testing). "Will you go over it once more?" he procrastinated.

"Look, I'm goin' to be sensitive here because..." explained the Badger. "But if you don't get this... I mean we're talkin' Elly Mental here."

"Please, just go over it one more time, for me?" Chris wheedled. "There are 10 players, but only nine spoons?"

Badger grinned.

"But that means someone doesn't get a spoon!" Chris protested.

"You got it, Sherlock," Badger replied.

"Ok, ok," Chris said uneasily, "it's kind of a mad scramble, isn't it?"

"Shocking," put in Thaddeus.

"Force equals acceleration," added Shep.

"I understand that now I think. But where do the cards come in?" Chris couldn't remember actually playing cards. The whole notion of whittling away the day over these strange magical things was quite vague. No thanks, Chris wanted only one mania, and he was afraid he'd found it.

"Is that right, Badge, bare knuckles?" asked Jake.

"There's never any shortage of warriors," offered Bergman. "Apparently, brute force maintains its appeal to a certain segment of the population."

"Athens, 360 BC," interjected Shep.

"God, I didn't know you were still alive," joked Tony.

"Wouldn't the Greeks just steal the spoons?" inserted Jake.

"And would they be wearing clothes?" asked Sutter.

"Anyway," Bergman continued, "before we commit to battle, can you tell us the aim of this conflict?"

"There ain't none," Badger replied. "It's just a test-to—"

"Mony," Tony interrupted.

"No one tests me mow-knee—nor me testicle—unless I let her," winked Jake.

"To cull the herd, is my guess," put in Shep.

"...To test whether certain changes may occur over prolonged drug use," proclaimed Badger above the din.

"By 'prolonged use,'" repeated Shep, "would you be referring to a population of heavy users defined as 'at variance with society, unwilling to participate in conventional reward systems and operating below their intellectual capability'?"

Badger paused. "It's a simple game, really," he promised, "you're dealt four cards. The idea is to get four of a kind by passing one card at a time to your left. Whoever gets four of a kind, tries to take a spoon."

"Fine, I got that but what I don't get is why?"

"'Why' is irrelevant!" shouted the Badge. "It's a stupid ass card game! Who cares? What's important is getting that first goddamned spoon because then everyone else can take one too."

"But there aren't enough!" pleaded Chris.

"Right, you've got to be faster than goose shit."

"What if you don't get one?" Chris persisted.

"You're declared a pacifist and shot!" Badge thundered.

"Mr. Badger, I put it to you again, what is this test testing? Are our reactions to be examined for your amusement only? If so, I must take strong exception," intoned Bergman.

"Yeah, me too. Whatever he said," added Jimbo.

Badger snorted. "Are you going to talk like that all the time now?" He carried his attention to the others; "Hey, I sympathize with you guys, floating along in your super-groovy world. I would too, if work wasn't needed any more, if planes flew themselves."

"Planes can fly themselves," cackled Shep. "Auto-pilots."

"But they can't land," Badger answered.

"Yes, actually, they can do that too. Drones land themselves," Shep added.

"Well, isn't that a kick in the head," laughed Minter.

"Hey, it is 1972," Tony popped up.

"Super groovy," replied Jimbo.

Badger had enough. "I will kill the next person who talks!" he screamed. "It's time to get on with the goddamned game!"

Chris watched the others tense as the hand was dealt. Cards sometimes drifted, sometimes jumped from player to player. Chris stared at his draw: a deuce, a nine and two queens. Thad discarded and someone screamed, the table exploding into darting fingers. Next to him, Jake and Bergman smiled, spoons clenched in their hands. But Tony and Ron were locked, cursing and spitting, in a desperate tousle, their fists struggling to gain control of the slender throat of a badly mangled spoon.

"Gimme that, you sonofabitch!" yelled Tony, pushing sumo-style into a stack of chairs which tottered and fell.

"Never!" said Ron tersely. He maneuvered among the chairs to bring his weight advantage into play.

"Five joints on Tony" said Jake.

"You're on, white power," laughed Thad, "my boy was a four-year varsity wrestler in Buffalo, New York."

"But mine has herbal power," concluded Jake. "Hell, my guy is all herbs."

At that moment, Ron adroitly fell on a pressure point in Tony's arm and he surrendered the spoon as if paralyzed.

"Ok, make that one joint on Tony," Jake conceded.

"What the hell did you do to me, man?!" Tony bellowed. Fire burned just below his elbow and only slowly did sensation return to his fingers.

"You mean, what the hell did you do to me?" Ron questioned, as a trickle of blood leaked from his wrist. "God! You slobbering animal bastard you. You bit me, you goddamned fiend, you!"

"Look!" said Bergman, "he's transforming; he's going over!"

"Goddamn, you're right!" squealed Jimbo as Tony, stooped and growling, snapped at them. "He's crossed over," Jimbo stared amazed, "he's all animal now. Of course, he didn't have far to go."

"Is this what you're after doggie?" asked Chris, casually lifting the remaining spoon from the table.

Tony eyed him, panting. "RRRuurrffffff! Rugggfffff!" he threw himself across the table at the startled Chris. The two landed on the floor, and in an instant the spoon rose, trophy-like, in Tony's small yellow teeth.

"Is that it? All the spoons in?" yawned Badger. "Ok, who got the first spoon, who didn't get one and how many cards are left in the deck? Quickly, children."

"White Power," Thaddeus addressed Jake, "you be deliver'n my five joints to the infirmary." Thaddeus contracted, stung by the sound of metal on metal. 'I jus' might be out of fluid' he thought. "Waiter," he shouted unsteadily, "bring me a beer!"

"Oh, no, not you again," rebuked the Badger, "I didn't think you had any more brain to scramble."

"Hey man, don't be talkin' that way to your employer. You jus' killed your tip," laughed Thaddeus. "Now, hurry on and get me a dobbie, or I be talkin' to the overseer."

"Oh, Jeeez!" Badger exclaimed; he crossed to the examining room where the dope was 'hidden' in a 300-pound floor safe. Crouching before it, he struggled to recall the combination. He began his fourth attempt when Wayne spoke: "Counterclockwise a complete revolution past 15, before hitting 32."

"Huhnh!? Wha' the—"

"Time for my vitals."

"Oh shit," Badger moaned. "Look, skip the vitals. We'll average; just git."

"Remember, counterclockwise."

"Scram."

"Hey man, my pot, my pot," Thaddeus demanded upon finding Badger at the safe.

Opening the vault, Badger extracted a brown cigar box. From it, he pulled an envelope containing 10 clear plastic tubes slightly larger than a jumbo cigarette. Within each tube, a white worm of wonder held from its work by a green stopper.

Thaddeus watched in fascination—all this organization—if they legalized today, we'd have world peace tomorrow!

"Hey, what's—Yowie Zowie! Look a-a-a-a-a" stammered Jake.

"Wait—anybody else want one while I'm here?"

"Yeah, me," said Jake.

"Um-me," grunted Shep.

"How much is that-t-t?" asked Jake awestruck.

"You heard you got maxed out at 10 joints a day, right? So there's 10 times you guys times 20 days."

"2,000," said Shep.

"Wow," said Jake.

"Minus consumption," Badger corrected.

"Wha'dya do with the unsmoked stuff?" asked Jake.

"We're gonna dangle it in front of your faces as the door hits you in the ass."

"So much for gratitude," said Wayne.

"Yeah, well. Hey, what the hell are you doing in here? And the rest of ya. Git the hell out. Authorized Personnel Only!" hollered Badger.

As they crowded out, Jake cut Wayne off, "Gratitude? What does that mean?"

"He needed some help."

Jake's eyebrows gathered above his nose in a straight, prominent ridge. "Yeah? Help with what?"

Wayne raised his biosensors. Jake was so good at being who he was, he couldn't be a forgery. "Oh, with the combination," he replied.

Jake's mind raced: If they had enough for 10 j's a day? Well, how many does Birdbrain smoke? Or Chris? 1-2, if that. Right now, he only needed five. That means a surplus... Jake's pearly smile emerged. He draped his arm on Wayne's shoulder, "I feel we have something in common. What do you do?" he asked.

"I'm not employed, right now," Wayne answered.

"Well, what do you do when you are employed?" Jake continued.

"I design flying saucers," Wayne confided.

Jake pulled him down the hall. "Far out! That's exactly what I've always wanted to do! Tell me about it."

* * * *

Thaddeus took a long draw off what remained of the joint and exhaled, following the smoke from the tiny ash as it danced upward in sinuous, dreamy ripples. A heavy breath severed the delicate, sensual columns with the ends of the upper piece scrolled up like a blanket. But a very light breath, and the sooty formation only stumbled, pitching sideways into the most original features, daring, risky curves, and strange yet familiar shapes, as beautiful as they were brief.

'Air is life. Air touches all things, all things touch air. Men and objects outside them are not really divided,' pondered Thad during a bout of indivisibility. 'That is an illusion formed by our inadequate senses; all is bound together with tiny hands, unseen kisses.'

Thad knew he was stoned. He split in two, one portion acting out his life, the other caught in reflection; one doing, the other distant, watching. Thaddeus pictured drawing on his marijuana cigarette only after he had done so, found his head in his hands after a five-minute search, felt the vibrations of sound before the sound materialized. His mind probed deeper into the crannies of understanding. He willed, he focused: 'I am home to many dimensions; my thought is silk and my actions touch the world.'

The room spun and fell but Thad squeezed into a corner with visions of mountains carved from eternal snow. He felt caressed by his chair, felt it come to life. Far from an object of abuse, it was a creature of great sensitivity, heroically silent. We should apologize to our chairs for the treatment they receive from the assholes of the world.

He chuckled and it grew to a harsh, searing cough. He shook in pain, but his coughing laughter yawned and stretched its legs.

He noticed Ira beside him, inhaling his own joint. "Do a lotta reefer?" he asked reflexively.

Shep smiled. "This is heaven, man. Pot is so much better than booze. I like the mellower high, better on the takeoff and landing."

Marijuana was a leap into his softer side, the one less hassled by a world of urine-leaking alpha males on a territory-marking binge. Stoned, he understood the mysterious muted voices within, heard the colors of the chorus.

Marijuana lifted him like high-test coffee into a state of 'being on.' He energized, impatient to use the muscular alertness he'd plugged into. Racing through a cloud of nuclear material, he came out enriched, 'hot.' Yet, strangely, he was also calmer, less tense than his sober self. 'Power, and sometimes,' he broke up, 'control.'

"Oh god man," Thaddeus lamented, "I swear I get so horny when I'm stoned. Can't hardly think of nuth'n but sex."

"Sex," said Shep "dominates the organism to a degree that boggles the mind. Man's brilliance unhorsed by a finger-length wand of carnality. The irony of the Phallus: so powerful and yet so reviled, and ever more enjoyable because of it. It suggests a divinely-inspired sense of humor."

"It's all Greek to me," said Thad groggily.

"My problem is chocolate. I would give anything for a Hershey's bar with big, crunchy, salty almonds—and a Coke!—right now."

"Aww, don't do that to me," giggled Thaddeus, "my twin weaknesses—women and choc-o-lat."

* * * *

Nicholson recalled the passage: "Detectable psychoactive effects occur when the amount of the drug reaches threshold levels in the brain. The body processes THC—the psychoactive component of marijuana—through the lungs generally, as smoking is the typical ingestion route. Within 15–30 minutes of entering the bloodstream, marijuana smoke achieves maximum psychoactive stage. Only about 1% of the dose is delivered to the brain where it attaches to a specific set of receptors.

Remaining THC is distributed harmlessly throughout the body (reducing the amount available for binding with brain cells), until it is broken down through the process of biotransformation into simpler compounds which are then excreted via sweat, urine and feces. Some two hours after introduction, THC concentrations in the brain fall below a range of 2–25 nanograms (billionth of a gram) per milliliter (thousandth of a liter/quart), terminating psychoactive effects."

If, in order to create a greater splash than previous marijuana investigations, it might not be necessary to capture the genie *out of the bottle.*

Using a cigarette delivery system, the THC dosage could not be increased beyond the 'marijuana' threshold. So, reasoned Nicholson, the only way to boost the 'effects' of the drug into new research territory, was to exaggerate the conditions, or setting, in which the drug operated.

The idea was disarmingly simple: Most marijuana intoxication was by this time routinely understood; so too, were the effects of relatively long-term incarceration. Unfortunately, a good deal of the marijuana effects were canceled out in the deprivation of confinement. Faced with a rigorous schedule and loss of freedom, marijuana smokers seemed to restrict their intoxication.

To see what marijuana could do, would do in a *natural setting*, Nicholson would have to open the gates of the prison. Any clown with a lab coat could catalog the physiological effects of the drug. But to capture its essence, it would be necessary to free it from clinical boundaries.

There was an obvious risk to changing traditional research alignment. For one thing, it tossed out the window any hope of duplicating results. But the early data was so 'normal,' so not interesting, so predictable, that if anything new were to materialize, it would require a dramatic realignment of the research paradigm.

Some in the field had proposed such a departure in the case of drugs whose subjective value to the individual, is not easily captured by standard testing. But many opposed the idea as an attack upon Science itself, through its insistence on objective, repeatable, measurement. Scientists, it was said, could not abandon Science, even in the quest for truth.

Still, Nicholson toyed with the idea. Imagine one tiny experiment that could shed light on a key variant in the case of pot? We know there are many *perceptual* and *behavioral* changes that occur during marijuana intoxication. For instance, time expands. Everything happens in less time than one estimates; stoned drivers slow down so as to have additional time to maneuver safely. On many of these measures the stoned individual's state is altered though not so much as to endanger themselves or others.

But the key question for those who will make the decision whether marijuana would continue to be an outcast, is whether they feel a stoned individual will make a good citizen? Will they go to war for their country? Will they work hard and honestly? Will they raise good citizens? Will they go that extra mile to develop the care and concern that are essential to society?

Simple: Does it do harm to the user? Does the user do harm to others? Hard: Will it make them a better person? Worse? No affect?

To date, there existed a consensus among treatment professionals, that marijuana fostered estrangement from society and its goals. Its use, therefore, had to be discouraged, ethically. Nicholson felt that it was here, on the ethical issue of marijuana use, that his project could be most telling. As dangerous as it was to his career, he felt he had to undertake this risky assignment in order to pull Harvard to where it wanted to go.

Nicholson drew up a plan that would introduce certain 'anomalies' to the testing regime, anomalies that would be strictly forbidden in usual research procedures. The question now turned to how does the research subject react, and how much marijuana did he ingest while he made his decision? How does marijuana effect one's *ethical* decisions? is not a question that's been seriously asked and tested. Nicholson would ask it, Nicholson would answer it: Does marijuana promote *altruism:* engagement for the common good; or does it lead to hostility, opposition to the common good? Here at last, was the kind of research endeavor that one could sink their teeth into!

# 8

# *"I Just Wish..."*

Custer smiled, "It's a drug, Mr. 'no permanent address': 'psycho-active.' You know, mind altering?"

"C'mon," Jake drawled, "pot never killed anybody."

"I'll give you that. Animal studies show no toxicity at 100,000 times active dose. But somewhere, sometime, someone bought the farm thanks to Mary Jane."

"Big deal. You don't ban a medicine just because someone ODs."

"But marijuana isn't a medicine."

"Think again," argued Jake.

"Oh, so it's a medicine, now, too?

"You feel ok, and what harm does it do? It's not like it permanently fucks-up your brain?" asked Jake.

"There's a space/time distortion that some find pleasurable, others panic."

"Not many," Jake gushed.

"A small per cent, it's true."

"Less than a percent," Jake insisted, "and they're not paranoid because of marijuana, but because of 'the drug.' They're terrified they're gonna be busted."

"If you're looking for permanent mental impairment, dial psychological dependence among heavy users."

"But they're not criminals or psychos."

"So you're arguing that this side of the border with Homicide, there's a lot of room for folks who just want to be high as a kite all day long?"

"Dude, I'm not going to make you smoke it, if you don't want to," Jake laughed.

"Some report an increase in aggressive, violent behavior. Others, severe or permanent loss of psycho-motor control."

"C'mon Columbus, get to the point!"

"Very heavy use—several times a day—produces strong psychological dependence."

"So what are we talking here: D.T.'s, heroin withdrawal, the bends? Will my kind kill for reefer, doc?"

"Well," admitted Custer, "more likely, you'd suffer restlessness and insomnia, just like quitting cigarettes."

"So, if pot doesn't hurt me, and I keep some nearby for withdrawal, then I'm in the clear, right?"

Minter relented. "It's a funny drug. It doesn't leave traces in the blood like cocaine, alcohol, or heroin, and it isn't really observable that someone is marijuana intoxicated.

"We check pulse rate, time estimation, short-term memory and shooting gallery skill plus the ability to improve with practice and they're all unaffected! But you tell us you're as high as you've ever been? I don't get it."

"I tell you what," Jake offered, "you toke?" he asked.

"I- ah, what? Partake?" Custer demurred.

"That's ok, man," responded Jake. "Sometimes?" Jake drew a joint from his pocket and handed it to Minter.

Minter took the joint and sniffed it. Their grass was grown on a well-fertilized plot in tropical Mississippi, and was marked by a penetrating, resinous odor. "I believe this is one of ours?"

"I'm giving it to you," said Jake.

"Yeah, well, thanks a lot," replied Minter. "But how did

you get it?"

Jake stared into space. "Good question."

Badger entered, batting the thick pungent cloud of smoke Jake created. "Do you want any more of that?" he asked, pointing to the spiral of ash on Jake's joint.

Jake didn't hear the question clearly as various melodies played though his head in a kaleidoscope of enriched sound. While he followed the music, a sensation in his hand flowered: "Wheee-su!" he whistled, flicking away the roach that melted thumb and forefinger, "I'm zonked!"

Badger seized the moment, swabbing Jake's arm with alcohol. The rapid cooling hit like a summer squall. The needle approached. "You gotta do that?" Jake stiffened.

"Well...yeah, I gotta do it," Badger replied, jamming the thin rod into Jake's arm.

"Bummer!" said Jake loudly as the needle pierced his skin. Watching the ampoule fill with his blood, Jake became talkative: "So you're taking blood how often now? Every two–three hours? Or, is it more oftener?"

"'Vonce a night—a day, yess, vonce a day," replied Badger, withdrawing the syringe and applying a swab to Jake's arm. "T'anks for za blo-o-od."

"You know, doc, just between you, me and Herby, that's the third time today you've sucked my blood, hell, I'm damn near anemic thanks to you."

Beddiker felt a stab of conscience: The Experimental Protocols required blood taking, regardless of the 'normal' testing cycle, if subject ingested the equivalent of one 100 mm joint at one sitting. Why more blood samples? Would they have anything new to add? "I'm just a small cog in the wheel," said Badger.

"And how did Chris do?" Jake exclaimed.

"Fainted."

"See. That's what I wuz say'n for crissakes. Ya take a guy like this, and ya jus' yank his chain. I mean what Berg-brain did to him and they go bananas. It's not the drug, it's the god-damned needle!"

"Who?"

"My point is, ya got all these people locked into your dead-end jobs and you won't even give them the right to close their windows? Why the big deal about what a person does in the privacy of their own home as long as they're not hurt'n anybody. Why do you have to stick them with the needle?"

"In the priv-a-cee of their own homes, women rule and men become children," dropped in Shep. He'd wandered by, warmed by the strangled rhythms issuing from the human voice at 1 am.

"Oh, another marijuana Ph.D.—Pot head Defender," observed Badger.

"If I was as anal about 'total control' as you are," Shep challenged, "I wouldn't do drugs either. But if I can't chose how I want to live, in the absence of any danger to others, I'm being coerced. And not by the substance some are trying to control, but by the effort at control itself!" Shep yelled in a voice from a tiny, hairy dog.

"You don't notice changes?" Badger quizzed.

"Changes? Why, yes. It's obvious our constitutional protections have eroded in the face of a right-wing attack!"

"Is that what you think?"

"Exactly what I think. You've taken a harmless plant and demonized it in order to terrorize our own population into handing over more authority to conservative zealots," Shep wheezed.

"And you've got to have it or you can't be sharp and detached?"

"You know, you're right," replied Shep thoughtfully. "I guess I am addicted. But my stoned self doesn't trust my sober self. My stoned self says, 'You know, you're a lucky guy. It could be meth.'"

* * * *

Wick listened in disbelief. Nicholson planned to abort the whole experiment in just the second week! Nicholson's ambition no longer passed for news. But til now, he'd been judged to be sober. Wick wondered if he might be dreaming.

"Jon, we're going nowhere with the old data," he thought Nicholson said. "We are caught in a paradigm shift: the old paradigm needs rapid evolution toward a new paradigm."

Wick thought Harold's words might be a product of his dream imagination: Nicholson, searching for the means to his own greatness, began to get off on big, pot-like ideas, until he was hooked. Now an addict to the prospect of glory, Nicholson marched on in a trance. Wick mulled over his responsibility to turn a deranged Nicholson over to authorities?

"Jon, I insist we adopt Article A of Planned Protocol Revisions, 1971," Nicholson bellowed. If I remember correctly, Wick thought, that cancels all the others. Only a fraction of the existing tests would be maintained at a level guaranteeing their accuracy.

"Jon," Nicholson stormed, "we don't want to duplicate the results of 1944!!"

"But if we do repeat the results, how much clearer could indications be?" he heard himself call out.

Nicholson ignored him. "Jon?" he hollered, "we have to

take a radical approach, It's not about what we knew then, but what we can do now."

"I don't follow you," Wick screamed as if a hurricane stood between them.

"Jon, Jon, focus on now," he lectured. "It's a simple matter of altering your ethical code to prevent these ethno-botanists from taking over the field! We're going to win this thing, we're not going to let Psychology, or Harvard, down." Harold Nicholson bent over him, gave him the full personal treatment, the winning style and the convincing handshake. He signed something. He remembered a cold white face mumbling, "Uncle Sam needs you!"

* * * *

Ron Green, 27, two-years Biological Sciences, courtesy of Arizona State; two years biological extermination courtesy of the U.S. Army, stewed in a plastic cocoon and willed a new world. Lurching from the wreck room, he ventured onto a windy, tumultuous sea. He watched as icy drafts constructed sleek towers of eons-old air reaching toward a gray ceiling run through with luminescent flashes.

When it wanted, the Atlantic could put on quite a show. Using this discovery to keep his mood aloft, he struggled to put aside anxieties, and seek a fragile joy. The mammoth sea swells off the North Atlantic, with wave after giant wave pounding the shore into colorful vapor, helped. The simple enormity of the ocean commanded respect, but the crisis of survival in its depths left him exhausted.

He always wanted to explore the harsh truth of life in the sea from the slug to the shark, with knowledge of its awesome secrets flickering slowly in his mind until it sparked into brilliant flame.

But first the hard academic work, large amounts of math and biology until he panicked. Leaving his past life like socks behind him, he struck out to the see the world. Europe turned out to be too much like the US; Chicago, Las Vegas, Philadelphia —they were interchangeable. He retreated to Mexico, where the dollar was still appreciated. But even in Mexico, you need income. He went back to the States so he could work to free himself to live the way he wanted.

Sometimes when stoned, euphoria gave way to paranoia—the feeling of wasting time. But he learned to handle differences, until he could 'maintain' and appear sober by 'floating' and reaching deep for the inner consistency which is self.

Ron didn't want to get too stoned, a 'freak-out' where he was just too frazzled to concentrate. He aimed to be just loaded enough to drowsily absorb music, feel-good vibes and the temporary elimination of crushing boredom. This was the simple plan.

A lightness stole through his limbs, burning bright holes in the stress that often enveloped him. He rejoiced in that familiar contradiction: excited, yet cool, composed.

Ron got a kick out of this weird emotional deal with pot. At first, it feels like you were really getting off, going some place foreign and new, thanks to the weed. But it isn't real. Stoned, you don't do anything different, you just feel differently doing it. Nothing on the outside changes; it's all on the inside. Being stoned, you seem always to be listening for that missing voice, forever on the verge of some terrific, unambiguous conviction. You sense the arrival of great knowledge right around the corner—but the message of pot is that there is none; there's no horde of revealed truth, no insight beyond 'a peaceful, easy feel'n...'

He knew there was an impression among non-tokers that a pothead is unwilling to do anything unless stoned, and then, when stoned, is unwilling to do anything.

* * * *

If you were to ask me, thought Wayne, while manning the point, 'I'd have to tell you that something is mighty suspicious around here...' For one thing, it was supposed to be a 'marijuana' experiment, yeah? Yet, you don't have to smoke it if you don't want to. 'Want to?' In a marijuana experiment?! How clever is that? He'd obviously stumbled into a top-secret Ghost Army Op. here in Boston, the Commie heart of America. There existed a tiny few he could trust with this information; it would be up to him to figure out what the Army's Ghost Division really wanted: were they rehearsing a cover-up? Or were they asking these stoned imbeciles to participate in the cover-up of the rehearsal of a planned cover-up?

# 9

## *Assassins Round Table*

Custer controlled 'Round Table 2,' another Group meeting, forcefully, aiming his questions to those that looked the most stoned. "Shep, what does pot intoxication do for you?" Shep opened his mouth to answer when Badger added, "Be specific."

"First of all, weed makes me more tolerant of people in general," he said, smiling toward the Badge. "Normally, I'm skeptical of the human species, believing we break down completely around 50,000 miles." He spoke easily, confident that a continuous stream of luxuriant coherence would flow like light.

"Reefer makes you feel good about yourself, so you're disposed to feel good about others. I call it, the 'Reciprocity Principle.'"

"The Golden Rule, huh?" Custer interjected. "Everyone agree? Anyone disagree?" he laughed. "You, Reese?"

"Mellow."

"Explain that," Custer zeroed in.

"You're excited, you know, kinda like you're on a fourth-floor balcony. The 'view' from pot is 40' above normal."

"Riding the ol' endorphin train, eh?" smiled Custer. "Anybody else wanna talk about their high? You?" he asked, pointing to Jake.

"Yeah, wella. It's high all right." The others laughed. "Higher than shit!" More giggles.

"It's high and outside," broke in Tony.

"It's 'O-Hi-O," Thad went on.

"It's 'Hi and Good-bye'," said Ira.

"How 'bout you, what's your story?" Custer asked Ron. "Are you stoned?"

Ron yawned, "Huh?" The room roared.

"How 'bout you, how much have you had, one, two joints?" said Custer, switching his inquiry to Thaddeus.

Thad accepted the attention solemnly, then a smile slowly unfurled across his broad, expressive face, "Damn!"

"It's simple. People want to have a good time," said Tony.

"Certainly less obnoxious than it's opposite," Bergman cited.

"Drugs are a rite of passage, they're a pathway into the brain, a window to another universe," hollered Shep.

"And their importance might be crazily exaggerated by susceptible people," Bergman qualified.

"Drugs," explained Shep, "are the means of our existence!"

"Funny to hear you say that," Chris deadpanned.

"It's true!" shouted Jimbo, "the world is ruled by drugs, good drugs and bad drugs, drugs that lead to peace and understanding, and others that lead to death."

"Ooo, going deep, are we?" exclaimed Bergman.

"It's self-evident," said Shep dismissively, "You got tension? Bingo—mama's little helper, Valium. Overeat? Tums. Hangover? Bayer. Heavy? Dexedrine. Hungry? Fritos."

"Wanna party?" broke in Jake, "Budweiser."

"Lonely? ABC Sports," spouted Jimbo.

"Taking drugs is official policy," continued Shep. "Self-medication is the rule, not the exception."

"Then why is marijuana ill-eagle?" asked Chris.

"Because western society has accepted alcohol as its signature recreational drug," answered Shep, "it must reject other, similar drugs to demonstrate that tolerance is not license."

"That's what you call 'tolerance?'" mimed Thad.

Bergman interjected, "If I catch your drift, you're saying a drug which kills 400,000 a year in the U.S., can out-compete another drug that kills no one?"

"Precisely. The fear of promiscuous drug use—a drug perceived as a threat to the status quo—is stronger than any desire to judge competing claims except in experiments like this one."

"But all sort of similar drugs are being introduced by the pharmaceutical industry all the time," exclaimed Jimbo.

"Not entirely similar—mood altering versus psychoactive—we'll lighten the mood, but not too much," conceded Ira. "The pharmaceutical industry is constantly pressuring the Food and Drug Administration to set up trials to 'ok' its patents. Well, you can't 'patent' pot so why push for its acceptance; it's just another competitor."

"Why don't we just launch a letter-writing campaign until Congress passes a law saying that since it's no more dangerous than alcohol, it can be sold like booze?" asked Tony.

"Such naivete," Shep laughed smugly. "Pot smokers aren't going to come out of the weeds and admit they use an illegal substance. They won't go to party caucuses and put the issue into play. Where's the payoff to a politician to stick his neck out on this one—for the sake of 'fairness'? You gotta be kiddin'.

"Government protects the property of the elite, anti-marijuana laws protect their authority," expressed Shep.

"Excuse me, your genius-ness-ness, what's your plan?" yawned Jake.

"Think for a moment: what's the world's largest religion?"

"Catholicism," answered Jimbo.

"Why do you say that?" Shep countered.

"Cause I just heard it last week in Church," Jimbo explained.

"Another distortion," Shep commented.

"Islam," said Bergman.

"Yes," Shep admitted. "And why are those billion Muslims different than Catholics?" he asked.

"They don't believe Christ is a God," Jimbo supplied.

Shep's shoulders sagged. "That's a bit too obvious," he instructed.

"They can't drink alcohol," Chris ventured.

"Indubitably!" Shep's eyes lit up. "But," he gleamed, "the prophet never condemned ganja."

"Excuse, me your most highness," squeezed Jake, "I don't get it. Muslims can't drink; Catholics can't smoke."

"Or masturbate," put in Ron.

"Can't' masturbate?" laughed Thaddeus. "Boy, that's some religion."

"Wait a second, w-a-i-t a second!" Sutter jumped in, "you're going to push pot on a bunch of drunken bigots, and alcohol on a swarm of religious zealots—"

"Exactly," said Ira as he feverishly scratched. "It's brilliant. Don't you see? The distilleries come up with this new hootch which is part alcohol, part THC! They sell it as a new blend '*derived from cannabis.*' License it as liquor in the U.S., as 'food' in the East."

"Where's Wayne, goddammit?!" yelled Tony.

"I'm keeping an eye on things," said Wayne, appearing silently.

"My man, you gotta be riding that perimeter, or we gonna get some strange frick'n ideas in here!" shouted Jake.

"Did he, or did he not, talk about chuggn' THC like it was Everclear?" asked Thaddeus, gagging.

"I've got a deal—just for you," gushed Ira. "We'll market the THC product with a psychoactive ingredient at 2.5–3.5%. Same as beer!"

"He is smart," sighed Green.

"Smarter than the average bear," grinned Chris.

"Your Gu-ru-some-ness," asked Sutter, "why don't you get into politics and get this done? Your Godfather wishes it."

"I considered a political career. I've got the fire in the belly, the IQ. The National Organization for Reform of Marijuana Laws would supply the money… Of course, I'd have to sharpen my people skills a bit."

"Is it just me, or is any one else troubled by your use of 'sharpen' and 'people'?" Jake wondered aloud.

"And I explored other issues besides legalization," Ira argued. "Alas, that's when I discovered the common man and I could not abide the same rate of evolution."

"So you took yourself deep because you weren't the best standard-bearer for the 'What do we want? POT! When do we want it? NOW!' crowd?"

"Approximately."

"You too busy smo-kin' weed, smo-kin' weed, smokin' weed," Thad whistled.

"Who gives up their whole life for a goddamned plant?!"

"So instead of the politics of marijuana, what did you go into?"

Ira coughed, "Pornography."

Chris cleared his throat.

"Not as a performer, I'm guessing," Bergman insinuated.

Thad broke from his too-small desk as it ever so gradually

increased its constriction to the point where if he didn't run, he'd be dead. He made his way to the infirmary with a sketchy idea of striking up a conversation, snoopin'to see if Melody were working. He thoughtfully retied his robe.

Despite his care, Melody seemed wary. Thad noticed the maneuvering and snickered. "Yes?" she asked.

"You remind me of my exy," Thad reflected.

"Oh, how nice!" she mocked.

"No, no," he giggled, "you're taking it the wrong way."

"Well, ex-cuse me!" Normally, Melody found herself at the mercy of these dreamy stoners. "Tell me," she asked, "just what do 'moi' and the 'ex' have in common?"

Thaddeus laughed even more, "Well," he mused, "you're both beautiful. Thaddeus never has anything but the best."

Melody allowed herself a smile, "Yeah, and how am I unlike your ex-wife?"

"She wanted control; she had to be on top. You're not like that," he said, staring into her eyes.

Melody bit her lip, buying time. He was too heavy and too cocky. "You're right," she said crisply. She found herself entranced by the sinuous movements of Thad's hands, which, despite their size, displayed an extraordinary flexibility almost amounting to fluidity. "I don't want control. I demand it!"

"You, on the otha hand," Thad continued. "Hunh!" He slumped over in violent laughter, "You kill me!" he screamed.

"Think'n about it," she replied.

"Oooo-oo," Thad chirped scuttling out the door.

* * * *

Jonathan Wick went to great lengths to maintain a professional distance between himself and the subjects of the current drug research. Physical separation not only assisted this design, it suited him personally. After 10 consecutive years of college he was about to receive his doctorate in a field rife with obscure historical fact, lurid biographical detail, and compulsive searches for great, transforming events.

Studying Psychology, it was hard not to make the discipline itself the focus of study, carving out a rich career for oneself without ever venturing from the encyclopedic reach of the Subject. Actual research, with real, live people, often mentioned, appeared troublesome in the details. But given Nicholson's strange directive calling for 'interactive association,' Jonathan was oddly excited, the kind of guilty rush felt when the UPS truck pulls up.

It had been determined that the subjects were to be handled 'proactively' in a series of Group encounters of a deliberately provocative nature, in order to raise the pressure on the smokers who would then be scored on their leadership, communication, partnering, sociability, etc. The aim was to separate the leaders from the would-be leaders, the tactics they used—and how much marijuana they consumed. A test of stoner leadership essentially.

Today's topic, 'The Assassins of Hasan-i-sabah, The Link Between Marijuana and Violence,' had been suggested by Nicholson himself.

"Ok, settle up youse guys," Badger mugged, "today we explore the strange case of Hasan-i-sabah, the marijuana drug lord who made a career of kick-ass kif and clever killings. The words 'hashish' and 'assassin' come from this dude.

"We want your, ah, opinion, on what you think of the link between, ah, weed and this cold-blooded murderer," finished Badger.

"Hey, tell us more, 'tell the people what she wore?'" Tony

giggled.

"Tony?" Jake asked, "as a native Californian, no more beach songs unless by the Beach Boys."

"The point," said Badger loudly, "is this dude Hasan gets his thug gang hopped up on a really pure form of marijuana man, and they dream a sort of perfect existence on the drug man, so to feed their addiction, these 11th century camel-mounted killers plundered modern day Iraq from Baghdad to Basra.

"Now, the question is-"

"The question really is," broke in Ira, "you haven't established any link between marijuana and murder. All you've got is hearsay—1,000-year-old hearsay."

"We have it on pretty good authority, really—Marco Polo," put in Wick.

"Marco Polo?!" shouted Ira excitedly, "he was a goddamned fraud! Half of what he claimed is made up by his own admission."

"Well," Wick temporized, "Marco Polo was one of the most successful travel writers of all time."

"That's my point," Ira said vehemently.

"Anyway, the Marco Polo version says Hasan Sabbah was an Iraqi warlord who drugged his soldiers into kidnapping and murder in a kind of Paradise for Profit scheme.

"Another version says al-Hasan, a Sunni Muslim, was a general in the armies of Islam during the Christian Crusades. He developed a strategy of targeting certain leaders of the invading infidels, and eliminating them. The soldiers who carried out his orders weren't stoned zombies, they were paid pros. Hasan paid them in heavy-duty marijuana—that would be *cannabis indica*—because it was so desirable, it was as good as money."

"Let me get this straight," broke in Tony, "this dude invent-ted primo smokage, and offed his enemies with ninja killers?"

"It's possible," said Wick.

"Cool," replied Tony.

"What do the rest of you think?" asked Wick.

"Speaking for the 'rest of us,'" said Shep, "this is meaningless claptrap. What's the sense in arguing a non-event. It's legend."

"But Hasan must have existed or else why are 'assassin' and 'hashish' linked to him? If it's false, why is it false?" asked Bergman.

"Why does it matter? It's false. It's not a question of how false," said Shep.

"Did Marco Polo exist?" Jimbo questioned, "if he did, maybe Hasan too, is real?"

"Polo did visit Iraq as a diplomat for Kublai Khan around 1,300," claimed Wick.

"Hasan was earlier, wasn't he?" asked Bergman.

"A problem faced by many historians, including Homer, and the writers of the Christian gospel. It's 100 years after the event, that's not reportage!" Shep hollered. "If you don't know which version is true, they're equally untrustworthy."

"That doesn't follow," Bergman argued, "both stories put Hasan high on the food chain; for most of our history there's an accurate record if you're willing to look for it."

"Right, his name is associated with drugs and violence, but there is no proof he merged marijuana and murder. It's a fairy tale. It didn't happen. But, yes, it could have. Someday pigs will fly powered by pure ethanol; what difference does it make whether Jack hit the beanstalk with his ax three times or five?"

"Right. It still fell down on the gingerbread kids who were sleeping with grandmother in the wolves' castle," said Ron.

"Ok," said Jake rising, "court adjourned. Everyone must leave; further discussion prohibited by order of sunlight and fresh air."

"I think there are a few more issues here, people," Bergman joshed.

"That's it, Berge!" cried Jake. He pointed to Sutter. "Forcible removal." Jake and Sutter began to prod Bergman toward the door.

"I must protest," Bergman laughed nervously.

"Now!" Jake shouted. Bergman relaxed into the arms of Jake and Sutter who carried him out the door into the hall and promptly dropped him. "First sun in a week and we're stuck with Socrates," said Jake as he and Sutter rushed for the outdoors.

Inside the exam room, Badger began to score his subject evaluations. He felt a hand flop onto his shoulder and flew into the air, "Jes-es-es!" he hollered.

"I didn't mean to scare ya," offered Wayne, his arm extended. "I just like that story so much, I had to know if there was more, especially about those ninja guys?"

"Oh God," said Badger.

# 10

## *Pot Doesn't Make You Do Screwy Things; Pot Doesn't Prevent You from Doing Screwy Things*

"Wow!" exclaimed Badger, "Look it these aggression levels in Berge and Jake. These guys hate each other. If we could get them on different teams."

"You're suggesting?"

"There's much to be learned here, my friend," winked Badge.

"Normally, protocols are pretty explicit," mused Custer, "but the latest note from Nicholson challenges us to 'independently' design our own experiments."

"Based on what?"

"Well, based on Science, of course."

"For Science!" Badger toasted with his ginger ale.

* * * *

Later, during Group, Custer announced: "We're forming a competition. This will be a team exercise and will require some fitness and exertion."

"Not interested," barked Shep.

"With all due respect, Mr. Stern, to your acknowledged slothfulness, this is not a voluntary exercise," Custer reproached.

"Just for that outburst," sniffed Badger, "I'm putting you on the losing team."

"That's for certain," snapped Jake.

"Now, gentlemen, we're going to let you talk freely—"

"On any subject you choose," accused Bergman.

"You wanna be on his team too?" warned Badge, wagging a pencil.

"Let's just say," ventured Custer, fingering a line of stiff red bristles running along his jaw, "that we want you to talk about your reasons for smoking marijuana. Be candid," he paused, "remember, everything you say is strictly confidential."

"Until revealed in a paper you're writing for Psychology Today," Bergman sniped.

"That's it!" stormed Badger. "No more candy bars!"

"Don't do it Badge," wheezed Jake, falling to his knees, "I won't last, I'm a goner if you taka waya da choc-o-lat..."

Custer leaned into his knowledge of body language, and singled out Tony 'D' for the 'What's it like?' query.

"It's movies, man," said Tony, "pot turns your life into a movie; like you can stand next to your real self and watch it act. The pressure's off. It's a feeling of power. It's cool man, different, like being swept away in a tidal wave."

"Tsunami," corrected Shep.

"That's what I said," Tony retorted.

"No, it's not what you said!" Shep insisted.

"Wh'ad I say then?" Tony asked.

"You said 'tidal wave,'" Shep replied.

"Yeah!"

"Tidal wave?" repeated Shep.

"I said—hey, wh'd you all call it again?"

"A tsunami," announced Shep. "It's a killer ocean wave

triggered by a shift in tectonic plates; tides are entirely different."

"No kidd'n?" Tony wondered. "It's a what? A 'pot-sumi'?"

"Yeah," broke in Jake, "pot swept me away too, in a giant petunia."

"Well, pa-too-ey on you-ey too-ey," Tony responded.

"Poor Dewy and Huey," mumbled Bergman, "so much they didn't knew-ey."

"Ka-blew-y," smiled Jake, slamming his fist into his palm.

"See, that's it, that's why I smoke grass, it's that anger deal," stuttered Shep. His bloodshot eyes were fixed and penetrating as fossils.

"Wha' you talking about?" puzzled Badger.

"You sir, your threats of cruelty and deprivation in order to coerce us into obedience to your frick'en will!" thundered Shep.

"Time for some, ah, serious revolution here," added Thad.

"Yeah, I'm pissed as hell," said Jake.

"Oh, Jesus!" Badger moaned, "no one's forcin' you to do anything you don't want to do."

"Marijuana is the only drug that can fight the plague of aggression that terrorizes us!" Shep proclaimed in a reedy voice.

"It makes me forget the little 'me' in me, and makes me see the bigger picture," said Berge.

"It's like flying a kite on the beach," Tony beamed.

Badger and Custer conferred. "Are we being sandbagged here?" Custer whispered. Badger pinched his ear ritually; Custer teased his beard.

"Ok," Custer began, "suppose marijuana does cancel out aggression?"

"It doesn't cancel out anything," Bergman argued.

"Says who?" jeered Jake.

"Least of all aggression," Bergman finished.

"I thought you said, 'pot neutralizes aggression'?" asked Custer, turning to Shep.

"The short-term memory retains only 10% of the information it absorbs. You didn't remember what I said so you substituted some hodgepodge you invented."

"Something like that," Custer acknowledged.

"Your 'Assassin' discussion suggested a connection between marijuana and aggression. So now we're being pushed to respond to that same old chestnut," Ira insisted.

"We're listening," Badger teased.

"You've got pot pinned with this 'Prove it doesn't drive you to kill,' challenge," explained Ira. "What if you asked if marijuana has ever prompted anything positive, something good?"

Chris focused, deliberately pulling himself back from the hole in the floor, a window of blue-black stone… "Phew!" he said, "that's the thing about weed. You focus on one little item to the exclusion of all else until just being able to stand seems like an incredible achievement."

"You're right," said Jimbo, "Let's toke up to all the aggressive, me first pricks who turned it around thanks to the herb!"

"I'll lift a leg to that!" Sutter cried out.

* * * *

Chris caught himself napping, nailed to his chair. He tried to move but couldn't. And he wanted to start doing push-ups today. Work on his arms would relieve his self-consciousness. Amazing, isn't it, so much of life is vanity! The rituals we perform to purify our lusts.

He felt his heart racing, chest throbbing like a hummingbird. He pushed his chair back, folded his legs and searched for clues behind closed lids. A pinwheel of distant lights glowed suggestively. He spiraled into the great, warm embrace of a seamless universe. 'There are no individuals, we are one. Independence is an illusion; we are not creatures in space. We are space.' It was all so simple!

A world pushed to starvation in a time of surplus; the fragile joy of life an early casualty to an explosion of greed ripping through the social contract. He fled outdoors.

Ah! The moon appeared as a giant pearl against cobalt blue curtains; Chris imagined he was certified 'moon glow' grown on a farm not far from here.

His life to this point didn't amount to 'a fart in a can,' Uncle Willie said. He couldn't hit a curve ball, was bullied into quitting his beloved Boy Scout troop, and spent his grandfather's coin collection on a huge sugar rampage to impress some 12-year old classmates. He could cook and sew but the barbells he bought were useless because he was afraid to go into the basement by himself. He was an 'ok' student because he spent too many hours daydreaming about girls he couldn't have because he daydreamed too much. They called him 'introspective.'

How'd it get this way? Was there some kind of key, or was it just unrelated chaos?

He suspected he should shoot for something higher. How high? Too high, and he might get discouraged; too low and he wouldn't grow. The whole of life was a blur, raining cats and dogs all the time.

Chris nodded, his head on his chest as the last light bled from the sky. He seemed to be sleeping when his head popped backward: tiny brushstrokes burned their way across the ancient canvas of night: Stars!

He gaped at the thousands of visible infernos stretching

across the horizon, marveling at the rich assortment of colors: violet and turquoise strands, there a glowing golden diamond; here, candles of amplified blue and techno green fused into a warm beacon. The lights of Boston were only a tiny bloom of fire in the corner of the room; the pulsing stars ruled the sky with confidence. The stars knew everyone.

He could feel their heat, the subtle power of gamma and x-rays over an endlessly deep and forever ocean; he suffered the thunder of screaming alto and deafening bass as every turbine in the universe looked his way.

Suddenly the naked skin of a pregnant giant, a 747 megaliner ripped into view. Massive as a train, it dropped into nearby Logan airport like a polished aluminum fruit bat. Chris stared into circles of blue fire while the silvery bullet tunneled out of the granite night.

* * * *

Not that he was afraid to die. Jimbo remained an optimist, confident that death would lead to an easier clothes selection. Life, death, acid reflux—it was all subtle machinery in the hands of a foreign teaching assistant.

But imagine for a moment the smorgasbord of disasters awaiting in a state like California: crushed to death in a trashbin; swept to sea in a massive stormwater pipe? Sharks, crossfires, food poisoning epidemics, landslides, foggy freeways, stalking, overdose, bear attack, snakebite, blowout, obesity. The 'Eureka!' state was virtually a transitional zone to the Eternal Life.

It was all about staying within the lines. If you stayed within the lines you would enjoy the greatest probability of a long life. Everybody, of course, knew about the lines, one way or another. You might overhear your parents talking, or more probably, you have direct experience, something you quickly lock away because the first meeting with the lines is apt to be very painful. No matter how it happened, the lines would become part of your life.

You see, there are lines everywhere, angles you have no choice but to follow. I mean who, after all, chooses the trajectory of their life? Yeah, you can avoid California, but wherever you go and whatever you do, the lines will do the steering. Some lines are parallel all the way to infinity. Others bisect, intersect, connect.

Everyone is propelled in a certain direction according to the lines drawn for them. Oh, I know your question, yes, you can kinda *bend* them a bit, but it's a lot of work and they don't move much: the lottery winner that promises few changes: 'Maybe spend more time with the grandchildren.' The doctor that can't stop doctoring; the ex-jock that will watch any game... They're tracing their lines.

The lines kept things organized, defined. Without them, people would start to accelerate and lose control. They'd fly ever faster until they collided or simply exploded like firecrackers, spilling debris and tragedy in all directions.

It was only natural to keep within the lines for another reason: a sense of place, a belongingness that people, like the lowliest mutt, must have. The lines keep us powerfully, invisibly bound, capable of withstanding the meanest winds.

But if you don't follow the future that's drawn for you, if you go *outside* the lines... Well, some serious shit is gonna happen, that's for sure. Maybe not the end of the world, yet very strange crap-ola nonetheless.

That's what Jimbo liked about weed. The lines didn't feel so tight, so limiting. No, the lines are still there, but they're harder to spot, like monofilament.

* * * *

"You know,' said Jake as he and Sutter left the Wreck room after sharing a joint, "I'm way stoned, this grass is so hot-t-t! How much you think this shit'd go for on the outside?" he asked, "$200? $250 an o-z?"

"Goddamn," replied Sutter, "yeah, easy $250, maybe three bills."

The pair paused at Jake's door as he surveyed the hall. "And how much do we get now, on a lid?" Jake asked as he opened the door and entered his tiny cell. He took the bed, stacking up pillows behind his head while Sutter perched on the plastic desk chair.

"Let's see, we get 20%," Sutter answered.

"So we sell an ounce at $100, it cost us $80?"

"Yeah."

"So $20 bucks on a c-note. Now, if we were selling this shit, we could get...maybe $300 an ounce, and..."

"You're not thinking—"

"Right," Jake revealed his pyramidal smile of glowing enamel, "we go for 30%."

"No!" Sutter cried out in disbelief.

"30%—easy—with this stuff?" Jake summarized.

"That's a, ah..." Sutter tried to calculate but he was off the rails with Jake's latest idea. Jake's 30% was radical, man, radical.

"Better stuff, better percentage. It's reasonable," said Jake matter-of-factly.

"Let's see, 30 on 300 equals 90…"

"Make it a hundred."

"Wow! $100?" wondered Sutter.

"$100 on an ounce and everybody's happy. We get stuff like this, no prob," Jake concluded.

"Sure, stuff like this grows on, on, weeds!" Sutter broke up, coughing.

"That'll be your job," said Jake, his ice-blue eyes set.

"Hunh?"

"We're taking some of this shit with us," Jake explained. "We'll see how it goes, if we can get $300, even $250."

"Yeah, then what?"

"Yeah, well that's when you go to work."

"Me?" said Sutter.

"We're gonna need a steady supply of high-quality shit."

"High-quality shit, eh?"

"Yeah, HQS: From Early and McClellan, purveyors to the Queen of Fine Smokables," finished Jake.

"Brain food, man." Sutter laughed but Jake didn't.

"We're gonna need a supply, man. We gotta have a dependable source; we can't go on with this outside growing deal, with the bugs, hail, drought, other growers, *policia*—dig?"

"Yeah," Sutter replied.

"Suppose we get $100 an ounce, that's $1,600 a pound, five times what we turn now. And if we could grow it ourselves, in a safe house, so we could sell as much as we wanted, we'd pick up another 20% and we'd be getting half of the street price! Man, that's some money, and say we could deal 10 pounds a month at $250 a lid at the low end say."

"That's $20,000 a month!" gasped Sutter.

"Yeah," said Jake.

"But grow'n man, that takes lights, power, fans, feeding. Hell, it requires freak'n genetics."

"What?" asked Jake irritably.

"You know, plant science."

"Yeah, that'll be your worry."

"Jesus, thanks."

"Don't mention it."

Outside, a cool mist invaded, thickened, neutralized the yard lights then recording the shadowy appearance of the first large droplets of the coming deluge as they streaked in from the north-east. Soon the *arbor vitae* were dancing tightly with well-suited young gusts, their shapely branches bending to an ever-faster tempo.

# 11

## *The Ghost of Fiorello*

Minter donned his cleanest flannel shirt and applied wax to the tips of his mustache. Prowling behind the steel desk in the conference room, his lengthy, angular frame, taut freckled skin and stork-like bent sent a comic message to his mandatory audience. Anything to distract and de-energize the fearsome 'collective dissent.' Minter wanted to know if respondents under the influence of marijuana could act in deliberate defiance of the powerful myths about cannabis?

"Gentlemen, get your programs right here!" yelled Badger, thrusting an eight-page fact sheet on the subjects as they filed in.

"Today," Minter intoned, "I'm going to ask you to identify any statements about marijuana that could be 'unwarranted, unsupported or biased.'"

"Tell me it's not the same old tired bullshit we get every day?" challenged Sutter.

"By no means," responded Minter. "This is different than the exhausted do-do we've been feeding you, what is it, these long years."

"Yeah, today it's strictly fresh catch dung," said Badger.

"Just so it's organic," asserted Berge.

"Don't worry 'bout a thing," cajoled the Badge, "grab your marijuana thinking caps and dream yourself up a place to groove."

"Hey, Badge," cried Tony, "when they cut out your heart,

did they put it in the freezer to warm it up, or did they put a plant in it because it was hollow?"

"Geez!" snickered Jake, "Badge, he seared you man! That's like arc welding, dude."

"Badger, what did they do with your brain, did they use it for rope because it's so twisted," asked Berge, "or is it in teaching because it takes four months off a year?"

"And if the cat got your tongue, why didn't he bury it?" said Sutter.

"Oh, El lame-o," Jake chipped in.

"And did the Hampshire get your arms?" Chris called out.

"And those awful, short, bowlegs of yours, and that weird head," laughed Jimbo.

"And your penis," yelled Wayne, "what—"

"Ok, ok!" Minter intervened, "Today, we'll present excerpts from a major scientific study of marijuana, the Mayor of New York—Fiorello H. LaGuardia's—now that's *Italian!*—Committee on the Marijuana Problem in New York. This study was conducted by the New York Academy of Medicine a year after the federal Marijuana Tax Act of 1937.

"The blue-ribbon committee asked social scientists: Who used marijuana, what were its physiological and psychological effects, and whether it led to either mental deterioration or criminal behavior?" Minter outlined.

"The Report's findings are spelled out in Info sheet #9 which you now have. The La Guardia Study was the largest, most comprehensive examination of pot in 2,000 years.

"The Mayor's Committee conducted tests and interviews over a six-year period 1938–44, in response to the marijuana hysteria that led to the weed being outlawed. The Committee conducted a sociological study of marijuana users, and the relation between its use and criminal or antisocial acts. Likewise, a clinical study was undertaken to reveal the physiological and psychological effects of marijuana, and whether it causes physical or mental deterioration.

"The selection also contains evidence of bias, unwarranted assumptions and unsupported conclusions.

"Your job will be to identify five such statements… That's right, I said five. Hey, you, Ira, knock it off!"

Shep had begun reading. "Sorry, can't help myself."

"Yeah, right. Anyway—yes, you can do this as a group, you don't have to do this individually."

"Really?"

"Really," answered Badger decisively, "so hop to it!"

As the subjects turned to the readings, Badger shot a meaningful glance to Custer. Given the standard of the times, the LaGuardia Committee tooled around the sociological world in a Bentley. The brief summary actually contained no examples of bias, unwarranted assumptions or unsupported conclusions. Every statement came straight from the Report unaltered.

It's assumed most marijuana users would select those portions of the document that question marijuana smoking as being 'biased, unwarranted and unsupported.' Users would also be less likely to tag any pro-marijuana statements with the 'bias' label. This pattern would demonstrate predictable 'outsider' thinking.

The opposite response, the 'it's too good to be true' path, with respondents skeptical of positive claims made for marijuana, would bolster the conclusion that marijuana at least didn't hinder the construction of intellectual honesty.

**Major LaGuardia Conclusions**

1. The consensus among marijuana smokers is that the use of the drug creates a definite feeling of adequacy.

2. The practice of smoking marijuana does not lead to addiction in the medical sense of the word.

3. The use of marijuana does not lead to morphine or heroin or cocaine addiction.

4. Marijuana is not the determining factor in the commission of major crimes.

5. Juvenile delinquency is not associated with the practice of smoking marijuana.

6. Reactions which are natively alien to the individual cannot be induced by the ingestion of the drug.

7. Those smoking marijuana for a period of years showed no mental or physical deterioration which may be attributed to the drug.

8. Under the influence of marijuana, there was a slightly freer flow of associations. Men talked more easily, confronted each other more directly and manifested a state of well-being at times amounting to euphoria.

9. The publicity concerning the catastrophic effects of marijuana smoking in New York City is unfounded.

"God, can you beat that, they had all this down in 1944!" gasped Jimbo.

"The Mayor had guts. You gotta give him that," said Ron admiringly.

"We always get the shaft," put in Tony.

"We're shaftees, designated shaftees. What'cha gonna do?" asked Berge.

"Ok," Badger shouted, "who's on first?" He paused. "You," he indicated Ron Green, "Poindexter. What's up?

C'mon, give."

Ron picked up the papers and read until he found something that confused him. "It says, 'The feeling of well-being may be the predominant effect of the drug, but respondents also indicated an undercurrent of irritability and anxiety; fully 88% of regular marijuana users considered themselves 'aggressive' after they had had the drug as compared with only 42% in the undrugged state. Thus marijuana releases repressed unpleasantness as well as euphoria.' This I don't get. I mean I agree with the 'well-being' bit, but I don't buy this 'irritability/unpleasantness' stuff."

"Biased, unwarranted, unsupported conclusion?" asked Custer.

"What's it to ya?" Ron said sternly.

"Fear not, friends," Custer smiled, "just trying to get your answers. Now, anyone else go along with Ron?"

"C'mon folks," Badger encouraged, "no pot until you get hot."

"Yeah, ok, whatever..." Jake chipped in. "I'll vote for whatever he said."

"Anyone else?" demanded Badger.

"Yeah, me too," agreed Tony. "Why the hell not? We'll get out of here faster."

"Anyone opposed?" cried Badger.

"Well," said Bergman slowly. He thought about it and decided he had to say something about 'the process' regardless of the dirty looks. "It seems to me we should list the questionable statements before we vote. What if we come up with more than five, what if they're all biased, what if none is? Shouldn't we try to get the big picture first?"

"Five is all we need; five will do," countered Jake.

"Imagine discussing all the possibilities and choosing the best..."

"Five. That's the number we need here. Keep it simple, stupid."

"If all you want is five, have Shep do it."

"Hey, that's not a bad idea, considering the source," said Sutter.

"Shep, you got five?" asked Thaddeus.

"Woof, woof!" Ira barked.

"We gotta draw a line at this species swapping!" moaned Bergman.

"Give him a bone!" Wayne shouted.

"Give 'um yours," Jake smirked.

"Gentlemen, gentlemen, I don't think having Ira do all the work is what we're looking for here. Let's put the question back to you, Bergman. Do you have another one the Group can vote onto the list?"

"Here's one, bottom page six," replied Bergman. "It says, 'In both long-term and first-time users, subject's confidence in his verbal capacity enhanced by marijuana use.'"

"Yeah?" Jake said. He ran the edge of his fingers down the wide soft wale on his corduroys attacking a piece of bothersome grit lodged under his nails.

"According to the handout," argued Bergman, "long-term and first-time users don't have the same reactions to pot."

"Except they all want to play horn in the Big Easy," said Thaddeus.

"Or look like they play horn in the Big Easy," said Chris.

"Yeah!" laughed Thad, "it all works."

"You know Bergmeat, you're just so negative! Somebody has something good to say about the weed and you gotta go off!" cried Jake.

"You feeling increased confidence in your verbal capacity?" Bergman asked.

"Hey, Shep?" called Tony.

"Arf, arf!" answered Shep.

"You may look and smell like a large canine, but that's the weakest bark I've ever heard," Jimbo proclaimed.

"Unsupported, unwarranted and biased!" Ira snapped.

Minter brought them back to the issue. "Ira. Analysis, please."

"Interesting. These results come from a prison population. Who else could smoke post Marijuana Tax Act of 1937? That's a bias right there. Prison is not, at least not yet, a cross-section of America. It's just the opposite 'normally.' Ha, ha—a prison population is made up of persons who lack verbal skills. That's why they're in prison."

"They can't talk their way out like you," put in Tony.

"Couldn't think their way out," Ira corrected, "if you can't think, you can't talk."

"You're talking yourselves in, the both of you," cautioned Wayne.

"LaGuardia repeatedly mentions the user's 'lessening of restraint,' and 'confident, 'know-it-all' attitude," Ira went on briskly. "It isn't physical aggression as we think of it, but an acceptance of life that becomes a mandate. That's why you're wrong, Berge," Ira concluded, "the subject population was biased toward the lower strata, but it doesn't say their verbal abilities actually increased, only their sense of confidence and well-being grew."

Minter accepted their silence for agreement. "Ok," he encouraged, "you need a few more. Anyone? How 'bout you,

Chris?" It was about time they stopped treating this guy like he was a crêpe.

"I'm glad you called on me," Chris said with a straight face and the room howled. "I have been thinking about this passage on page, ah, three, beginning: 'The ability to estimate short periods of time, and ah, short lin-e-a-r distances are not significantly affected by ingestion of marijuana.'"

"That's the Bellevue memorization test, repeat digits in forward and reverse order," offered Minter.

"Yeah," replied Chris, "well, on page four it says, 'marijuana has a dele-ter-ious effect... on mental functioning... the extent of impairment—in reversed digits—related to the amount of drug taken."

"Un-huh," coached Minter.

"But on page six, it says that, 'Although eager to be 'high,' there was always a point beyond which no amount of talking or cajoling could make them continue smoking...' So my question is, 'why, if the subjects limited their smoking on their own?"

"Sounds 'unwarranted' to me," chimed in Jake. "Three down, two to go."

"Hey, check it out—page 4," Wayne broke in, "'Subjects were asked to draw a human figure. With marijuana ingestion there was an increase in the percentage of subjects who remembered to give their man ears. This may indicate 'heightened awareness' or 'greater sensitivity to others.' Wow, now that's sweet."

"Yeah, right, Wayne," Jake shot back, "good to see you're on top of things. Now get back on the roof and look for those black helicopters."

"How 'bout you, Jake," asked Badger, "can you come up with one?"

"Yeah, ya son of a bitch," Jakes whispered, "I got your one right here," he added, giving Badger the middle finger salute.

"C'mon," Beddiker challenged.

"Ok, ok," said Jake pouring over the fact sheet. "Yeah, here's one says: 'Those smoking marijuana for a period of years showed no mental or physical deterioration which may be attributed to the drug.'"

"What page, what page?" cried Bergman.

"That would be page KMA: kiss my ass."

"Is that what you want, someone to kiss your ass, maybe caress it too?" Bergman responded.

Jake tensed and for a second looked as if he might leap from his chair.

"Page eight," Jimbo called out.

"Thanks."

"You had more?" Minter asked Jake.

Jake looked distracted, "Yeah—same page: 'Marijuana does not change the basic personality structure of the individual... it does not e-voke—What the hell kinda word is that?—responses which would otherwise be totally alien to him.'"

Minter hesitated. "So you're saying this is what? Biased?"

"No, no, no, nothing like that. I agree with it. I like it. I think it settles the whole goddamned argument, don't you?"

"If not biased, unwarranted, or unsupported," put in Bergman.

"What the hell is that supposed to mean?" said Sutter, "he's agreeing with the statement, how can you challenge that?"

"The point isn't to find stuff you agree with," Bergman explained, "but stuff that's not substantiated."

"Here we go again!" cursed Jake.

"Berge, look here," directed Ron, "page five: 'As a group,

the marijuana users tested show very even functioning, not marked irregularity as would be the case in mental deterioration. From this we may conclude that the marijuana users suffered no mental deterioration as a result of their use of the drug.' That's what Jake's been saying."

"Look, I'm trying to help Group find a fourth misleading statement."

"By being a colossal pain in the ass," said Jake.

"Actually, Berge has done us a service," offered Shep.

"Hunh?" Sutter replied.

Ira shifted in his chair as if trying to shed his skin. "Page seven: 'While smoking there was a decrease in the subject's ability to think in line with the group. The increased number of responses on the Rorschach Test was due to the subject's greater awareness of small, extraneous details which in his undrugged state he overlooked,'" Ira continued reading.

"In other words, during drug intoxication, one sees the obvious and commonplace differently, more richly, than in the normal state."

"So what?" asked Jake.

"Berge's probing proves that we are being set up." Ira turned to Custer and the Badge. "The document is internally consistent; there is no bias, or unwarranted or unsupported statements. You're peddling a hoax." Ira threw his sheet toward Minter. "Am I right?"

Custer smiled.

"We're not finding contradictions, just confirmation."

"But what about this, page three: 'In general, it appears that those functions most closely associated with higher intellectual processes are more impaired by the drug than are the simpler functions,'" charged Bergman.

"Hey, it took Ira an hour to put this together, so I guess it proves that one's right too," said Tony.

"I'll be goddamned," said Jimbo.

# 12

# *Casino Odds*

After the morning tests, Chris noticed a professional-looking notebook lying on the ping pong table. His instincts told him to pass on; any involvement was sure to lead to unpleasant complications. And yet... He edged closer. It had to belong to staff —or maybe Bergman, his habit of jotting things down irritated Jake no end. Thaddeus thought he did it just for that reason. Berge probably wouldn't mind him peaking if that was necessary to have it returned. Chris opened the notebook and began reading:

"Ira (Shep) continues his juvenile isolation from the other patients. When addressed, he stubbornly refuses to respond until you have raised your voice. Even then his answers are oblique and evasive.

"If you refuse to play his childish games however, and insist on a straight answer, his smiles and boyishness disappears and he seems quite hurt." A general description of the testing period followed, signed by the assistant in charge, David Minter—Custer!

Custer had seemed to be one of us! Wick was totally inaccessible, as spacey in his own way as someone on pot. Badge was, well, just like a real badger—a shaggy, burrowing cousin of the weasel with a chip on his shoulder. Melody had her own problems with Thaddeus. Custer was the only one to show a genuine interest in the subjects as people rather than as just another step up the academic ladder. What in the hell was going on?

Of course, there was no way he could inform Shep of what had been written; it would just kill him. What was the purpose anyway, of this, this spy book? This wasn't 'Science' was it? He felt a chill, a sudden anxiety. Call it paranoia about the whole undertaking. Trapped in a condemned barn, shut off from friends and contacts; deceived, ignored, frustrated. They couldn't help but respond with cynicism and belligerence. Ghetto conditions in, ghetto attitudes out. Yet every act was dutifully put down to the workings of that all-powerful, mind-altering drug: marijuana!

Were they still people, or were they products of the drug? What came next, would the Establishment, convinced that rebellion adhered to the leaves of a plant, market a slew of legal pharmaceuticals offering near similar antidepressant effects but without the political boost? And without marijuana, would youth abandon their quest for a better society, the end of the war, equal justice?

Chris stared at the joint in his hand burning with slow, smoky deliberation. Wasn't this how they handled dissidents in the Soviet Union, put them on powerful drugs, keep them confused, disoriented, unable to form the iron resolve necessary to take the dangerous steps of opposition? As a cloud of pungent smoke snaked up his arm from the burning joint, he was visited by the uneasy suspicion that maybe the powers that be wanted misfits to smoke themselves away in dreams and dissipation?

He pushed the burning ember into his hand and waited for the message of pain to reach his brain. Ahhh! Underneath the black, dime-sized smudge was an angry hole. Chris buried his thoughts in the hole. He scrunched the rest of the joint under his foot and kicked it under a chair...

* * * *

Custer spread the discussion papers around the large masonite table as the subjects filed indifferently into the room. He watched as Wayne 'accidentally' knocked his sheet to the floor and stepped on it; Sutter folded his into an airplane and launched it toward Jake. Custer began reading in a loud voice:

"In the next half hour you will be asked to discuss the following situation and arrive at a unanimous agreement as to how the group as a whole would advise Mr. Z. After you've talked over *how each of you feels about the situation,* come to an agreement as to the **minimum** odds of success you would require before recommending that the more attractive alternative be chosen.

"The situation: Mr. Z., a 24-year-old steelworker, has been mistakenly imprisoned under a life sentence for a murder which he did not commit, despite overwhelming evidence which convinced the jury and later appeal judges that he was guilty. Having nearly exhausted all legal means for retrial, he now has formulated a plan of escape.

"If the escape is successful, he will be able to fly to Brazil, a country without an extradition treaty with the U.S., and live a full and free life. If the escape plan fails, however, he will never be paroled and there is a strong possibility that he would be killed during the escape attempt. On the other hand, if he accepts his sentence, he will be paroled in 15 years or, in the event that new evidence turns up, sooner.

"Imagine that you are advising Mr. Z. Listed below are several probabilities or odds that the escape will be successful. Please check the lowest probability that you would consider acceptable for Mr. Z to attempt escape:

"a) There is a 10% chance that the escape will be successful; b) 30%; c) 50%; d) 70%; e) 90%; f) Place a check here if you think Mr. Z should not attempt the escape, no matter what the probabilities."

"This is a piece of shit!" Tony snorted.

"An ever-lov'n, 'not for individual sale,' humungous slab of gravy-covered crap," sputtered Thaddeus.

"Fie! Fie, on both of you," mocked Jake, "how dare you call this manure a piece of shit? Don't you realize some poophead excreted a lot of his inner stool into this feces-filled turd? Let's have more respect, after all, some assholes are just born full of shit, right, Berge?"

Bergman studied the paper before him. "I don't know," he responded, "when it comes to excrement, I don't have the experience others do."

"Oooowwweee!" Jimbo clucked.

"Ah, it would seem that you people are ready to begin?" Custer ventured.

"Ok, let's start this shit off. Everybody put 10%? Fine. Group decision is 'Yes' the poor bastard should run for it with a 10% chance," said Jake. He rose looking for agreement.

"I'm with you man," agreed Tony.

"Great discussion; meeting adjourned. Interested parties to the smoking lounge!" Jake shouted.

"Guess I'm a bit more conservative," broke in Bergman. "10%? Is life that cheap? I wouldn't think of running unless the chance of escape was at least 90% in my favor..."

"90%!" Jake choked, "Wha' the—? Anybody else? Hey, let's vote this sucker. Chris?"

"I'll go along," Chris whispered, "though…"

Jake smiled. "Shep... Shep?"

Shep bit his lip and squinted, "Me, huh? Gimme a second," he belched. He dropped his chin heavily into a cupped hand, "Hmmm." Scrolling a finger down the page he mumbled, "Yeah, here, 70%."

"Way to go, Shep," Jake winked. "We'll put you down for 10%. Ok, everybody! 10%. Let's hear it! Raise hands! And god, whatever you do, don't fuck us over, Bergdroppings!"

Bergman assumed as stony an expression as he could. "I think discussion raises interesting questions; I'm sorry Group seems, ah, disinclined to pursue them. Frankly, I didn't know 'stoned' meant 'numbed.' For my part, I wouldn't advise Z to attempt escape under any circumstances."

"Are you gonna screw us again?' Sutter fumed.

"I don't imagine screwing you under any circumstances," said Bergman. "But you're killing a guy for what amounts to casino odds."

"Oh yeah, well you're letting an innocent guy rot in the pen when he could be having the time of his life in Rio," Sutter hissed.

"Could be."

"Berge, you just don't get it," said Jake. "This isn't a real situation. Z does not fuck'n exist! This whole thing is irrelevant; you're objections are irrelevant; you're..."

"Anything's better than being locked up for fifteen goddamned years," argued Tony.

Bergman studied Custer's impassive face. "Is it? Is death better?" he asked.

"But he's innocent!" Tony insisted. "He shouldn't be there in the first place. He's got a right to escape."

"Actually," Sutter interjected, "Z should take a fuck'n gun and shoot every one of the goddamned bastards!"

"Objection, your honor," said Shep sleepily, "we left the eye-for-an-eye standard somewhere BC…"

"A 10% chance of getting laid in Rio vs. a 90% chance of clearing my name?" argued Bergman.

"Why should he give a shit about his frik'n reputation. He's already dead; straight society has passed him by," Jake retorted.

"Z's fate certainly has aroused all sort of noisy speculation," joked Jimbo.

"If Z is innocent, there must be some shred of doubt that he can muster into a new trial, a reduction of sentence, early parole — something," Thad speculated.

"Bullshit!" declared Jake. "It says right here, he's 'exhausted' all appeals. Don't you guys know how to read?"

"'Nearly' is the modifier in place there, friend," added Shep drowsily.

"In the jug he's one of a million—all of them innocent—who cares? But a fugitive in Rio... Why, he could get his own television show."

"Yes, yes, I see it now: slow dissolve to one-armed man fleeing the scene with a fruit basket," said Chris.

"Hey, mistakes are made all the time!" Bergman conceded. "Injustice is real. The point is..."

"What's the goddamned point, assuming you've got one?" challenged Sutter.

"You've got a responsibility to fight wrongs or..." Bergman searched for traction, "there'll be more victims."

"Screw ancient, dead, old man society!" laughed Jake. "Society is still in bowler hats and monocles when it comes to marijuana! There are thousands of sorry bastards in jail for smok'n weed, or refusn' to fight this fuck'n war. They're victims; they don't owe the ruling class jack shit!"

"Berge: super-patriot. Who woulda thunk it?" laughed Sutter.

"Utter bullshit," Ron said tersely.

"Interesting notion, community responsibility," Shep drawled.

"Crap," Wayne cackled, "the man don't let you get away with nuthin'."

"Z has to fight, not only for himself, but to restore to the world the confidence of its good intentions," Bergman explained.

"If that's the case, Mr. Society fighter, the Jake dude has got it. If you're black, there's one intention: guilty! Only a bloody, Attica-style escape gonna put reform on the map," offered Thad.

Bergman hesitated. "Change requires martyrs, that's why it's so slow."

"The difference between what should be and what <u>is</u>, can be spelled s-h-i-t," chimed in Ron.

"Yeah," gloated Jake, "lock all these pseudo-intellectuals in the slammer and let them think their way out!"

"Yeah," Sutter added, "Berge—'turd' man of Alcatraz!"

"He was dealt a bad hand," replied Bergman. "Z still has to play through, he can't go out of bounds."

"Ain't that a fact!" rocked Thaddeus.

"Ooops! Mixed metaphor, can we accept that judges?" jibed Jimbo.

"C'mon Berge, check the goddamned 10% like everybody else so we can get the hell outta here," Ron ordered. "It'd be different if anybody agreed with you but they don't. Wake up, get it."

"No, I'm not going to counsel escape at any odds."

"'Play by the rules,' he said; 'majority rules,'" he said. "C'mon, cheese head, make it unanimous," instructed Jake.

Bergman folded his arms across his chest.

"IIleeeiie!" shouted Wayne, grabbing Bergman's sheet, marking '10%' and thrusting it at Custer.

"Dip-shit," muttered Sutter, stalking out.

Bergman remained in his chair as the room emptied. "Hey," Chris called from the door, "it's only make believe."

Bergman smiled; maybe it was the pot after all?

* * * *

Wayne was impressed: stoned out of his mind, clinging to his alpine redoubt, he nonetheless managed to appear straight to Wick. They talked for the last 10 minutes—was it 20?—and he had maintained though his head was reeling and any moment he might explode. It was all too weird! Wick was talking biking, yeah, biking on 'toast'n desert roads.' Ah, the desert: thrusts of red and yellow muscle rippling across the valley, air coiled like a spring under an awesome heat burning purple in the hills. What? Wick didn't say 'toasting roads,' he said they were 'roasting toads!'

Now, what the...huh? He stared at the small adobe stove where Wick, a joint in one side of his mouth and a toothpick in the other, grilled frogs.

'I am way out...' he thought proudly. When Wick motioned to the shooting gallery, he had to be led.

Grabbing the M-16 styled weapon, Wayne aimed confidently at the video screen. Wick eyed him narrowly, "You don't object to this test, do you? I mean there's no racial problem here is there? I'm supposed to ask, after somebody..." Here his mouth rippled like old paint.

"Turn it on!" Wayne yelled, anticipating a frenzy of light. There it was. The electronic battlefield. What a trip! And the incredible part was that Wick couldn't appreciate any of it. It was like Wayne was invisible: a stunning secret hiding in plain sight.

Wayne moaned softly. The lights were phenomenal—like Christmas at New York Edison—bright and so many that, broken by his squinting, they formed a universe of fractured radiance.

On his left, a camouflaged missile launcher charged over the hill. A miniature soldier on the launcher sighted him and aimed the ordinance. Boom! Wayne was too quick, letting off three accurate rounds—fwet, fwet, fwet—the missile carrier disappearing as if sucked into a sponge. His eyes recovered to the center of the field picking up tank movement from behind a dune of woody desert plants. The tank aimed its long barrel at him when—blam!—an unconscious power pointed, squeezed, a blast of deadly firepower striking the doomed vehicle. From three separate rock piles sprang scowling infantrymen armed with machine guns. They had just come to a stop in order to shoot at him when Wayne, turning his rifle in a graceful arc, mowed them down. 'Gee, this is great fun!' he thought excitedly. He could feel the battle as if it were fought on this very ground.

Wayne noticed that Wick was talking to him. At least he knew Jonathan was talking, but he didn't know it was to him. It was like watching film without a soundtrack, plenty of lip movement but not a lot of sense. Wick laughed and shook his head, shook his head and laughed. He wasn't talking anymore...yes! He was going to speak, Wayne was going to be able to hear him at long last, he tuned in to: 'trigger.' Yes, he'd heard the word correctly: 'trigger.' He leaned closer.

"Pull the trigger!" screamed Wick.

"What?" Wayne searched for meaning. He looked at Wick; Wick was pointing at the gun. Wayne examined the weapon:

'trigger'? He followed his sleeve down to his finger, squeezed tensely against the... the trigger guard! "Hmmm," Wayne moaned. "Maybe I'm stoned."

"No!" Wick deadpanned, "you're absorbing weed like a 200-pound finch and guess what? You're stoned!" He paused to add weight to his words. "Now put your finger on the damn trigger and shoot."

Wayne turned to the shimmering box and slid to attention. Aiming at a personnel carrier, he pulled back his arm as if drawing a bowstring. Blam! A loud report startled him, then he saw the red flame of his strike. 'The sonofabitches!' he muttered, ferociously scouting the field. There, right there—blam! Another electric beam sliced into the vital undersides of a missile launcher, throwing bodies into the air and raising a small black mushroom cloud. He simply aimed, and deadly fires sprouted amongst his enemies, *heh, heh*. In rapid succession he pointed at a bazooka-carrying soldier, two jeeps and a tank, twitching with satisfaction as they blew apart: 250, 300, 500 points!

Suddenly, the noise of the battlefield exploded like a fireball, singeing his hair and sending him rolling into a trench. When he tried to rise, bullets whined narrowly past his head. He rolled again, under control this time, into a second foxhole, as a tank bore down on his former position, its big gun ripping the earth with powerful claws. The vibrations of his coughing machine-gun shook him to the bone. Suddenly, he felt a shadow and a cold sweat gripped his heart: above, a tiny sliver of light streaked toward him from out of the inky sky.

He pulled himself as low as he could, digging loose dirt with his bare hands and tossing it on his head. He watched in terror as the jet squirted through orange skies toward him, its guns tattooing the turf with ugly holes. Panicking, Wayne leaped to his feet, and strafed every object in sight with deadly fire. On his right, a peasant popped into view, arms raised in surrender. Wayne squeezed off a round sending the slim figure toppling backward, then swung his rifle on a group of five more peasants, women and children, their conical hats indicating their enemy status. Wayne drilled them too, 50, 100, 150, 200, 250 points!

Sensing movement on his left flank, Wayne wheeled on a small woman, a girl really, carrying a baby toward a bridge... Wayne blasted them, their headless torsos tumbling through the air like flakes of cereal, when, with a loud concussion, the machine went black. "5,300. Not bad," Wick sniffed. "Crazy. A better shot when stoned."

"Yeah," Wayne mumbled. He kept seeing the woman and child blown into so many parts of a puzzle. But where in the hell was that goddamned plane?

# 13

## *The Mayor of Pottsville*

After showering, Jimbo ran his fingers through his hair lightly massaging his scalp. He'd heard strong scalp muscles would hold onto hair follicles—the oily pits incubating hair roots —more tightly, slowing their rate of loss. Sadly, the family genotype squandered few resources on maintaining a healthy coat. His hair was thinning so quickly he scanned 'off-beat' magazines for those new products that promised "Astounding Breakthrough In Hair Health!" (next to "Enlarge Your Penis!"). He learned to avoid mirrors or close his eyes, sometimes too well. As he worked his fingers delicately through a woodlot of slender filaments cut fashionably long, he wished himself into a deadman's float, a deliberate cerebral flat-line over a labyrinth of commonplace detail.

The pot was called in as a for-hire defensive backfield that would bottle-up most of the annoying distractions, so that he could slip out unnoticed and gain first-class yardage. He concentrated on emptiness, imagining it in its deepest depths, trying to visualize it in its vastness.

That's when he heard it, a single tone, repeated painfully slowly as if awaiting a response. It seemed to come from very far away, very deep in the earth. Each repetition grew louder, more insistent. As he concentrated on the echo-like tone, one synapse after another linking in a kind of dance, he felt himself resonate. Entranced, he listened to the steadily growing sound:

da-da, dum-dum, da-da dum-dum, da-da-dum-dum.

It appeared as a small black dot no larger than a period at the end of a sentence. Soon the pleasant harmonies swelled, absorbing energy until it was the size of a baseball; no, a basketball, a..ah...wheel. And the dot-turned-small planet was singing to him. Meek at first the music gained in volume until he could make out the words clearly. It was a kind of chant, aimed directly at him in a sing-song address, chanting at him, chanting: 'Mar-ee-wa-na, Mar-ee-wa-na, Mar-ee-wa-na, Mar-ee-wa-na...

Next to him, Chris again pondered the meaning of his life: was it all a game? Was he winning? Was he losing? Who's side was he on? Each day he got ripped, he struggled to accomplish the smallest things. Mentally, a spring run of salmon-colored ideas on melting snow; physically, immobile, happy, glued.

He relished the relief from physical tension pot gave him, where 'the world' shrank to 'his world,' overcoming the haunting suspicion that life was a game—an orchestrated competition of bristling, lethal intent, with sharp edges, long, narrow passageways and blitzing trap-doors, a 30-day pass before certain death due to a rapid succession of worn parts.

Marijuana too, compressed the empty hours, crushing menial tasks under a barrage of high-fidelity sensation. Time ballooned a thousand-fold, spiriting him away on a bubble of extra seconds thanks to a normal dose of an illegal pharmaceutical.

But the feeling of well-being, a glow of increased mental activity, eventually disappeared, overcome by a knot of brief, tumbling feelings spinning in and out of retrieval until lacerated by a pile of faces, places and yearnings he just couldn't fix. He knew the drug figured in his frustration, and that frustration could only take so much before it collapsed into anxiety, which would then pass, slowly, stealthily, to Fear. "If I let it," he recognized. "What I need is a substantial distraction."

"Mr. Conner—Chris—why do you smoke the chronic, man?" asked Badger, dipping the eraser of his pencil into the oily corners of his nostrils.

"Because," Chris whispered, "it's the pathway to Truth."

"Ok, Pathway to Truth. Tell me the truth, are you addicted to pot?"

"I believe there are seven levels of marijuana use on the Pathway to Truth," Chris replied, unable to prevent a broad smile.

"Don't fight the weed man," offered Jake, "if you fight it, you won't get off."

"You, Jimbo, what's your excuse?" asked Bedikker.

"You against pot, man?" said Jimbo. "And you're collecting data with that attitude?"

"Nothin' personal, I just got better things to do. Hey, where ya goin?"

"Nothin' personal, but so do I," muttered Jimbo, seized by a sudden zeal.

"Okay, okay, let's be cool," offered Badger. "So? Why do we smoke, hmmm?"

"So he won't be type-A like you," Ira shot back.

"Oh, Jeez," Badger responded, "ain't a bit of prejudice here."

"Ira's right. He could be a star in an academic counting house somewhere. Like you, a whore for Big Business. We know you'll turn this research into something modern consumerism can use to prey upon the little guy. Every time you cooperate with The Man, you're drawn further into their agenda," Jimbo ranted.

"Why should we violate our principles to join a powerful

elite busy back-dating stock options or pouring waste into trout streams? It's too high a price for getting ahead!" he thundered.

"You already gotta a head," said Sutter.

"And don't you be gettn' no more. Not here anyway," added Thad.

Jake leaned his way—"You ain't on the same shit we're on, are ya?" he asked. "Not the same shit at all I'll bet. You got your own stuff, hunh?"

"We've got plenty of Thorazine," said the Badge, retreating a step. "Not a bad high but it takes some getting used to."

"Thorazine?" replied Jimbo, becoming all itchy. "'Here, take this drug, but don't take that one.' Everybody's working to escape to their own time, drink'n, smok'n, figur'n how to attack the fox next door."

"The difference smarty, is between medicinal and recreational use," inserted Badger.

"I don't think so," Shep sneered. "There's marginal medicinal value to tobacco, alcohol and coffee. This a retail war between the artificially created products of the chemical industry, and the natural foods and drugs of traditional small-scale agriculture."

"I can see you haven't thought much about this," interjected Jake.

Jimbo circled the room. "This moment marks an historic turn. Marijuana has to come out of the closet. We can't hide it like it was masturbation or baldness."

"Baldness!" laughed Jake.

"As the founder and chief smokesman for 'PPP': 'Pot, Potheads and Progress,' I urge you to let marijuana join its rightful place as a legal, tax-paying, mildly-psychoactive, privately-consumed substance like alcohol—only better," Jimbo polemicized.

"Did he say, 'mildly-psychoactive'?" Jake sniffed.

"I thought I was the founder," put in Sutter.

"No, you're the flounder," said Jake.

"Suppose you tell us what you mean when you say current drug policy toward marijuana is immoral?" broke in the Badge.

"Marijuana was legal for years, government reversed itself so the FBI had something to do after Dillinger was killed. Now that's immoral!"

"Government can declare an item illegal; that's their prerogative. How's that immoral? You're implying some moral code that requires smoking marijuana."

"Rastafarians," smiled Thaddeus. "My people are way out in front of the white devil on this one."

"Right on!" snorted Shep. They exchanged high-fives.

Jimbo calmed himself, "Immoral because this wasn't a normal government act. Many deadly devices—knives, guns, acids, fertilizer, gasoline—can be purchased OTC."

"You can leave chicken on the counter for a week, take in 100 stray cats; you can guzzle raw fish and juggle chain saws!" Bergman jumped in.

"But what you can't have is can-na-bis," chanted Shep.

"You can park cars," Thad laughed, "you can close the bars, you can even buy a Mars."

"But what you can't have is a little bliss," came Shep's reply.

"You can't tell a spy until you look him in the eye," said Wayne suddenly.

"Thanks ah, Wayne," said Jake grimly.

"The reason it's immoral is because marijuana is not a dangerous drug; the weed hasn't killed!" Jimbo argued.

"It might have melted a few," pleaded Bergman.

Thad let out a hoot. "I'm tell'n you—it's a dangerous drug! You can't drive a shopping cart on that stuff, you can't grab a steak and put it down your pants without going tickly wild; you can't steel no copper or go after your wife's better look'n sister on that damned weed. It's ruining poor folk lives."

Shep erupted in a manual of flapping arms, flaring eyes and flecks of gelatin-like oral fluids mustered in raspy support. "Illegal marijuana is a middle-class marker; without prohibition, there is vulnerability, mortality. But you have no science!" he screamed in his strangled-animal voice, words careening wildly off the high-gloss walls.

"I'm with you, man," agreed Tony, "I never cared for science, either."

Jimbo continued, subdued. "Pot is not a high-octane mind-bender linked to overdose, permanent brain damage or violent, unpredictable behavior like alcohol or methamphetamine.

"Pot's a 'friendly' drug, a mild sedative designed to bring peace to a life of toil and disappointment. It's what they want. How izzit any different from hundreds of other mood-altering drugs which will be prescribed for my 'temporary depression' if, and when, they ever succeed in ending my dependence on Mary Jane?

"Shit, its god's drug, why should we be afraid of it?" Jimbo continued. "It's immoral to take a blue-collar drug from a blue-collar people!"

"Here! Here!" shouted Shep.

"It's racist," piped up Thaddeus.

"Classist," agreed Berge.

"Druggist," Chris offered.

Jimbo paused, spent. "If you chose me as your candidate, I will work tirelessly to legalize the herb. Thank you."

* * * *

Shep restrained himself; he was after all, a 'je-knee-us' claimed his mother, a thin woman, hard to remember not all pruned up. His father, thick and dark, led a mysterious traveling life as banjo for The Northern Jazz All-Stars of Time & Space. "Huh! If he's such a 'je-knee-us,' why ain't he got a job?" asked the musician on one of his rare appearances in the tiny sun-filled flat.

"Don't you worry," she admonished, wagging her finger at the stranger-like musician, "he'll show us all up. He'll be bigger than Roosevelt."

"Bully," said the itinerant father.

"Not that one, FDR." 'Big-gah' than FDR. Imagine. That's what she had said. Of course, he wasn't in any hurry he was only 29 for Chrissakes. But FDR! When he was outta here, he'd call his contacts in the adult film industry, get the ball rolling. He got a rush just thinking about it.

Film producers are today's heroes. They are rich enough to be listened to, smart and well-connected enough to have direct influence. They make a call and a stretch of coastline is protected 'in perpetuity,' a clinic for the poor is placed in a festering neighborhood, a golf tournament rakes in $5 million for youth athletics.

Cinema occupied a much loftier position than mere rat science, thought Shep. Custer and Badger—livestock tenders—faceless Ph.Ds working for the pharmaceutical industry to place yet another expensive, unnecessary, artificial, potentially-dangerous money-maker into the public domain. Every week he'd be wheeling and dealing for 10 times their salaries.

Maybe he could make a movie about pot? No, not the silliness of Cheech and Chong, but a real film, sort of like a documentary, but better paced. The more he thought, the more Shep wanted to scratch the dark body hairs turning in on themselves, auguring under the grease-filled follicles and scabrous skin. He'd call it... (the title was very important) Grass Grabbing High in God's Green Eden? He wanted to get that in there: God. Pot was a natural product. The first aphrodisiac perhaps? The first stimulant, certainly.

The plant was recognized about the same time man's consciousness was declared independent of the deity. Man on his own ('Dominion' over creation) and with pot to guide him? That too, had to be in there, fully researched of course. Interviews with famous druggies? Maybe a different approach altogether... (Evidence, off-camera voice-over, generous use of graphs, charts, etc.) Definite connection between pot's effects and religious awakening. Yet pot has refused to set the course of the celestial imagination. It doesn't appoint martyrs to legitimize the cause.

Other cartels: The WASPs, Freemasons, Jews. Wait, I'm a Jew—Italians anyway, and Greeks, the KGB, Vatican, CIA/NSA/FBI, Hara Krishna, Motown, the Mob, Red Cross... It was all about power, you had it, you used it; you didn't have it, you pined for it like a hungry animal.

"So you're a movie producer?" asked Thad.

"That's right," said Ira proudly. "Sold nearly a million feet last year to an outfit outta Van Nuys."

Impressed, Thaddeus asked, "How'dja get into that racket?"

"I had a New York moment," Shep whispered, "I found $75,000 in a bag outside a hotel."

"In a bag?" wondered Thad, eyes rolling.

"Ok, maybe it was a briefcase," admitted Shep.

"But outside the hotel?"

"W-e-l-l-l, almost."

"Damn!" exclaimed Thad. "My people don't get many those opportunities— or we all be rich!" he laughed.

"Whydoncha come down, you could star, yeah," Shep offered.

"You serious?" wondered Thad.

"Sure, we use lotsa black people," Shep answered.

Thaddeus chuckled. He peered at Shep—the stubble and the beady eyes cracked him up—they were an absolute howl. He stumbled to his feet. He continued to giggle. His lungs ached but he couldn't stop. "You are the biggest goddamned bullshitter!" He stared at Shep trying to apprehend a clue to his true mind, "Bullshitter!" he hollered.

The pronouncement stirred Shep to a state of mind where he too, found humor and oxygen depletion. "Bullshitter!" he sputtered. They struggled to say something final. Thad thought he heard the voice of Melody calling him to 'vitals' and managed to peel off toward the door. "Bullshitter!" they squealed at each other over the growing distance.

* * * *

As he hefted himself onto the examining table, Thaddeus toyed with the tassel on his robe. Melody refused to bite. "Open your arm and make a fist," she asked evenly.

"Hmm," Thaddeus flinched. She looked at him and he smiled. She stuck in the needle. "Wha'dyya do in your spare time?" he asked.

"My boyfriend and I go to the police shooting range," she said, biting her lip.

"A fellow NRAer!" Thaddeus laughed. "Naw, c'mon," he exhorted her.

"What? Oh, ok, I work in a clinic treating sexually transmitted diseases. Oops!" she yelled suddenly, fighting to keep the needle centered as Thad convulsed with laughter.

"Don't do that," she scolded.

"I can't help it," he giggled. "That's funny."

"It's the pot," she said matter-of-factly.

"No," he insisted. "You've got a helluva sense of humor. You should be doing sketches."

Melody blushed. "No, it's true. I work with young people on STD issues."

"Are you going with anybody?" he asked abruptly.

"Are you?" she countered, tilting her head.

"Hunh?" Thad lobbied.

"Stop it, you're kill'n me," she mocked.

"No, really. I've wanted to move out for a long time." He stopped to address her frown. "I know what you're thinking," he interrupted. She busied herself with changing the blood sample cartridges. "It's one thing to recognize that you aren't talking anymore, aren't having much fun, but you still love this person so that it's just too painful to, you know, get around to it."

"'Get around to it?'" her eyes widening.

Thaddeus studied his hands. "I see myself as a man who can tell the truth, but it's getting harder. That's troubling. I'm not sure what's happening."

Melody sniffed. She couldn't tell if Thaddeus was putting her on, or was so intoxicated with pot that he didn't know what line of crap he was peddling. She allowed herself to study him. His head was squarish with well-defined features and an air of defiance like the statue of a make-believe king. Body a bit too thick for heroic; she'd have to know him a lot better. "There you go," she said breezily, forcing an alcohol swab against his forearm. She bent his elbow to secure the swab, being careful not to linger.

Thaddeus didn't move. "Well?" he asked.

"Well? What?"

"Hunh?"

She eyed him clinically. "How often do you make love?" She straightened her arms along her sides.

Thaddeus looked at her astonished, "You can't ask me that!"

"I just did," she responded.

"Ok, ok," he said overcoming his embarrassment, "maybe twice a day?" It was an exaggeration.

Melody smiled, her short rounded hair glistening. "Better stay put, you won't find that downstream," she winked, gathering up her samples.

# 14

## *Everybody Must Get Stoned*

It was a fine cottony autumn day, stoned or otherwise, thought Wayne. Low clouds emitting gilded light parked haphazardly along a broad azure boulevard leading to a gray horizon dimpled with seagulls gliding. A gust like a stiff brush stirred cicadas deep within their trenches. Frosty feet fighting warm wings, his thoughts flew clumsily beyond government-issue walls.

In order to remain in the neutral October sun, Wayne sat against the iron door to 'B' ward, second floor. This potentially exposed him to the new 'recon waves'—long-range tracking radar being developed by the Navy; said to be so powerful it could read cup sizes. Fortunately, Air Force objections to this large program donation to a service rival had brought the appropriation to a standstill in Congress.

Cooperative weather and the fact that he'd cut down to two j's per day, allowed Wayne to smolder: three so far, it was almost 1 p.m. wasn't it? An amphibian dwelled in his head; his head was a big, red flower. The flower lay at the base of a mighty tree draped in vines; a path grew from the tree. Was this good shit or what? He went indoors as clouds blew out the sun. It was a sorry sight: complete unpreparedness for an enemy strike.

Wayne shook his head at the group sleeping around the tv. "Well, if it ain't the 'Nod Squad,'" he scoffed.

Shep raised an eyelid. "Mmmm?" he grunted.

"Is that garbage putting you to sleep? Or is it like, trying to reach you at like, your level?" goaded Wayne.

"I don't mind you slandering the mindless mish-mash of maudlin mediocrity that mesmerizes millions, but you ought to confine your attacks to the medium, please, lest you anger a potential litigant," warned Shep.

Wayne doubled up, belching smoke. "I can trash the media, but I have to respect you, the mole rat?"

"Of course, there is a great deal of vacuity in television," conceded Shep, twisting posture to its limits, "but your criticism is harsh." He splayed his chubby fingers, greasy black nails and all, in the public airspace. "In a historical context, the medium is in its infancy. Are these early motions wasted or are they the essential play required by this new form of communication? Shouldn't we be giving thanks this surfeit of slapstick and situation comedy is balanced by commentary and on-the-spot reportage, cowboy drama becoming human drama; hillbilly becomes Capitol Hill?"

"What does it matter," said Wayne, "it's all propaganda."

"Advertising pays for a more sophisticated system than could otherwise be obtained. That's not all bad."

"It conditions the audience."

"What? Are we to exit the realm of free speech for a political flight of fancy??"

Wayne pushed his cerebral cortex until it puckered. If he could mind-warp Shep, he'd have the whole tribe.

"People are told what to buy, what to think, how to pray, in exchange for Entertainment," Wayne whispered.

"Information enables free choice; consumer choice informs the economy."

"Our enemies are using this against us," countered Wayne.

"Ya gotta stay on point," yelped Shep.

These guys are all stoned, thought Shep. Yet they insist on acting straight, like I have the time to follow their footprints. Because reality no longer offers Reality; because reality is only the serendipitous discovery of the past, not a concise record. We could be making colossal mistakes trying to scrape together tiny, insignificant moments into a colorful record, a pleasing series of reference points meaningless without an interpreter with complete knowledge, position currently unfilled. And we are 'reality' junkies, hooked on believing every half-way plausible map. We take on each day as if the bank made an error in our favor. Life is easy as pulling on one's socks. Instead of a complicated puzzle requiring deep-cycle batteries, karma, camouflage clothing, the secrets of negotiation, prayer, shop class, Thank You letter writing, and jumper cables.

Most people are really not up to the complexity. They seldom move beyond the class they're born into. They feel antagonism because of life's fixity, but they don't know what to do with their feelings. They don't mind the world as it is, they just resent their place in the arrangement.

But if you smoke man, you're cool. You're not going to get bent out of shape by things you can't control. You get along with injustice, unfairness; they're functional parts of our world, natural outgrowths of incessant competition, the need to create order, the essential turnover of the aged and infirm.

Stoned, you're in on the joke, the sacred humor of being able to create something out of nothing, where mono shifts into stereo and stereo accelerates into the left lane.

He lit a match to ignite the joint, his sixth: a triangle of soft blue blame flared up at him and died away, a campfire dancing across the dunes, all shadowy arms. Exhaling: fire and soot, jet exhaust, blast furnace heat, incipient lung disease...the *rush* of sudden comprehension.

Mind caught in traffic, he gave up thinking, moving reflexively, composing little pictures, making every idea matter. Slipping into ephemeral conversation he explored the geography of things not owned, pondered the necessity of doing *with,* foresaw impossible events, welcomed the onrush of the grass taking root, producing an immediate harvest of pseudo ideas, tiny switchbacks thin as veins that were actual mirages sprung to purple life by the sun striking the walls of the brain.

* * * *

Tony noticed only five chairs. Good. Five was easier to take than 10. He nodded as they sauntered in: Sutter, Jimbo, Chris and Wayne. Oh, well. They were doing something funny to the lineups but he wasn't sure what it was. Seemed like they were trying to break up Jake and his buddy, Sutter. Good news —weekend sessions abandoned! A new personality, a Dr. Kunkell, was introduced. Kunkell, thick and ruddy, with a broad scar across his nose was an ex-ski champion, phy-ed teacher; mountain-tamer, etc. - almost his own species. When he said he was *'excited'* to be here, Wayne went into his Cheetah routine, running across the floor on his knuckles while screeching a high-pitched alarm call. "You came to see us freaks?" Wayne challenged, straightening his knees enough to become a Hunchback, a chimpanzee-like Hunchback...

Kunkell stared at them as they read, 'ESP: Thought Transmission/Premonition!' Pretty airy, thought Tony. The message: Interesting, but we need more study. Kunkell was fidgeting, eager to begin assessing this vegetable-based cult in the Sodom of the East Coast.

"Now, some of my colleagues," he began, his words like smooth stones, "claim that all this Parapsychology stuff is just a lot of bull. What do you think?" he challenged.

"I think your friend is right," replied Sutter.

Kunkell threw another punch: "Let's assume there is something to this ESP stuff for a moment. Let's say people do send and receive messages by ESP. How common do you think that is?"

"Pretty common, I'd say, but then I'm nuts!" snickered Wayne.

"You might be 'nuts' Wayne," said Chris, "but you're not common."

"You're uncommon," yelled Tony, "King Toot Uncommon."

"Well, I don't think being 'psychic' is that common," Chris resumed. "I remember when Uncle Bill was chopping down a tree, and Uncle Henry said that if he kept cutting, 'the whole damn thing is gonna fall on your stupid head!' And he was right. Now, was Uncle Henry psychic?"

"More psychic than Uncle Bill, apparently," volunteered Tony.

"Yeah, you want to be more psychic than that," added Jimbo.

"Is 'psychic' the same as parapsychology?" Kunkell continued.

"They're spelled differently, you idiot," Tony whispered.

"Does anyone here believe in thought transmission?" Kunkell counterattacked.

Sutter yawned, "Depends on how many miles you got on it, but I'm down to a goddamned roach and how the hell you expect me to transmit with that?!"

"You aren't much help to your own case," Jimbo spoke directly to Kunkell.

"What you mean by that?" Kunkell bit.

"Well, I been sending you all sort of telepathic messages, but you still talk'n!"

Custer averted his face; Kunkell conceded. "Perhaps you would like to tell me why you have such resistance to this article?"

Maybe tell you how much we resent patronizing behavior? thought Jimbo. Perhaps let you in on the fact that when you impose your will, you create resistance, not cooperation? Or that certain easy data is really useless? That it has nothing to do with weed, it's just the way we've been treated? Naw, we can't tel'um all that.

"Yo, Skip," said Sutter, "sorry, but it's just not the maze we rats were hop'n for."

"Yeah," added Tony, rising, "give us more cheese next time."

"More cheese, more cheese!" they chanted, and left.

Kunkell turned to Custer: "Are they always this cantankerous?"

"It's the captivity," Custer shrugged.

"But they've got all the marijuana they could ask for!"

"Apparently," chuckled Custer, "you can't have enough."

Nerves had become so frayed, thought Custer, any group activity could set off a dangerous train of emotions. Subjects assumed an alibi of disinterest, but engaged in frequent minor rebellions. He dug out his goody bag, appearing on the ward with comics and games. "Hey! Squirt guns!" shouted Tony.

"I gotta have me that Monopoly game," gasped Jake. "You,

you and you, come down to my room for Monopoly!"

"Wait," Sutter cautioned the retreating figures, "you don't have any dope! How can you play stoned without pot?"

"Right, how stupid of me. I must be strung out. Hey, Custer, bring some numbers down to my room, si vous plais?"

"Hold it you ungrateful creeps! You can't smoke in your rooms because I'm the only one on duty so that means the tv room!"

"Aw, c'mon," Sutter pleaded. "It's too noisy in the damned tv room! C'mon, join us."

"Yeah, joint us," teased Jake.

"No more fart'n around," Custer, agitated, retorted.

"Well, if you won't let us smoke in the rooms, let us bring our tv down here?" asked Sutter, indicating the Nurse's Station.

"Ok," Custer sighed. "But no smok'n unless I'm there!"

"Abso-fuck'n-lutely yo' honor."

"Incidentally, I could be usin' one of those merry-joe-wanna-bees myself," said Thaddeus, adjusting the diaper-like loin-cloth he'd been wearing of late.

Spying the Monopoly board under Jake's arm, Bergman asked, "Mind if I play?"

"Well, now that you put it that way," answered Sutter.

"Can't Berge; Custer's the fourth," broke in Jake.

"Umm..." mumbled Berge, "that reminds me, Minter's wife is on the phone."

"You know," said Jake, "I've always wanted to play three-person Monopoly—the Trinity and all."

"That's ok," said Bergman, "threesomes aren't that odd anymore, especially in California I'm told."

Bergman felt confident he could handle the drug, customize marijuana. Smoke it to smother boredom under a blanket of dreamy pauses and sudden, motiveless enthusiasms and refrain when driving or when forced to do some 'serious' business. He realized he was hosting a dangerous experiment, but some dark force refused to let him stop. As he struggled to name it, he was compelled to take more marijuana, seeking the upper limit of stoned as proof he could take it or leave it.

* * * *

Chris struggled for breath, swimming hard to remain on the crest of his own wave. A brief attack, one of several since Bergman zapped him, weakened his constitution just enough to render him susceptible to... Oh, shit.

His youthful, artistic, competitive, charming, gay psychopath dad Gary primped for another appearance in his best public shade. Ever since a cold September morning at the lake, Chris measured his life in moments stolen from a serial disaster known as Gary: Gary mocking Chris's inability to swim at six years old; Gary pushing his head underwater, the scrawny kid sputtering, gasping, wondering; Gary demanding he water-ski behind the massive smoke-belching old Johnson Sea Horse; Gary's third girlfriend since the divorce days before her suicide; Gary's war of annihilation; the fish king's handsome leathery face going suddenly blank when Chris finally agreed to ski; Gary sneering, 'No, you don't deserve another chance, you're a quitter.'

Every pathway since led to a mass extinction of hope at the feet of this brilliant, terrible man, this torturer of bright teeth, obedient hair and pupil-less radioactive blue eyes. Chris began to drink heavily when he realized its effectiveness as a sleep potion. Pot was a whole lot better: he could watch his life as if the role of Chris was played by a confident actor giving life and meaning to a clever, well-plotted script.

That is, he could until Bergman took the stage.

# 15

## *Just How Much IQ Is Needed To Pass An IQ Test?*

'A catastrophe, if it expects to be taken seriously, would come gunning for me first, don't you think?' Chris mused, his attention again drawn to the odd-looking birthmark, a many-fingered lake, stamped on his right shoulder. Chris knew it was the unique strands wrapped into his character like steel cable that made him completely different from anyone else. When stressed some of them failed and, well (there was no manual) Chris would feel freakish, unclean. He once tried to explain this to a friend, but she turned on him and called him 'depraved.'

He wondered when it was all going to get untracked. He seemed to be sliding through life, supine as an otter, moving rapidly but with limited view. He wanted to sit, stand-up, leap but he was held down, pushed to the ground by a mighty force pressing on his shoulder.

Stoned, he could explore, go upriver in his own mind without fear the carefully bundled sinews of his own one-of-a-kindness would snap, lashing him with their broken, screaming ends. He relished the quiet feeling of being salted away like something precious.

* * * *

Sutter grabbed the doorknob and pushed his way inside. Jake was bent over, his back toward Sutter, his whole body quivering. He was moaning something. 'Oh, no!' thought Sutter. "Oh, ma-ma!" moaned Jake. Sutter coughed. Jake turned, "Jeez!" Sutter stammered, "Sorry man, oh," his face reddened. "I didn't know you were, ah, waxing the bishop." "Gotta get that cum outta there somehow," Jake replied. "Hey," he said, motioning, "get me some kleenex. Whew! Sonofabitch! Ahh."

* * * *

Chris stood out, he knew that—'a cold fish': thin, aquatic-looking with milky, red-veined eyeballs. But what the birthmark taketh, it giveth too: He truly loved people; loved to listen to their stories, lives which he could see take place before him as if through a wisp of curtain. Sometimes, not every time, the pot made him want to interact with these people in the living rooms and kitchens of their words. But the great clarity he enjoyed in his sympathy for others was no protection against insult; Bergman showed him the error in his thinking. Bergman didn't mean to attack him, he was just hungry.

* * * *

"Jesus Christ!" Wayne shrieked, "that mutha-fucka was one a hard test."

"Hard test!" Shep guffawed, "haw-aw-r-r-r-d-d" he repeated helplessly, locked in painful ecstasy. His right hand picked up the pace, rooting deep in his hairy chest for any vermin bold enough to risk encampment. "Ha-ha-ha... t-t-tesssst!" he gasped, slipping out of the Great Chair.

Ron approached casually, the sight of someone on the floor laughing wasn't the magnet of former days, "What's his problem?" he asked.

"I dunno," replied Wayne. The two of them stood over the

crumpled figure of Shep, left leg shaking violently inside his filthy slacks.

"Maybe he's having a seizure?" offered Ron.

"Could be," observed Wayne. "Saw a seizure once," Wayne went on, "guy's head bouncin' aroun' like a 4x4 in mud. Went rigid as a plank alluvasudden; fell straight backwards like this. Konked hisself on the c-ment real hard. Started to twitch...bled like a kotex. After that, had to wear a football helmet wherever he went. Called 'im 'Crash Kelly.'"

Ron helped Shep to his feet, holding him up until he could breathe. "What happened?" he asked.

"All's I said was, 'It was a hard test, man, and he gets a frick'n seizure!" explained Wayne.

"'Hard test. That's delicious!" wheezed Shep. "It's a fuck'n IQ test!"

"Yeah? An IQ test?" Ron said warily, "like how smart you are?"

"Exactly," Shep shot back. "It's not Pass/Fail. The number of correct scores indicates where you'd fall in the general population in terms of intelligence potential."

"Even so, it wasn't easy!" broke in Wayne. "And we didn't get any time to study." If only he'd had his weapons box, he'd fix that test good.

"My God!" Shep yipped. "You can't study. It's native intelligence."

"Well, what if you're not a native, what if you just moved here?" asked Wayne.

Shep corkscrewed into a giggling, asthmatic crouch. "I love this guy!" he said, gripping Wayne by the waist. Wayne pushed him away.

"What's your IQ?" Ron asked Shep.

"What's yours?" came the rejoinder.

"I don't know; I don't know if I've ever taken one."

Shep's mouth twitched.

"So what's your IQ?" Ron asked again using his best diction.

"It's like this, your IQ never changes much," replied Shep with brittle honesty. "By this time, you've taken at least three IQ tests. The fact that you don't know yours is an IQ test in itself. If you can't guess your own or someone else's IQ within a few points, well then, grab a broom and start practicing your trade," Shep laughed. Suddenly, he lurched to his feet, and breathing heavily, staggered down the hall.

"Thanks, thanks a lot." Ron mumbled.

* * * *

Wayne's father, son of an Air Force general, determined during the 1950's nuclear arms race, to raise the first 'peace baby,' keeping the infant with a cascade of soft white hair gushing down his forehead, from the 'vampirism' of the media. Oh, there was a television, but not tv; there was no time for the Mertz/Ricardo shtick, or *Bonanza* (especially *Bonanza*). Instead the recent 'image replicator' blinked open to live PBS theater and, of course, nature documentaries featuring ravenous wild dogs, thirty-foot serpents, killer crocs, poisonous goldfish and deadly, vengeance-minded insects. Radio was outlawed: 'not that god-awful Charlie McCarthy!' (except for Sox games); magazines were scrutinized: *Geographic* was 'ok,' but *Time* 'A Luce publication? Never!' Even children's books were censored: talking birds were alright, but witches and magic got the ax.

Imagine Mr. Hammer's surprise one morning—he who struggled so valiantly against the toy gun, the cartoon anvil, the celluloid pratfall, as the quiet, obedient three-year-old suddenly seized a crooked stick from the walk, aimed it expertly at his father and hollered: 'Bang-bang-bang, you're dead, you sonofabitch!'

Afterward, little Wayne got every tool of random mayhem his black heart desired. Even the successful patent lawyer questioned the results as the Grand Campaign overseen by Wayne spilled into the neighborhood turning harmless kid encounters into flash points of mass destruction.

Adjoining homesteads were littered with five and six-year-old bodies that Wayne, official battlefield referee and ruthless warlord, refused passage home after they'd been slain. Slaughter of course, was obligatory as Wayne armed his cowboys with grenade rifles, exploding horses, seismic sea-wave generators; his Indians possessed tomahawk radar, paralysis-inducing eagle feather bonnets, kidnapping teepees, dogs sneezing fatal bacteria. There was no object in Wayne's strategic view, that couldn't somehow be bent toward homicide.

As Captain Rellik ('Killer' spelled backwards) of Space Warrior Squad, an elite extension of the High Command, Wayne's mission was disturbingly simple: wipe out the enemies of the U.S. of A, meaning anyone, from the UN to the Professional Librarians Association, who challenged the Supreme Command.

Some day of course, the Supreme Command would turn on its premier assassin and he would become the hunted. Wayne expected the final, violent confrontation any day now.

* * * *

Jake's father, Arnie, of ***Arnie's A-1 Used Cars***, had turned him on to the sexiness, the skin-clearing potential, the excitement of wads of untraceable, untaxable, unbillable bills. Arnie went to the edge of town and paid $2,500 for 1/2 acre along Highway 21. Another $1,000 for a front-end loader and Arnie brought tarmac to sumac, gouging from the hillside the farthest commercial outpost on the road to Kenyon, S.D., Population 11,370.

It was all about money; Arnie's 'profit' was what he could hide from the government. Arnie bought cheaply and sold below $1,000 to maximize his cash flow. He did his own books, burying somewhere within the web of lines that made up the graph paper enough cash to cut a swath through town larger than his vocation would normally justify. Jake learned early 'build a stash, don't flash the cash.' Jake began selling weed at 15; he was smoking so much that he had to cut back or find a new source of revenue. It was a natural fit, he filled the demand but didn't 'flash the cash.' He and others in the trade, bought land and diversified.

The day drunken strangers knocked on his door imploring him for a nickel bag on credit: 'C'mon, man, for the Revolution!' were long gone. He sold it by the brick only now (kilo: 2.2 pounds = $2,000, $57 an oz.); he had a good front in the paraphernalia distribution business. It cost him 22 months at Bridgewater, a medium security country club, but he'd moved up to an untouchable role, he'd done his time. There was $60,000 in his freezer ('cold cash'), 15 acres on the chalky green waters of the Eel River outside of Garberville in the tall trees, $25,000 in Kruggerands buried on his girlfriend's uncle's farm, and several grand in these new computer stocks.

Oh, and it was like snagging spawned-out fish when it came to chicks: the quantity of young women who'd blow you for a quarter! In fact, that's how he met Sutter—the annual Humboldt County Grower's Bowl. They traded ladies, Sutter was dating Kath, his ex; he was tight with Sutter's former squeeze, Kristi.

Yep, Arnie had it right. Long hair? Bell bottoms? *'Do you stand or squat, Missy?'* All the resentment, all the backwoods in-breeding, the logger macho, melted into 'GOAG,' (Good Ol' American Green) at the cash register. Pot money would soon run the country, not the first time empires were built exploiting the space on the other side of the wall. Whatever their politics, Americans grew tolerant in the presence of cash. More than one thoughtless old skinflint claimed respect as 'frank,' or 'frugal,' thanks to their wealth. And there was no end of new ways of becoming old money.

Jake had a plan involving 'muscular capitalism.' 'A dollar earned, is a dollar fresh from someone else's pocket,' Arnie hooted, as he set about applying black shoe polish to the tires and Vaseline to the trim.

## 16

## *Addicts Are Their Own Best Friends*

As he was about to speak Dr. Nicholson noticed a rough brown line of grime creeping around his cuff. Had he put a dirty shirt back on the hanger—no! It was simply amazing how the body did its work. Again, a lesson in humility. Whatever steps one took to erect a marker of humanity's aspirations, Nature threw herself in the opposite direction. No matter how strong the detergent, body oils and soot stood ready to annul the effect.

"Yo, Doc," Sutter's voice ending on a high note.

"Yes, Mr. McClellan? Say, before we begin drug usage questions in this one-on-one session, I'd like to ask you a personal question."

"Go ahead Doc, shoot."

"Well, what I'd like to know is why has your generation proved to be so rebellious, so annoying—attacking everything traditional—beliefs, institutions, authorities?"

"Hey," said Sutter swiftly, "you don't know there's a war going on?"

"Is that it, the war?" inquired Nicholson.

"Damn right. The war, and other shit, too."

"Tell me about your opposition to the war."

"It's not right."

"Elaborate, please."

"You don't kill people just because they're communists. I

mean I wouldn't kill Baptists, either. And I've got a lower opinion of them."

"I think it's about whether the Vietnamese want to be communists—there's a big difference."

"Bullshit. You don't murder people in little far-off countries whatever they call themselves."

"Don't you believe in self-determination? Shouldn't the Vietnamese decide between the bullet and the ballot?"

"Some decision. They stand to get shot either way. It's war, man. We brought the war to them. It ain't like it's gonna be a fair vote. Peace ain't on the ballot.

"It's the same with your take on pot, man."

"By 'me,' you mean my generation?"

"Yeah," said Sutter, "you guys—the older generation—have this thing, right, this World War II idea that force has to be met with force. Ok, sure, if someone was trying to take away my Harley, I'd fight. That's not the same as killing Vietnamese because we want to rebuild their country into something we can be comfortable with. But we're driving the peasants into the hands of the local communists with all our bombs; I mean who's going to be there for them in the end?"

"How does your opposition to the war translate into the marijuana debate?" asked Nicholson.

Sutter jumped at the question. "See, it's this attitude that you know better because you're older and more experienced and you've studied the facts and they're on your side. But that's bullshit, man. It's not true. You're assuming all this shit."

"How so?" broke in Nicholson.

"Well, you are older," Sutter conceded, "but you grew up when pot was 'wacky tobacky,' the source of madness and mindless violence. But those aren't facts. They're prejudice repeated until it passes for fact. The real facts are just the opposite. Your generation's 'knowledge' isn't based on fact at all.

"The facts are that marijuana is harmless. It isn't addictive and it isn't strong enough to make you a psychotic murderer, or even an accidental killer. But you've conveniently buried these facts. They don't fit your so-called knowledge. So now you're doing another study, another search for 'facts' that will fit your comfort zone.

"But now booze, man, your facts say, it's ok—in moderation. But when it's abused like it always is, you accept it, you make a joke about it. Of course, the truth is, alcohol is the most destructive drug of all, it kills half a million people a year just in this country. But it's funny man, when someone's drunk."

"Yeah, well, I think I get your point," Nicholson interrupted, "though you're way off if you think this experiment is fishing for red herring."

"Yeah?"

Nicholson located the creases in his slacks and pulled downward. "Suppose we take a look at the claim that cannabis is not addictive," he aimed. "How often do you smoke, I mean not just in here, but as part of your daily routine?"

"Man, I don't know," replied Sutter, pausing, "everyday, I guess."

"But it's not addicting?" challenged Nicholson.

"Hey man, I don't do it, like because the mar-i-ju-na genie is whispering, 'E*at me, eat me; I'm good shit and you need another hit.*'"

"Then why do you smoke daily?"

Sutter fidgeted. "Because I get frustrated you know. Tired of waiting 'til the world gets its shit together. Like all this bad karma from the war, and these ancient attitudes about work, sex, politics and pot, you know?"

"'Our' ancient attitudes frustrate you?"

"Yeah. Like everyone's so stubborn man, change is too slow, it makes me depressed."

"So you light up a doobie to give you the sense of being someone doing something?"

"Right on, man!"

"You have your own little antidepressant."

"Yeah. Just like you guys."

Nicholson smiled. "You may go now," he said quietly. As Sutter got up to go, Nicholson took off his glasses and massaged his forehead. Bergman entered and scouted for a chair that was not directly across from his interrogator to no avail. Nicholson waited until Bergman, born to the air like a fly-catcher, found an uneasy perch in which to alight.

He pulled a sheet from Bergman's file which charted his drug usage. He passed it along. "Says here you ingest nearly six full cannabis cigarettes per day."

"Is it that low?" Bergman replied, trying to make light.

Nicholson stirred in his chair. These goddamned pants were definitely too tight. His nuts felt like they were in a sling-shot. "Do you, ah, worry about addiction?" he asked.

"No, I'm not a paid psychologist; I let you worry about addiction," Bergman responded.

"Galen, maybe it's time you started to worry?"

"Addiction?" Berge repeated, "what's addiction?"

Nicholson nodded. "The addict doesn't conform his behavior to reality. He distorts reality to fit his behavior. When his doctor tells him he must stop eating or he'll have a heart attack, the non-addict concludes, 'Ok, I can do that.'

"But the addict says, 'Med school, schmed school, what

does that kike doctor know anyway?!'"

"C'mon," Bergman replied, "you can't lay every problem at the doorstep of addiction. Everybody's addicted to something but the world doesn't stop.

"Sex, power, pills; some are addicted to danger, others to safety. Isn't there something known as 'religious addiction'? Isn't a 'good employee' addicted to their work?"

Nicholson shot back: "A common trait of addiction is denial. Your background survey indicates you drink alcohol everyday. Now, most people don't drink alcohol and smoke pot everyday. To most observers, you're a heavy user of drugs and that suggests a problem."

Bergman tried to stay calm. "Ok, how do you define a problem?"

Nicholson scowled. He preferred not to waste his time with baby steps and didn't anticipate them with someone of Bergman's intelligence. "My simple test: is it getting in your way? Tell me, could a professional athlete do what you're doing and perform at the top of his calling?"

"For a while, I suppose," Bergman dodged, "it ain't like it's a needle habit."

"The fact that you view some addictions as limiting tells me you do understand the problem," Nicholson argued. The two of them eyed each other.

"Galen, ask yourself a simple question: Where do I want to go with my life?"

Bergman studied the question as if it were an agate. "Where do I want to go?" he repeated.

"In cases of drug dependency, the individual does not achieve their goals," Nicholson answered. "They substitute drug-seeking behavior for goal-accomplishment. The drug experience repeated regularly replaces life's accomplishments."

"I think you mean 'rarely' achieves their goals," Bergman replied. "You're substituting sometime drug outcomes with slightly motivated people, for predictable outcomes by highly motivated people," Bergman responded.

"There's an absence of motivation to go forward," Nicholson insisted.

Bergman remembered taking a beer out of the fridge but couldn't remember where he put the squishy to wrap around it. He felt good he couldn't, thinking it might mean he wouldn't have a beer after all. He wandered about the apartment until he found the squishy. There was a recently opened beer in it, his fourth. No food. Already stoned. It's just noon. He needed a regular job.

Maybe he should quit the booze and pot. That would mean moving out on Dierdre, her gray eyes like hawk eggs, her freckled vanilla yogurt skin, her slim, smoothy legs. Beautiful but frail, she needed organizing, a push out the door. Their dependencies were starting to clash.

Nicholson, sensing an opening, continued: "You don't think you're affected by pot and alcohol because you're always affected by them. It's constant, therefore it's harmless."

Bergman asked, "How do you stop?" The words surprised him.

"Realize you drink and smoke because these are acts of independence," Nicholson explained. "You change your mood because you can. But in the process of being drunk and stoned all the time, you lose your real life."

"How come you use pot and booze like they're interchangeable when the literature says they're not?" Bergman interjected.

"Alcoholics are bullies, basically," said Nicholson. "They

need to control and the alcohol assists them to do what is otherwise not permissible. And pot?

"I think pot changes brain structure. Normal impulses are blocked so the brain builds new ones permanently altering things such as the ability to track conversation, think logically, or face stress."

"C'mon, that's b.s."

"Not really," Nicholson retorted. "It's my experience that pot retards emotional maturity. Instead of dealing with one's problems, the pot addict refuses the possibility of change. They don't grow; it's too much responsibility. They're dishonest. They fashion a routine of inward looking self-medication. They claim they're being creative, but they're fooling themselves." Nicholson wondered if Bergman's silence meant he'd overdone it.

"What makes people smoke pot?" Bergman asked.

"I think they want to escape."

"Escape what?" Bergman wanted to know.

"Whatever..."

Bergman rose and shook Nicholson's hand. As he left Nicholson called after him, "Galen, you think you can do this alone?"

Bergman turned, "Doctor, trees do fall in the forest, regardless of what you may have heard."

Nicholson picked up the roster as Chris peaked around the corner. "Come in, come in," he implored.

Chris circled the only chair available. "Here?" he asked.

Nicholson nodded professionally. "Welcome Chris. Sit down, please."

"You wanna talk to me?" Chris asked.

"Yes, if you don't mind?" Nicholson replied, resisting the temptation to dig at the offending material constricting his hips.

"Well, actually I had hoped to start *War and Peace,* but I don't have to rush into it," said Chris.

Nicholson's eyes narrowed. "Chris, do you know why we have these personal sessions?"

"I think it may have something to do with the Experiment?" Chris offered.

"Exactly. Most of our data will be of an empirical nature, expressed in numbers and percentages. Of course, there will be questions: Why this? Why that?" Nicholson became deliberate. "People—very important people—with no connection to *cannabis,* are going to want to know why we arrived at the conclusions we did."

"And you are going to tell them?" Chris broke in.

"No," corrected Nicholson, "you are."

"You're not giving out my phone number are you?" Chris said in alarm.

"Chris," said Nicholson severely. "We have to relate our numbers to real, living people for them to have any meaning. It's all done anonymously of course."

"Of course—subject number six, initials C.C. went insane with drugs and grief after breaking up with his girlfriend of 10 years who opposed his going into free marijuana experiment—and had to be taken to Bellevue but his identity remains a secret."

Nicholson laughed. "You know, in addition to getting information from you that will help us round out our research, we're available at this time, to give you some insight into the nature of the drug you're asked to partake of."

Checkmate. Chris had to hand it to Nicholson, he knew how to hide the knife in a cake. "Ok," he sighed, "what do you want to know?"

"Well, it would appear you had a rather bizarre episode with the drug—for reasons beyond your control—on the first day of access. Since then your use of the drug follows no established pattern. Could you explain this?"

"Do I have to?"

"Hmm," Nicholson equivocated. "You don't have to. I can't compel you. But in the interests of science, of understanding, we would very much like to have some personal observations from which to draw upon in our analysis."

Chris searched the room for a clock, a painting—any distraction that might dampen the tension of having to supply an answer he knew to be mostly invention. There was no island either, on Nicholson's professorial appearance—not a scar, pimple or uneven tooth. Nicholson raised his eyebrows. He sat quietly waiting for Chris's reply, but Chris was back in high school where a metal shield descended from the ceiling to protect the precious gray matter locked within his skull from contamination. The teacher earnestly mouthed the appropriate learning matter but the words deflected off his steel cap like so many harmless bb's, leaving him perfectly aloof from academic infection.

Nicholson leaned forward confidentially. "Is there anything you'd like to ask me?"

There were a few things thought Chris, scouting for them even as they scattered across the bushy, overgrown landscape of his mind. First off, I'd like to know what I'm doing here, you know, in the greater scheme of things? Secondly, I'd like to know why I just didn't pop that asshole Bergman in the nose and feel good for doing it? This is not a rhetorical question. I'd like to have an answer, please!

Hello. Anybody?

Thirdly, I'd like to know why there isn't an echo to any of my questions? Huh?

"Well, I think we're finished here," said Nicholson, promising to let out his trousers within the week.

"Wait," Chris said suddenly. Well, it was now or kiss it all good-bye. He searched for the right words while Nicholson faced the prospect of reseating. "You know," Chris began with naked honesty, "I really don't know who I am. All my life I've imitated others, done what they did, not because I wanted to or thought it should be done, but because to follow someone else was easier than putting together my own plan. I mean, what would I put in my plan? I have no idea." The words oozed out of him like pus. It felt good to put down his big wet, smelly suitcase for a second.

"But that first day with Berge. Whew! Well, it was too much. I felt, ah, fear. I mean, it was always there, the suspicion that I was living a borrowed existence. I, I carried it off hoping the real me would suddenly show up and I'd be done with the false one. I'd have it then, you know, when the real me came back to town.

"But Berge blew it all up. He just said a couple words and I fell apart. Man, I should have said, 'Bull shit!' or 'Screw you!' but there was no 'me' to say it." Chris could feel tears mustering in his eyes, and that dry, pinched feeling in his nose, but he kept on.

"There was no big brother, no shot of adrenaline. The pot didn't help. It didn't fill my head with clever comebacks. It let me down. So I gave it a second chance, and a third... Because sometime, somewhere, it'll trigger me."

"Well," said Nicholson, standing, "I can advise you on one thing."

"What's that?" Chris shot back.

"Stop smoking *cannabis*."

"Why?"

"Because it's the one thing you can do immediately to make a major change in your life," Nicholson responded.

"To give up pot?" squeaked Chris.

"Yes," said Nicholson.

'But,' said Chris, to a portion of Nicholson's face where the skin appeared tighter, augmented by mortar and stone, 'that's why I started to smoke weed in the first place!'

# 17

# *The Final Frontier*

Jimbo had none too definite goals in life; mainly he pined for some form of acceptance and reward. How to get there was the problem. He'd never stayed with anything long enough to gain the edge. Eventually, this lead to the suspicion that he didn't have his shit together. Never would. Worse, he would sometimes find himself standing under a dome of cold light surrounded by a lurking fog of icy darkness. In the dreamy dyslexia of night, he awoke repeatedly to glance at the luminous symbols racing around a mysterious source of energy inches from his head, then slipped back into sleepless torment. In the morning, he felt upside down as if he hadn't slept at all. That's when he reached for the pot.

After a few hits, his life came into perspective as if focused by Leica. Now there was marvelous clarity: the intimacy and truth of the world revealed as in a close-up of the thousands of inter-locking scales on a butterfly wing.

He wondered if the 'fog' and cannabis weren't just different parts of the same system? Typically, the fog was brought on by the need to select some type of meaningful employment, a need that disappeared in the distinctive swamp smell of a good joint.

* * * *

"That's fa-diculous," puffed Jake, "I can't find my lighter. Look," he paused, "I bin in ev'ry state, and," he coughed, "includ'n, many times, the state—cha, cha, ca-ca-cahut!" he wheezed, the pot pounding his chest like a heavy wet wave, "of passion."

"They say the state of arousal borders the state of confusion," pitched Bergman.

"Only gearheads and polluters own cars," Sutter flexed.

Shep stepped to the plate. "Ecstasy inches away, but Topeka, that's another story! Howya gonna get there?"

"Git where?"

"Git to Topeka. Git to wherever in the Hell it is you wanna go?"

"We're not goun' anywere are we?" asked Sutter.

"Goin' to Hell if we don' pray," said Jake.

"How do you git from point A to point B?" squirmed Shep, "without the internal combustion engine?"

"Infernal what?" Jake responded.

"Who's points are we talking here, A or B?" asked Sutter.

"And does she have a younger sister?"

"Well, let's ask her."

"Better yet, let's ask her sister."

"So you need a car?" said Shep.

Jake eyed him curiously. "No, we've got a car you ol' pervert."

"That's my point, the car is the ultimate PDS: Personal Delivery System."

"Yeah, I know what PDS is," Jake winked.

"Well, then, you know nothing short of *teleportation* can match it. Whether you hitchhike, bus or carpool, you're still dependent on the internal combustion engine."

"What's your point?" asked Jake.

"Or are you just happy to see me?" put in Sutter.

"That's my point!" shouted Shep.

"Point... point... Haven't we been here before?"

"Yes, yes of course, there's my damn lighter!" cried Jake.

* * * *

A hysterical woman slapped Wayne awake with angry shrieks and a storm of tears. He sat up groggily as pieces of the dream sought cracks in the floor in which to hide. Wayne assembled as many as he could: *Down on his luck, out of work for months, on the verge of homelessness. He tried everything, made 20 calls a day. Always the same answer: 'Sorry, no work.' Finally, in a desperate move, he called an employment counselor. The counselor, a pleasant voiced 'Anne-Marie,' told him that 'from initial inquiries, we believe we have the perfect job. Excellent salary, fun environment, generous bonus, extraordinary vacation—all just for you! Only one question remains, that is...' But at this point, the voice of Anne-Marie, who for some reason he pictured with pigtails, grew weak. He could see her pale mouth form the words, but he couldn't hear them. She repeated the question but each time the sounds of her voice were mangled by the drone of a large fan necessary in the tropical venue of deep sleep. Anne-Marie eventually tired of his silence, her pretty face boiled from pink to red. Her hair became greasy and matted. Finally, with a climactic yell, Anne-Marie's message could be heard with fearful clarity: 'You're so fucked up on marijuana, you can't even answer the question!'*

* * * *

The reduction in hand clicking had not gone unnoticed. 'The crickets are dying like flies,' Badger noted in the Day Record. Minter read it and passed it along to Dr. Nicholson, adding, 'Will investigate.' Even before the reply he'd had the

Badger do a maximum press count: 2.5 hours. "You're certain?"

"10,000 clicks; 60 a minute, alternate hands, 3,600 an hour - 2.5 hours. But 3.5–4 is more likely. It's a pain in the ass."

Both agreed they weren't hearing much 'clickering.' Three days later, Badger wrote, 'No clicks, zilcho! 6 a.m. til 2 p.m. Draw your own conclusions.' Custer called Nicholson's office: Dr. Nicholson was out of touch in Atlanta. Badger suggested he notify Wicks, the next senior investigator. Custer pushed back in his chair, booted foot poised on the desk.

"What day is this?" he asked the Badge.

"God, I don't know, Wednesday...the seventeenth?" Badger answered.

"So the experiment is half-over?"

"Yeah, yeah," Badger caught on. He grinned, "But what would Nicholson say?"

"Oh, you know, 'you are Harvard, the school's reputation is at stake. It's reputation is the school's capital —you must be true —to Harvard! The only ethical behavior in this context is to, is to lie, lie, lie...'"

Badge burst out laughing, "That's great, that's great. Say," he continued. "I confiscated this from crazy Ira. He was claiming he 'accidentally' clicked over, you know, but he was leaving it at '0000'and coming around for credit every three hours. When I called him on it, he said it was broken."

Custer took up the clicker. It read '0000.' He rapped the finger-punch sharply: nothing happened to the tumblers. He opened the locked desk drawer with his key and chunked the broken Imp inside. He selected one of three alternates and, recording the serial number, handed it to Badge who stood stiffly in front of him, mouth agape.

"What's all this?" he asked, baffled.

Custer launched his chair backwards, "Don't worry about a thing, I'll take care of it."

* * * *

"Yes, exactly: Ego Maniac. Who would want to live otherwise!? To possess the secret powers others fear; to give meaning to words turned to mud in the maws of mumblers; to strut in finery while sparring with the most brilliant thinkers of the ages. To imagine yourself a Prince whose appearance is awaited with excitation, whose hair and eyes glow with romance, whose mere person blasts through a room like the scent of danger; yes, this is ego mania and I love it," said Thad.

"Ah, I couldn't help but think Mr. Maniac, during your speech, that a lot of you fellas... And I don't mean to single you out, Mr. Ego; but you are guilty too, of messaging the terrible lizard—the 'brute of the loom'—as you spoke? What's the deal with that, huh?"

"You mean hammer'n the nail right in front you?" said Thad.

"Yes, well, 'butter'n the corn,' 'cuffing the clown,' 'c'mon around the mountain'? Most of the time they've got their pants on, if you can call that a mitigating factor—I don't necessarily—There, you just did it!" Melody cried.

"Right, huh? Well," Thad fished, "it's still dry."

"That's disgusting!" Melody stammered. "What is this, this thing with the schwantz?"

"Public masturbation."

"Beg pardon?"

"The final frontier," answered Thaddeus.

* * * *

When, after an hour or so, Ron, sitting quietly by himself in the tv room, staring out the window, lost in a world of marvelous but temporary revelations, felt he was no longer high, a powerful urge overcame him and he trotted down to Emergency for another 'fix,' so he could come back to the tv room to stare quietly out the window while a rainbow of promise and reward tumbled about.

Stoned, Ron took the news better. Sober, he felt prickly, annoyed. The news was simple enough: he didn't make the grade, *nolo contendre,* second team. Ron hoped he would do something to make a difference; he thought he had good ideas, but might lack the feminine arts of persuasion. Now the message was getting through: he lacked warmth. He didn't appear sympathetic.

Ron got altered; got into the nature of being high on pot, wondered about the euphoria even though he knew he could only get so high, tried to define himself in light of his sometimes heavy use. He was puzzled, too: if McCartney and Lennon hadn't met, would they still be Lennon and McCartney?

* * * *

"Your're shitt'n me!" Sutter accused.

"No lie man. One six niner—the highest IQ ever to submit to drug testing."

"Shep?"

"Seems impossible. Overweight, sweaty, dangerous-by-any-measure New Yorker loose with a brain the size of Frankenstein."

"170? Wow, that's half my IQ."

"Que pasa? 'Half' my numerically challenged friend?"

"Huh? Ah, yeah, twice my IQ!" Sutter giggled.

* * * *

While the rich draft dodgers, the pot smoking, oversexed, liberal pantywaist college students protested the war by spending their loans on weed and gett'n laid, Ron fought the fuck'n war for them. Took a round at Ple Ku and went into anaphylactic shock: hair on end, sweating like a jungle rain, large welts erupting over his broken body accompanied by a terrible itch and then the gasping for breath... Pronounced 'dead,' he miraculously rallied and survived to hate those who didn't have the balls to enter another country to wipe out dictatorship.

After recovery, and a Silver Star, he was shipped stateside with a strong pot habit and a desire to go to college. The pot helped in the transition from corpse to collegian, from gung ho to Kung Fu. Like a pesticide, it went right after that shadowy black blotch that formed on the edge of his vision each time he opened himself to the smoky, shifting heat that cradled those caustic memories. Strange trip, man! Beauty and pain, opportunity and failure, power and humility, love and destruction. Still too terrible without weed to think on again, too many questions, too many active phantoms out there in the jungle ready to sniper every truth, every happiness.

His eyes scraped each limb to its cleanest, sharpest essentials. Vision was vital, an eagle's eyes would be useless, too slow-focusing. Reactions had to be precisely echeloned, sequenced by irrefutable logic. Without the feeling of control, of full power surging, you ain't going to make it.

* * * *

"But Thad, you have a wife and three children!" Melody exclaimed. She was sure of herself, certain that she had identified this intrusion. Keep it on a simple level: sacred/profane, love/lust.

"I'm a coward," he admitted, standing uncharacteristically still. "I'm not happy, can't remember a day when I was."

"You know, I'm not the one who should be listening to this."

"No, that's ok," recovered Thad. "I suspect Jenny is feeling the same tightness, the same shortness of breath. We live in a UN truce zone; we can't talk without lightning and thunder."

"Ahhh," Melody sighed, "I'm willing to listen if you think it'll do any good, but I can't get involved."

"And that's the great irony behind all of this," Thad burst, "I'm an actor, not a street nigger. I play heroes. Heroes, even dead ones, face the conflict that stalks every man. They're willing to risk all in order to live to the limits of their feelings. But I'm not. My life is denial. Go along to get along 'til I've disappeared. I'm not peddl'n or plead'n. Fact is, you're a catalyst to all this. It's like I'm finally breathing fresh air."

"I give you credit, you can sling it with both hands," she retorted.

"Yes, you're right," he laughed, "I've sown a life of deceit."

"I didn't mean it like that."

"It's true. Until I met you, I was just unhappy. Now, I'm inconsolable. I feel the exhausting weight of my own weakness!" he hung his head.

"Our relationship is strictly professional. I sense that you have serious issues at home. I suggest you solve that problem before you take on a new relationship."

"You're absolutely right, no, you really are." Melody's laugh became a snort and she had to cover her mouth. "I have to sort this out, this is my problem. But it's only a problem when I find myself here," Thad said earnestly.

"I'm going to need overshoes soon."

"I made a mistake, I own up to it."

"You're married. You said 'I do.' You created children."

"I feel, like, like, I'm trapped."

"Trapped in your marriage?"

"No, trapped in my parent's marriage."

Jake and Sutter passed in the corridor. "God, he's about as tight on her as a garter snake on a field mouse."

"Yeah, if he doesn't nail her, it won't be for lack of trying."

"You can guess what he wants from her," added Jake, "but what does she want from him she couldn't get from a large pizza?"

# 18

## *The Sounds of Silence*

Custer joked with Thad and Tony as Badger struggled to place a large reel-to-reel tape recorder on the table. "What the hell is that for?" asked Sutter.

"They gonna play sweet music to soothe your savage heart," supplied Thad.

"Yeah, what kinda music?" responded Sutter skeptically.

"For you, long-hair music," replied Tony.

"And for Berge," said Jake as the former entered, "they gonna play square dances."

"Ok you clowns, cut the b.s.," ordered the Badge, "we got work to do."

As Badger continued to toy with the knobs on the machine, adjusting for speed and tone, Minter outlined the day's program. "Ok, listen up. As you know, pot has a reputation for, ah, 'facilitating' humorous conversation. Hey, hey, hold it," he instructed at the raucous reaction to this observation, unwilling to give these reefer pirates the chance to completely scuttle the ship. "So today, we want you all to get high and treat us, and posterity, to your best, wittiest repartee. *Comprende*?"

Badger passed out joints, including two to Shep, but the latter's hand continued to flop above his head. "Ok, what is it?"

Shep wiped a chubby palm across his naked chest. "This tape recorder—it's a Wollensak."

"Yeah," said Bedikker warily.

"Well, you know, they murdered my people!"

"What the hell are you talking about?" Badger shot back.

"Wollensak," answered Ira. "It's really another name for I.G. Farben, the makers of zyclon—B."

Bedikker and Minter exchanged worried looks.

"Oh, come on, you didn't know?" Ira scoffed.

"Know what?" said Custer.

"This device was stolen from the Nazis after World War II —the same Nazis that used zyclon—B gas in the crematoriums to kill millions of Jews—my people!"

Badger examined the tape machine. "I had no idea," Custer admitted.

"Wait a sec, wait a sec," Badger chipped in, "says here—Made in USA." He attempted to turn the device toward Ira.

"Wha'd'ya expect it to say? Made in Auschwitz! It's German technology handed out after the War to government whores!" screamed Ira.

Custer felt a chill. "Is this really going to be a problem? I don't think we have another."

"Naw, that's ok," said Shep dismissively. "I just wanted you to be AWARE."

"Oh, we're aware alright," said Badger, "very aware." He raised his eyebrows. "Can we continue?"

"Wait a second," Thad piped up, "isn't this grass grown in Mississippi, land of Confederate slaveholders?"

Minter knew the proposed experiment was fraught with problems. There was no form, no structure to keep respondents on task. Results would be hard to codify and nearly impossible to duplicate. Ordinarily, this would be enough to sink it. Still, Nicholson didn't kill the idea. A good deal of documentation pointed to this part of the marijuana 'high.' Though subjective, numerous surveys turned up a feeling of giddiness leading to uncontrollable laughter. Problem was, such reactions appeared to occur more frequently among new users. Then there was the matter of chemistry. Groups of friends might erupt in laughter, but strangers; well, relative strangers? On the other hand, what if they kicked over just the right stone and got into new, radical territory? The terms of the study allowed for a lot of hands to be dealt, why not gamble on a couple? Badger had managed to turn the tape on and the wheels revolved silently and methodically as a maple seedling spiraling through a thin October sky.

Well? thought Minter. The joints were smoking yet conversations stalled out. Of course, the setting posed obstacles to the planned spontaneity. The subjects were arrayed around the tape recorder in a doughnut—too mechanical. They'd taken their places as if attending another tiresome battle with the 'Rules of Life,' or a worship service before a hallowed vessel. Custer needed a spark. Perhaps, if they weren't already miles away those dueling personalities Jake and Berge might be provoked into an exchange? "Berge?"

Bergman found himself trapped in a narrow isle of Schoenhof's Foreign Books, established 1856, a small frame shop just off Massachusetts Avenue, one of Cambridge's more interesting red brick streets. He had brought a woodcut, 'Road To The North," by Nora Unwin, purchased at the New England Print Exhibition in Sommerville for $50, the money sent to him by his parents for food in response to his urgent plea. He'd gone to the Print Exhibition because it was cheap entertainment but upon seeing the woodcut he was stricken with an overwhelming compulsion to possess it, convinced they'd be together for life.

The woodcut depicted a dark zig-zag road plunging through a naked forest of shadowy limbs from foreground to frozen horizon. The impression was of an austere universe, lacking color and heat, but nonetheless defined by purpose: a distant being leaving humanity a swath of hope.

Excited by the intricately detailed, if sullen, tableau, Bergman envisioned a colorful border, perhaps two or three different shades from red to pale rose with a shiny, enameled lacquer frame to offset the woodcut's cold black lines. While the 'canvas' was small, about the size of a paperback book, Berge expanded its footprint in relation to its importance, contemplating an immense, multi-layered matte and a thick, coved frame. Bergman felt support of his grandiose ideas flowing from racks of ornate and gilded frames on either side of the narrow aisles when the proprietor, studying the piece suddenly raised his hand.

"Ya shit!" he shouted in a heavily-accented voice. "I have framed Degas, Matisse, Monet and you," he spat, "tell me what to do." Bergman recollected that the gorgeous Fogg Museum was just across the street. Apparently, he and the proprietor shared that thought at least. "Yes, I frame for the museum," he said pointing, as a drop of spittle staggered down his chin, "the Masters—nothing but the best! I work 40 years, f-o-r-t-y years! I do hundreds, I do them all; they come to me. Never, never, they tell me what to do. You go home now," said the small white-haired man, infinite sadness twisting his face into a wrinkled quagmire, "I will take care of this. One week. Go."

"Huh?" blinked Bergman.

Minter shook his head, "How 'bout you, Jake?"

The desert easily sheds its charms when forced to slog through sticky, unforgiving sand without enough water, uncertain of direction and with questionable help. When Jake agreed to take on the responsibilities of 'the field' in the dope network, he didn't realize he'd be risking his life. It sounded like fun—and real wealth. Pay rose from 10–15% of a kilo ($35–$50) to 50%, or $175. And there were lots of kilos, enough to clear $25,000! All you had to do is pick them up in Mexico, somewhere not well-mapped, and transport them—undetected, of course–into the U.S.

He envisioned some serious money when he signed a contract of sorts—his name, address, and assets, along with a picture of his girlfriend and dog—receiving in return a gun, a .357 magnum pistol the size of a waffle iron with fake wooden grips and a nickel finish. The gun was loaded with illegal hollow-point 'cop killers' which expand upon impact inflicting fatal damage.

Getting into Mexico was the easy part; from there he was pretty much on his own. His buddy from high school, Sutter, joined him but was too freaked out by the whole idea to be a reliable source of advice. They drove Sutter's VW bus to Matamoras where they met 'Jose'. Jose was the guide, he got an added cut; Jake understood another mule was waiting with the stuff. With Sutter and he alternating, they'd get the third bag out. Jose brought them to a spot on the Rio Grande several kilometers from town where they were met by two others—Renould and Phillipe. Jose adamantly insisted that the three Mexicans were to be the carriers. Jose made as if he spoke no English and neither Jake nor Sutter knew much Spanish.

As Sutter knelt and examined the bags to make sure the shit was cool, Jake re-calculated the deal. Three bags of 175 pounds apiece meant 240 kilos, or $42,000 total ($14,000 per bag). He was to get $25,000 and he'd promised $5,000 to Sutter to accompany him. That left $7,500 to be split $4,500/guide, $3,000/mule on the other side of the border. But Jose was demanding a new order, an extreme one: $2,500 to each of the other mules, $7,500 for him! At 5 grand to Sutter, Jake saw his share shrink to half, and they were still in Mexico…

Jose wanted a handshake on his terms now, before, he argued, *federales* hit the area. If they were discovered, warned Jose, there would be very little profit left for any of them. Sutter was walking in tight circles; 'Holy shit,' he muttered repeatedly. 'Hurry!' Jose exclaimed. 'Alright, alright,' Jake agreed, secretly putting another proposal on the table. He had to get across the border, that was the first order of business, he told himself in agreeing with Jose. Once in the U.S. well, then, there was a whole new set of options …

The Mexicans lifted their packs and moved single-file up an arroyo and into a hot cactus-laden plain. Jake walked slowly, his sunglasses pressed close to his head, a shield against the smelting temperatures. Everywhere there was red: red sky, red sun, red sand, red-clay dirt pitted with spots of green and brown, the whole in a frying pan simmering to the hazy, purple horizon. In a frame it would be magical; in reality, it was hell. Jake sensed a new element, one that terrified him. His fate was completely in the hands of someone else, someone who'd just clipped him nearly 50%.

When they got to the river it was broad and brown, running shallow but refreshed, colder, after recent upstream rains. Suddenly, the heavy packs in the broad, powerful current were no longer a liability but an asset, Jose, Phillipe and Renould moving steadily thanks to the added weight. But Jake and especially tall, thin Sutter were at greater risk of being swept away as they inched over the muddy, treacherous river bottom. A couple of times Sutter's footing gave way and Jake had to dig in, dragging Sutter to firmer ground. The Mexicans pulled away ominously. They eventually sat on the river bank laughing and smoking as the 'North Americanos' struggled. Before they made it to shore,

Sutter's pack, the one with their drinking water, was ripped from his shoulder disappearing in the dark avalanche that surrounded them.

Jake was panting by the time he and Sutter gained the bank, but not from exertion. He knew something had to give. He couldn't take $7,500 for all the work he'd put in on this deal; no way, it just couldn't be done. Sure, he could lean on Sutter's cut of $5,000, but he'd still be out $12,500, and that was too much. It wasn't fair. The organization was only going to pay so much, that was it. Jake tried to reason with him, but Jose was adamant: he claimed he'd been stiffed on the last two runs he'd made for the Syndicate. Besides, if caught they'd torture him mercilessly. If he survived, he'd be a broken man. This way, the gringos get a 'guaranteed' crossing, 'Always ok, say Jose!' So what if their side lost a few points, he reasoned, it was the Mexicans who did the dirty work; in the U.S. they just handed out the stuff like candy and the money came pouring in. But in Mexico, justice wasn't camera ready.

When Jose did a run, he'd be 'hot' for six - eight hours as he met his contacts and steered them through the many reefs between the growing culture and the smoking culture. He was a grower himself, and, if in the States you weren't much concerned about exposure and punishment once you got your supply, in Mexico it was a different story. Everybody knew what he did. He had to act as a benefactor in his village, passing out large sums of money. But the payouts to local officials left him in debt, with a need to expand and become more involved in the growing of marijuana. He was thinking of buying a heavy-duty vehicle to cross the river further upstream but it would mean more bribes. He would have to cut out Renould and Philippe. So now a big check and then none, that's the way it goes. He tried to explain this to 'Senior Jake,' but the latter shook with rage.

Jake didn't handle frustration well. Once (he didn't know at what age) he'd seen his old man singing for drinks in a rundown saloon only he couldn't stand up long enough to fill his lungs. While Jose, a Mexican who lived among chickens and pigs, wanted to be paid like a rock star.

At a certain point, the whole ugly business was too much to review again; he wasn't going to be pressed to the wall. He had the means to wipe the slate clear, start over in a realm where the numbers met his expectations. Taking care of Sutter, crossing the desert without water, getting out alive—this was heroic stuff. And now this goddamned 'beaner' comes along to burn the whole mission. Worst of all, they were going about it like predatory businessmen, as if pot was just another commodity, like soybeans. It was a slap in the face…

* * * *

When Bergman returned, the little man handed him the framed picture in a tightly-bound brown paper wrapper. "I'm sure you'll be pleased," he said without a hint of pride or false modesty. Bergman took it with trembling hands and unraveled the package in front of the proprietor.

Upon first glimpsing the finished product an icy hand crawled up his spine like an insect: the experience, craftsmanship and inspiration of this tiny man with a forehead as wrinkled as the knuckles on his weathered hands had transformed the woodcut from a work of art into a finger pointing at Bergman's dark soul.

As he stared at it, the extent of his obtuseness seized him. The beauty of the deep, narrow, unvarnished wood frame humiliated him; the perfectly proportioned, simple white mat filled him with despair. While he had wanted clear glass to highlight the contrasting white-black ink strokes, the proprietor had substituted non-glare glass imparting to the whole a mystical union that lay beyond Bergman's imagination. His own plan was gaudy to the point of obscenity by comparison. He'd been so wrong, so completely, smugly incompetent that his initial ideas seemed not mere misjudgment, but some kind of wickedness.

The framer now appeared saintly and he, Bergman fell to that of an apostate. The picture was his, but its power lay outside his current reach. He could never own it honestly unless he were to grow in some spiritual way, chose a path that offered his first steps only terror. He mumbled his gratitude, paid quickly and left. Hurrying to his tiny flat, he put the object on the wall, studied it closely for a moment, stepped back for a better look, slumped to his knees and wept.

* * * *

Jake figured the Mexicans had plotted yet another division of the spoils in the half-hour they spent lounging on the sand. He was prepared. 'How far?' he asked while still in the river. 'Not far,' Renould answered nervously. 'Which way?' Renould again responded, pointing to the northeast before Jose bitterly rebuked him. As he approached the group, Jake felt for the pistol. 'Ok, let's move out. *Vahmenous*!' he shouted.

Jose grinned deeply. 'Senõr,' he advised, 'before we pick up the packs…' But he never finished. Jake raised the pistol and fired an expanding hollow-point bullet straight into his brain.

The bullet entered Jose in the frontal precipital lobe at a speed of 750' per second. Instantaneously, the bullet, slowed by skull bone, flattened into a broad 'spoon' as it plowed through brain matter. Enormous amounts of brain tissue and minute blood vessels literally disappeared in a flash cutting off consciousness as if were a candle flame. Jose's hands jerked upwards toward the wound reflexively; they were not guided by thought for that too, had gone, pulverized into oblivion. The pressure wave which accompanied the projectile, because of its large footprint, caused catastrophic damage to the brain. No known medical attention could resuscitate the victim. A small trickle of very dark blood, almost black, appeared at the wound as Jose toppled over backward, dead.

Renould and Phillipe recoiled in shock; Sutter's jaw dropped, his face went ashen as if he'd suffered a heart-attack. Jake pulled $5,000 in cash from his pocket. He tossed $2,500 to each of the Mexicans. "More when we get to the truck,' he said. The frightened survivors gathered up the money, grabbed their packs and hoisting them aloft, trotted away. Guessing he'd be taking the first shift with the pack, Jake handed the gun to Sutter. 'Keep an eye on those assholes,' he warned.

Immediately after firing the fatal round into Jose, Jake went 'ape shit' in his own words, jumping about like a rabbit, his system 'totally amped' with adrenaline, a hormone secreted by the endocrine gland to speed up the contractions of the heart filling the body with the raw energy of hyper-oxygenated blood. He felt invincible. There had been questions; now there were none. He'd gone from a man with a nerve-wracking dilemma, to a man who had the Force... Philippe and Renould showed respect, falling over themselves to create distance from the graying corpse. With the gun, things went smoothly again. He could feel a giant hunger depart. The desire to kill lifted, Jake felt the surge of excitement, a wave bigger and darker than the Rio Grande itself, steal away. Jake wondered if he'd ever feel that ripped again.

Philippe and Renould couldn't believe the size of the weapon that murdered their employer. It was as big as a cordless drill; and Jose as dead as if he'd dropped off a 50-foot ladder onto concrete. To survive, they said nothing though each resolved to give Jose's widow half of whatever they might get. Other mules talked of the 'crazies.' It was part of the deal. If you were Mexican and you heard of this kind of money, this quick, you knew it was smuggling, that meant *gringos* with guns.

By the time they got to the truck, Jake and Sutter were exhausted to the verge of collapse. Renould and Philippe nearly came to blows over directions until, half-dead themselves, they compromised on a course that eventually got them near the hill which Jake had picked to stash the truck. 'This is it,' Jake said for maybe the 10th time, but he was right, finally. He tore at the underbody where he'd planted keys. When he pulled open the door, he poured hot water over his face until the anger and hatred washed away. He had Renould and Philippe load the truck then handed them the promised money. Without looking at them, he climbed into the cab and squealed back onto the road. When they'd gone about 20 miles in silence, Jake rolled down the window and pitched the gun into the vast baking wilderness. 'Incidentally,' he coughed, 'that extra $2,500?' he said to Sutter, 'that comes from your share.'

# 19

## *Addiction is Relative, or a Relative*

Nicholson gazed at the latest data: not much splash in the results from the various tests, no evidence of significant deviation from expected norms. Nicholson was dismayed, he'd hoped to be on the trail by this time, mushing toward that one indelible 'something' that would launch his program, his team, to the head of the pack.

One anomaly stood out: Wick's report of less clicker activity was at odds with the maximum tallies for each subject that were coming in. The daily ceiling of 10,000 points, or $10, for the IMP exercise didn't appear to be a problem in the least. So far, no discrepancy existed in the motivator totals for the pre-smoking and smoking periods; both stood at the maximum. Would this be the big news of this cycle in marijuana analysis? With the sophisticated experimentation currently practiced in the profession, a breakthrough was a necessity. Everything possible had been thrown against the wall; what would stick?

Now comes word that counting activity from the subjective level of observation "appeared inadequate" to explain motivational maximum totals... If Wick's report couldn't be adjusted for bias, was in fact accurate, then—well—mmmm. They couldn't afford to let background noise drown out the Breakthrough that was sure to emerge if they could just keep their focus!

Then of course, there is this other issue. Jonathan Wicks is an intelligent man, and nominally second in charge. He is a useful tool to implement the experiment's overall strategy, but he lacks imagination and is anal to the point of distraction. He carries out every order with nauseating perfection but has no suggestions or fruitful input. Bedikker and Melody are functionaries (and now there are whispers about her); David Minter may be a problem.

Minter is bright, innovative, yet reckless, and yes, perhaps disloyal. He may have his own agenda. I should have seen this coming when I bowed to his suggestion that we incorporate a bi-polar leadership into the subject population. Normally, under conditions which exist, we carefully screen our participants so only one of the group will presume a leadership role. That way, the subject population can be controlled by manipulating their leader through various inducements or punishments.

David, quite persuasively I thought, argued that the single leader concept allowed the we-vs.-them formation which was typical of classic <u>narcotic</u> studies but did not fit the investigative mode required of <u>hallucinogenic</u> drugs. He rightly pointed out that marijuana, erroneously classified as a narcotic, was, in fact, a mild hallucinogenic, and should be tested as such. A bi-polar leadership construct, Minter argued, would lead to a kind of competition for the experiment's soul, an exercise of free will that was more apt to reveal truth than the traditional construct which was manipulated and therefore dishonest.

As Minter outlined it, this required a grant of subject identity unprecedented in substance research. Essentially, the subjects would be offered equal status, with the power to veto the results of any experimental feature they could organize to disrupt! Instead of bullying subjects to conform to a rigid experimental protocol, subjects would be 'invited' to participate. Yes, it seems preposterous; but there was an attractant: when subject behavior is rigidly controlled, the element of moral choice disappears. As a result, testing is automatic, at the level of animal response. While it says something, it does not offer a comprehensive view of the individual and may misrepresent subject attitudes, say on drug-taking behavior.

For instance, while the inebriated person can be tested for physiological changes relating to alcohol, he is not the best source for opinions or other thoughtful responses on the matter. If you really wish to know 'why?' people take drugs—and without this kind of question we can't get a real picture of drug-taking behavior, thus we can't affect, except by the crudest, most proscriptive methods, drug choice—you have to solicit their higher, best instincts.

David believes this is when they are stoned and in a positive mood of relaxation and response. In a way, he's demanding that the subject matter sculpt the experiment, rather than the other way around. This is too dangerous and cannot be allowed.

He's risking bad behavior for great history. I wish him well. If he steps beyond the boundaries of truth in his quest of the Great Unknown, the mystery head upon the wall, then he's no longer trustworthy.

One can perform any number of hypothetical exercises in the classroom, but this is a unique opportunity. Harvard would be a laughing stock if we emerged from a month-long trial with inebriated babble passing for fact. It shall remain a rule of this study that the inmates of the asylum shall be studied as asylum inmates rather than as living embodiments of exotic illusions. Pot smokers are people delusioned by pot; they are in no way ennobled by the substance they imbibe regardless of what they might profess! We'll have to take such steps as necessary to reassert control before the subjects sit on the board of the institution. I worry however, if it's not already happened?

* * * *

Custer realized that isolation was now as important a drug as pot itself. While it appeared that some subjects were tired of smoking, they persisted, even increased their dosage, because of dissatisfaction with the routine. Today's discussion was designed to take advantage of this propensity. "Ok," he said raising his hands to attract silence, "here's a quicky for you to discuss."

"You mean, 'disgust,'" said Jake.

"A half-hour of real discussion. No half-assed crap and you're gone," Custer offered.

"Yeah? I'll bite," cast Sutter.

"Good. Others? Ok, then, here's what you got. Most of you smoke, many of you drink. We've established that you're not unwilling to alter your reality for large stretches at a time. The question is: If you could design your own drug to do all the things you want from a substance experience, could you see yourself taking it 24/7, in effect obliterating actual reality for an artificial one of your own construction?"

"Fair question," said Thad with a straight face. The others began to laugh and he did too, slumping forward his wide mouth twisted comically.

"Remember now," said Custer, "you gotta be stoned."

"Oh god, not again," Thad groaned. "You'd think there would be an end to this."

"Once more we gonna pour charcoal in our lungs for the glory of science," Tony parodied.

"Hey man, drugs are gonna get better; they're mak'n new drugs all the time," put in Wayne.

"Yeah, soon they'll be able to take care of ya from birth to the grave with cool, crazy stuff that'll get you high with no side effects," alleged Sutter.

"Like pot, man," cried Jimbo.

"No, man," argued Tony, "better'n pot."

"Shit man, now you're talk'n drugs. Somethun'll get you high but won't smell like you're bak'n a rug!" exclaimed Jake.

"I read this book once; it was called *Island,* I think," said Chris quietly, "they had a drug called *moksha,* that helps people, you know, to grow, ah, more sensitive... knowing oneself on a deeper level."

Wayne shouted, "Hey, man, that's for me! How do I get tha-at stuff? Tha-at *mok-sha* stuff?"

"You can't, bird-brain—it's in a book," laughed Jake.

"Yeah? I thought you just said it was on an island?" said Wayne slyly.

"I got this one," broke in Shep, "See, it's in *Island.*"

"Ok, so how do I get into this here island?" Wayne asked. "I think I could do pretty good by this *muska* drug, well, all drugs really, but this *muska* stuff for certain."

"You know, I bet you could, that is, if you could find it," said Berge.

"Oh, I could find it alright, you just point me in the general direction, I'll do the rest."

"Hmm. Ya really wanna get to the *Island,* huh?" asked Tony. "Well, you gotta start at the library."

"At the library? Hey man, that's neat!"

"Just haul yourself up to that stocky librarian with the crew-cut and the denim jacket, and tell her you want to be taken to the

*Island,"* smirked Jake.

"That's Huxley's *Island,* not the Isle of Lesbos," Shep giggled.

"That's it, that's all there is to it?"

"Well, then you have to read it," Jimbo interjected.

"Read it? Read *Island*?"

"I'd recommend it, especially those pages on *mouska,"* answered Shep.

"I don't have to go anywhere?"

"Oh yeah, you gotta go someplace man," barked Sutter, "you really gotta get into that book."

"I'm outta here, man. I'm goin' for the book, er, the Island!" cried Wayne, stretching for the door.

"Ok, ok," countered Minter, "everybody back into your traces, please. Back to the question at hand. Would you risk addiction for a really good high?"

"Well, if you already smoke daily—pot or cigarettes—you're an addict. So what?" said Jimbo, excitedly. "What more is there to say? You're an addict, I'm an addict. Every sonofabitch in here is an addict!"

"Ok," said Jake slowly, "I'm an addict, so wha' the hell does that mean?"

"You're dependent," answered Ira.

"Yeah," Sutter exhaled.

"Geeze—dependent: the state of dependency, deriving necessary power from someone or something else," concluded Ira.

"Ah, whatever," cried Ron.

"If that means I wanna stay stoned as much as I can," admitted Jimbo. "It's true, I'm dependent on weed."

"Dependency—addiction—is normally viewed as a negative," Bergman smiled. "Addiction is moral poison outside these sacred walls. Thus the difficulty of the dominant species to accept marijuana."

"Well, in fractured prose, that's the gist of it," Ira summarized, sneezing into his armpit.

"But I see it as a positive," said Jimbo gleefully. "Yeah, I used to be afraid, but this here hemp makes one neat addiction. And there are healthy addictions: diet, exercise—stuff like that. I put pot up there in that group. It gives me a lift, helps tune out all the noise, the racket..."

"If pot is that good, that you wanna take it all the time," said Bergman, "you can't take it all the time."

"Why not, genius?" asked Jake, yawning.

"Because pretty soon there won't be any time when you're not taking it. Then you lose contact with the reality that was not good enough to prevent you from taking pot."

"What the blank-blank are you talking about?" laughed Tony.

"If it's all pot, all the time," Berge ventured, "soon you'll forget how good pot can be because everything is pot, stoned is normal. So being stoned is just like the reality you ditched in order to get stoned. Stoned is no longer any good because it's normal. Don't get stoned, it'll make it all better."

"Hey, he's starting to make sense," jibed Jake, "a coupla cents anyway."

"Supposing you don't join the criminal class," Custer smiled wryly, "the question of addiction is always: 'How does the 'high' of your choice prevent you from realizing your goals: are you the best 'you' you can be?"

"You know," said Tony sheepishly, "I always thought that pot got between me and my becoming a nuc-u-lar, a nuc-cler, ah, what do you call 'em, a physic?"

"A nuclear physicist," said Shep.

"Yeah," said Tony, "one of them guys."

"But suppose you wanted to become an apostle of pot."

"Or 'a pot sell,'" Tony broke in.

"If the addiction causes no problems?" Jimbo sketched. "As long as you use it for good reasons."

"Such as mellowing out to the point where you can take all of this bullshit crap that would otherwise cause you to flip out and take 10 people with you," interrupted Jake.

"Exactly! Yeah, then it's ok," Jimbo nodded.

"Ya, right, I stop whenever I can't afford any and all my friends know it," added Tony.

Bergman thought a moment; "I suppose there are *some* things I've done, and some I haven't, because I was stoned. But no matter what it is, I want to be able to put it down for a while; to smoke it everyday is kindova weakness don't you think?"

"I gotta disagree with ya," drawled Thaddeus. "I absolutely wouldn't make a decision without consulting Puff, the Magic Dragon. Stoned, I'm closer to my true feelings, I'm more honest with, ah, my, my-self."

"That doesn't surprise me," said Jake, "what surprises me is all sorts of things which I forget now."

"Your attempt at realism in reality is unrealistic," hurled Berge.

"What the heck are we talking about here, really?" interjected Ron. "I mean, of course we look like addicts. Dah! But I couldn't smoke this much outside, who could? It's an experiment: unlimited pot. Just put it on your prepaid credit card, help yourself, take as much as you like, get as stoned as you've ever wanted on the best stuff you've ever imagined. It's a joyride, not a frick'n vocation."

"No, wait, wait, you're wrong, you're wrong—not for me, not anymore. From now on I'm 'Mr. Pot'" Jimbo said earnestly. "From here on in, I stay stoned at least most of the time; just to prove to the Dominant Social Order that's it's no big deal about grass. Mar-i-ju-ana is not the prob-lem-o here!"

"Grass isn't the problem, lame-o," Shep broke in, "you're the problem, not hemp. Hemp just serves as a marker for those the Dominant—whatever—wishes to keep out of 'The Club.' It's like being Black or Jewish, you're simply not wanted."

"But I don't give a shit what they think," insisted Jimbo. "I'll smoke a doobie and completely lose my anger."

"I think you have more to lose than your anger," said Chris nervously.

"You got that right," Wayne said narrowly. "The DSO doesn't mess around; their goons are everywhere. They don't want anything to get out of hand."

"Are you happy now?" broke in Jake, "you opened Wayne's cage."

Wayne pushed his lips to one side in a heap of rose-colored concentration. "You know, we got to start hitt'n those clickers again. Recon says they may be getting wise."

"Who gives a shit, fuck'm," offered Jake.

Wayne pointed a finger at Jake, "That's just the kind of thing that the DSO listens for," he whispered.

"Oh god, I'm gonna have a cow," responded Jake.

"Better hope it's an acceptable right-wing, non-toker cow," said Bergman.

"Oh, you can bet on that," cried Early, "and he won't have no typewriter either."

"Well, without a typewriter," Berge rejoined, "little cow

will get no further than big cow."

"The point, gentlemen; the point?!" threatened Custer, checking his watch.

"I think the point is," Berge spoke up, "do some people sell out so they can pursue pot dreams?"

"Hey, I'm no sellout. I'm in full pursuit of my dream," yelled Jimbo.

"Aw, shut up Berge," snorted Jake, "Dr. Stern will deliver the eulogy."

Ira turned to Jimbo, "You're no sellout. You don't want to be in their dangerous, cash-obsessed Club. They want to be kings on earth, but on earth there is only one king—Nature. We are all equal subjects before Nature."

# 20

# *The Good News of the 20th Century*

Melody could ignore him no longer; like a puppy on a leash, he'd succeeded in wrapping her up. No doubt he'd lick her face, too. She removed the chart to her arm and washed her teeth with her tongue. She tugged her lab coat down where it had ridden up, pushed the door back with authority and marched right to Thaddeus. "So, hello," she said, black eyes slashing out from a curtain of coffee brown curls. "Staying good and stoned are we?"

Thad was momentarily flustered, but on second thought, he liked the approach. It didn't matter that he'd been looking for her unsuccessfully all week. She was much prettier than he'd remembered: her freckles less dark and bug-like, even the mole on her chin was smaller. "Well, my ladyship," he said enthusiastically. "I felt a loss of light in your absence, as if you'd cut the cables to our electricity," he fawned.

"Yeah, right," Melody chewed on her gum, "wherever I go, darkness follows."

"Perish the thought—the exact opposite of my sacred intentions," he mocked. "Darkness is a consequence of your departure, not an accompaniment to your presence."

"And see that it stays that way." She smiled at Thad's surprised reaction, bending her slender neck to reveal a trail of soft, shiny hair almost like fur slipping down her back.

"Well, I don't—" Thaddeus hesitated.

"If you seek some scrap of human kindness, you must amuse me or off with your head!" said Melody brightly.

Thaddeus stared at her, then his bearded chin gave way to a ribbon of singing laughter. "You had me," he gasped. "Had me think'n. Ha, ha, ha," he slithed.

Melody took him through the vital signs quickly; Thad remained absorbed by the dream-come-true quality of this opening. When she put him on the scale, he hesitated and she saw he'd gained a kilo—2.2 pounds! "Oooo!" she whistled.

Thaddeus drew himself to full stature. "Solid muscle," he explained, "I've toned up cracking heads to bring these, these law-breakers to account. Muscle," he repeated, showing off his considerable biceps.

"Fat," Melody said, pinching a roll around his tummy.

"Geez," Thad belched, drawing back, "that's my private zone!"

"Yeah, well, at this rate your private zone will be public right-of-way."

"Hey, that's what I missed. That terrific sense of humor," said Thad.

"Thank you," she replied. "Melody's comic stylings can be heard daily by the isolated pot-smokers of B ward."

Thad giggled. "Say," he asked, "you don't happen to have a Mr. Melody stashed away at home, do you?"

Melody didn't have to answer, truthfully, any personal questions posed by subjects during the experiment. But you were supposed to communicate with them in as natural a way as possible considering your position. David wanted a no holds barred, make it up as you go relationship with subjects. Nicholson encouraged it to a certain point, then shut it down. They worked out a compromise: whatever you do, don't write it down.

"No gentleman, unfortunately. Had one but he moved out, said I had too many cats. You like cats?" Melody asked.

"Cats—well, not a big fan unless it's catfish," Thad joshed.

"Oh," she said.

"How many cats you got?" he inquired uncertainly.

"118 ," she answered.

"Wha'? 118 cats?" he snorted.

"118 sick cats as of this morning."

"Damn that's a lot a cats! But that's ok, you like cats, I can too," he demurred. "Did you say, 'sick'?"

"It's an animal hospital," Melody pointed out, "we take it in if it's uninsured, or unable to keep its eyes open after testifying about its role in the development of a new lipstick."

"That's mean!" Thad exclaimed.

"Huh?" she reacted absently, wrapping Thad's stout arm in the blood pressure gauge.

"Well, it's mean to treat animals like that, and it's mean of you to treat me like an animal," he said. Red highlights in her hair, square white teeth and tiny ears which came to a point, combined in Thad's head to form just about the softest, most attractive glow imaginable... Oh, and how she smelled!

"Thaddeus, even if you didn't have three young children."

"We're not actually married; it's a convenience thing."

"How reassuring."

"No, you're right, put the seed in the ground, ya gotta water it."

"I couldn't have put it more eloquently," replied Melody.

"But then, you're the majority, aren't you?"

"What's that got to do with it?" Melody asked.

"The dominant race always tries to deny and exterminate the weaker race," Thaddeus alleged.

"Actually, the 'dominant' race is getting a lot of help from the 'weaker' race in this regard," Melody parried.

"Yes, that's the white version," said Thad quietly, "then there's our truth."

"'Your truth' as opposed to 'the truth?'" Melody challenged.

"'Our truth,'" repeated Thaddeus, "because the sadists who inflicted the pain, want to minimize their role: 'Hey, chin up! You're not dead, are ya? It was business. Git over it. Racism don't exist no more; don't let it drag you down.'"

"I don't share those sentiments," she said curtly.

"Of course not," he purred. "But you b'en ignoring me like I was from a lesser tribe."

"It's not..." Melody found herself in the middle of an explanation she planned to avoid. "Well..."

"See?" he observed with altogether too much enjoyment. "It's like I said, you just can't handle real equality."

"I think I could," she rebutted, "if I were to find it."

Thaddeus slapped his hands together, "Yeah!" he hollered. "That's what I wanted to hear! That cuts through all the bull-shit."

"It had better."

"No, really," Thaddeus backtracked. "I can't stand all the double-talk."

"You know, ah, I've never met anybody who made it, shaped it and tried to sell it as ice cream quite as persuasively as you. You got a lot 'a talent, but you're wasting your time. Not interested." Melody felt invincible; she'd put this bounder to sea for the last time.

"Ok, ok," Thad temporized, "you've been square with me,

so I'll be square with you: I think I made a decision here that will change my life."

"Oh, c'mon!" she cried. Melody began to laugh, "You've got three kids. When will you have time to do anything?"

"I got kids sure, but that doesn't define me," Thad explained.

"Yes, it does," said Melody, "in terms of your usefulness. Basic stuff, really. Unless you're willing to eat your existing children, I see no future for me."

Thad posed, hands on hips, then let out a laugh that sent the subway train fleeing for the safety of downtown Boston. He rubbed the short hair around his temples, "Ya got me! Yaw' al got me good," he snickered. "That's good, that's honest, I can get into that. You can gimme more a' that." Despite his usual optimism, Thaddeus was coming to doubt he'd get anywhere with this scrawny, brown-eyed tomboy, but he couldn't force himself to part with the sound of her laughter, *like the winds of spring...* This pot is so good he thought, maybe Melody reaped the benefit from that just-completed second joint of the hour. He'd smoked it as casually as an ordinary cigarette, in a series of hard, regular puffs, exhaling the smoke through his nose.

"I'm afraid I can't." She held his arm with both hands probing for a vein from which to draw a blood sample, when Nicholson walked in.

"Where's Wick?" he demanded loudly. He twisted left and right but his eyes remained fixed on Melody's hands until she dropped Thad's forearm.

"He's, he's in the day room, I think," she fabricated. Nicholson looked from Melody to Thad, scowled, and left.

* * * *

Custer separated the three essays into separate piles; subjects received bonus dollars if they beat their straight scores while stoned.

"How stoned you want us to be?" cried Jake.

"The stoned-er, the better," said Custer without batting an eye.

"Next question," Sutter sprung, "what can we do about Shep here, he'll win if we let him?"

Minter shook his head, "You are not competing against each other, you're competing against your own previous scores prior to the inebriation period."

"Yeah!" they cheered.

Minter lowered his head, 'Still crazy after all these years?' he muttered. "See, Shep can get 100%, and you can get 100%."

"Wait, a sec..." Tony broke in, "it ain't fair. His chances of getting 100% are better than mine."

"He's right," screamed Bergman, "the man is a menace, he has to be hobbled. This is no place for intelligence!"

"Yeah! Let's brand him," Thad joined in.

"What!?" squealed Shep. "You're supposed to be my friend?"

"SSShhhh!" Thad whispered, "I'm trying to save your life."

"I think you have a point there, Tony," Custer laughed. "We could handicap Ira. No, not physically, but pointwise," David mused.

"Yeah, yeah. Exactly," Chris chimed in.

"Because Ira is in a rare IQ zone, we could give everyone else, say, 250 points to start."

"I say we geld 'im," said Jimbo.

"Is that farm talk for what I think it is?" cried Ira. "If it is, I insist I be ravished beforehand."

"There will be no forehand, no backhand, no hand job, while I'm around," Jake insisted.

"Actually, a gelding—when you're in the middle of the darn thing—is not the attractive sight many visualize," Berge suggested.

"God, you guys are way out!" sneezed Ron, induced to light up weed at last.

"You should see me when I'm sober man," said Wayne, "I'm awesome man, I really am. But when I'm stoned, I've got powers that are normally repressed." He winked at Chris and Chris smiled back awkwardly.

"Step right up," Minter instructed, "beat the house for a sizable daily bonus." As he distributed the essays, he explained that each passage would be followed by five simple True-False questions based on the material. All questions had to be answered correctly in order to earn the $10 bonus.

"Hey, what about our 'Shep' points?" yelled Jake.

"Ok, ok, you only need an average of four accurate responses on each essay in order to earn full credit," Minter corrected himself.

"Hey, that's not fair!" Ira objected.

**Essay #1**

For several thousand years—*cannabis* as active psychotropic ingredient, and *hemp* as a widely-grown natural fiber resistant to heat, water, insects and stress—were celebrated as vital, crucial ingredients in medicine, industry and society.

In the ancient practice of patient's rights to pain-relief, *cannabis* potions, elixirs, and patent medicines were widely used for treatment of menstrual cramps, rheumatism, fatigue, migraines, glaucoma, asthma, anorexia and depression.

Hemp seed oil was used in virtually all paints and in many

precision machines as lubricant. 'Canvas' sprung from the word *cannabis*, and because of its strength, was used for sails and rigging of all vessels before the advent of power. The Gutenberg Bible, Alice in Wonderland, and the initial draft of the U.S. Declaration of Independence all appeared on hemp paper.

An inexpensive agricultural product with a thousand uses and numerous strengths, hemp was monarch of the vegetable kingdom in the 19$^{th}$ century, and its uses were just beginning to demonstrate themselves in the 20$^{th}$ when hemp was felled by superior capitalism. History reveals a clear conspiracy on behalf of the chemical giant, Dupont, and the recreational drug industry—tobacco and alcohol—to oppose the hemp/cannabis industry as essentially and seriously competitive with their own. Hemp may have been a wunderkind, but today it serves as another 'Think' sign along the free-market road.

**Essay #2**

William Randolph 'W.R.' Hearst, inherited a fortune in real estate, gold and silver mining (the Homestake, Comstock and Anaconda), and used it to control some 35 major newspapers and magazines in a desperate gamble for power. Hearst invented yellow journalism: corruption, comics and killers; his presses spewing innuendo, distortion and concocted events so Hearst Inc. could attract readership while 'WR' attacked a list of enemies he felt stood between himself and the U.S. Presidency.

One of those enemies was Mexico which Hearst felt should be an American protectorate, like the Philippines. Hearst's father had procured immense acreages in Mexico during the disgraced dictatorship of General Porfiro Diaz who was accused of selling the store to the *gringos* and deposed in 1911 (Mexico owned only 1% of its oil by 1925). The center piece of Hearst's multi-million dollar Mexican holdings in chicle (gum), minerals and timber was Babicora, an 8 million-acre estate in Chihuahua. In 1915, Mexican revolutionary Pancho Villa raided the ranch, kidnapping a number of its employees and driving off 50,000 head of Hearst's cattle. Portions of the property were later 'expropriated' whenever leftist zeal seized the nation.

Hearst counterattacked, relentlessly constructing a caricature of dirty, marijuana-crazed Mexicans puffing across the border to deflower American female virtue and lock white civilization in 'dope slavery,' (Hearst's journalistic career revealed a fondness for the alien drug-demon using it disparage the Chinese (dagger-carrying opium addict), and Black Americans (machete-wielding cocaine 'fiend'). Hearst's potted Mexican campaign lasted 25 years and was so bigoted and pervasive that it still affects Anglo-Hispanic relations. Hearst's goal: foment war with Mexico so invading U.S. troops would safeguard his properties. Eventually, he went so far as to fake 'secret' plans of a Mexican invasion of the U.S. Finally, Hearst popularized the slang 'marihuana' (Mary and Jane) for *cannabis sativa,* legend has it, because Villa's men reportedly indulged while on the premises.

**Essay #3**

Pittsburgh's Andrew Mellon owned the sixth largest bank in the country and served as Secretary of the Treasury for nearly a decade (1921–1932), a period in which he saved both himself and pal Hearst a million dollars a year by lowering rates on large incomes. (Hearst responded by offering to back Mellon for President.) At Treasury, Mellon selected an ambitious new head for the Federal Bureau of Narcotics, Harry Anslinger.

Anslinger's subsequent onslaught against pot reached Hearstian hyperbole in the years prior to the Marijuana Tax Act of 1937. His overblown rhetoric, his omission of valuable, but contradictory data, his willingness to site Hearst's lies as evidence, had an unseen purpose. By threatening a moral and racial crisis upon the nation, he cleverly used marijuana's 'high' reputation to doom hemp thus clearing the field for new, petroleum-derivative synthetic fibers trademarked nylon, orlon, and dacron.

I.E. DuPont de Nemours & Company, Civil War gunpowder makers, experimented with plastic fibers drawn from oil and coal using forfeited WWI German patents. If DuPont, which supplied the lead for leaded gasoline, could suppress the use of cheaper hemp, the company stood to gain enormous wealth in plastics (about 75% of its post-war earnings in fact). DuPont then crafted a secret deal with the U.S. government to ban hemp.

Anslinger's phobic excesses stormed Congress, while low-cost oil was supplied by Mellon himself, chief financial council to DuPont, and owner of enormous Mexican oil leases. If any more help was needed to blow smoke in the face of John Q. Public, it was supplied by competitors to *cannabis'* pain-reliever role: alcohol, tobacco and the pharmaceutical industries who continue to sponsor anti-pot PSAs.

**Essay #4**

The marijuana widespread in the Unites States today is stronger than any known previously. Many first-time users have been hospitalized because of terror or fright responses to the mind-altering effects of the drug. Confusion, distracted thought and feelings of regret often accompany the 'high.'

Because of the danger it poses to the young and impressionable, marijuana remains a pernicious influence despite its reputation in some circles for inspiring gaiety. Teenagers face enough difficulty in their lives without complicating it by bouts of unreality.

In addition, marijuana smoking as popularly practiced, exhibits the same dangers (even more tar) as regular cigarettes.

Claims of marijuana's medical properties have been wildly exaggerated by marijuana's fanatical following. Thousands of lives are lost to marijuana every year as promising students tune in, turn on and drop out, while others sink into routine smoking with lots of big talk but no action.

Rather than taking a drug that knocks you out in order to 'feel better,' why not take a doctor's prescription for a specific remedy that doesn't waste your whole day? It's a sign of weakness to take a drug, any drug, regularly unless it's to regulate a medical condition. You can't relax by taking a foreign substance into the temple that is your body. At every moment you need to be vigilant against all those substances and groups that would rob this great nation of its vital essence. Marijuana not only weakens the individual, but undermines the strength of god's most cherished democracy. Everyone has a duty to the higher power which guides the universe to live drug-free.

Answer all 20 True/False questions (five per passage). Or, submit a brief essay (100wds max) describing the main point of the offerings, and how you feel about them.

Essay #1 True/False?

1. Hemp lost out to a superior product. 2. The story of hemp in the U.S. is yet another example of upper-class bullying. 3. *Cannabis* is a dangerous drug. 4. Alcohol and tobacco industries feel marijuana, if legalized, would hurt sales. 5. Dupont is a theme park in New Jersey.

Essay #2 True/False?

1. The wealthy can't be trusted. 2. Hearst owned seven castles. 3. Hearst didn't mind a war, as long as he could start it. 4. Pancho Villa and Hearst owned a cattle ranch in Mexico. 5. Hearst inherited 125 miles of California coastline, murdered a rival aboard his yacht and was known for his extravagant ways.

Essay #3 True/False?

1. Marijuana was outlawed because Andrew Mellon was worried about the country's moral character. 2. Anslinger shared Hearst's respect for factual accuracy. 3. The real aim of Anslinger's anti-pot campaign, was hemp. 4. Pot is harmless and gives relief to millions. 5. The modern light-weight nylon camping tent justifies a ban on hemp.

Essay #4 True/False?

1. Marijuana could take down America. 2. Half of all crimes in the U.S. are for criminal possession of marijuana. 3. The police could clean up the pot problem if it weren't for corrupt politicians. 4. Someone has to be oppressed if government is doing its job. 5. You smoke pot, but you don't want to be called a 'pothead.'

Minter planned the True/False answers carefully. Recent drug history being to some degree the subjects' history as well, he introduced the Alienation Scale. Some of the questions concerned facts not in evidence, others were mere assumptions, but appeared to be true depending on the degree to which one distrusted, even feared, their government.

The Alienation Scale begins at negative three '-3', or Destruction, a state of alienation so severe the person wishes to violently end himself *and society*.

'-2' asserts a very real demand for Vengeance as the individual is stirred to minor destructive acts not against society's institutions, but aimed at neighbors, friends, and himself by real or imagined slights.

'-1' indicates Paranoia: 'delusions' whether of persecution, or grandeur. Normal functioning recedes as suspicion and distrust on the one hand, and exaggerated self-importance vie for control.

‘0’ means Apathy, normal activity except for a chronic unwillingness to become involved in any enterprise requiring sacrifice.

‘1’ spells Engagement, at least philosophically, as one offers opinions, beliefs, ideas and commitment.

‘2’ is Action, i.e., concern made motion in a positive way; volunteers for active stewardship role, i.e., taking care of others.

‘3’ demonstrates complete self-sacrifice, eagerness to take on hard work with little chance of personal recognition.

Minter was surprised by the results among the seven who chose the True/False option: +1! This meant that despite the cynical tone, they’d responded positively and honestly with a careful reading.

He got three written essays: Ira, Jimbo and Bergman. Ira wrote: “Your reduction of the marijuana situation to a simple triangular conspiracy manipulating the lives and fortunes of millions, depleting air and water, imprisoning thousands, lying on a colossal scale, undermining faith in the highest offices of the Republic, all for a little more power and money is, well, plausible, but I don’t give a shit. This itching is killing me.”

Jimbo wrote: “See! If you know the politics, the history, the economic angle of the whole deal, there’s only one way to see the weed situation: we’ve been scammed, big time! It makes sense I suppose, pot being so much better than the competition, you had to take it out. You couldn’t let it compete. But still, the sonovabitches!

We have to keep at um. Got to organize, march, pamphlet, lobby and outshout them. That’s the only way; we can’t be bullied any more.

We got the good news of the 20th century. We gotta act like we want it.”

Bergman wrote: "I've heard the drug companies are trying to make a medicine out of cannabis that won't make you high? It's the 'high' people want, that heightened sensation, the illusion of calm and control, the feeling of being in synch with a different stream. At least, I do.

"Hearst, Anslinger, and Mellon represent the past: I resent the past. But you gotta rep the future you want. Gotta admit to taking a drug that could cause you to lose your job, or more. You're asking people to make this heroic effort for a little earthly pleasure, not for a place in heaven.

"If you pull my marijuana, I'll pull your Chevy Suburban. Nuth'n personal, just politics."

# 21

## *The Land of Nod*

Bergman couldn't get through to his own brain! Locked out. No key. He tried to concentrate: giant stone walls rose up before him, his stomach churned and that hard to reach area between the shoulders milled with biting ants.

His mind was useless of late, perpetually out of whack. It had been his greatest entertainment, an endless avenue of invention. It was a catapult, powering his escape from boredom, a powerful gardening tool that could level just about anything, an archeologist's pick, prying away weaknesses in face rock. But suddenly his mind was inaccessible, a gated community.

Maybe that's why he liked pot so much, because it could find the tiniest openings in just about anything, snaking its way toward the brain. He simply waited and jumped on board, allowing him to kayak into his own head. Once the gears bit, he was back in control. Concentrating when high, he used the stone's energy to go beyond the apparent to the gist. That was it, *bringing the energy.*

Pot had been helping him concentrate a long time figured Bergman, he'd been smoking it almost daily since junior high. Some days he'd forget what it was like to be straight. It started as an experiment he conducted on himself: What's the real difference between stoned and straight? Did being stoned give him focus, or did it change his focus? Were his thoughts his?

When he proposed the idea to his Psychology advisor, Dr.

Nesbitt, the old Professor rocked back in his chair. "Well, Mr. Bergman, you're either a fool or you take me for one." But he worked hard on his grades and when they met after spring semester, Nesbitt asked, "Now, let's hear about this asinine idea of yours."

Explained simply, Bergman would become an experimental chronic pot smoker, audited by himself to view the long-term effects of marijuana usage. He'd get stoned for two-month periods, alternating with two-months sobriety. He would keep a journal of his 'experiment' for a full year, after which he would have...

"What? What would you have, Mr. Bergman? That's what I'm having a hard time with. How the hell would this add up to anything? And don't call it 'Experimental Psychology!'"

Bergman could still feel his ears burning, boiling juices right under his scalp. "You'll have a personal eyewitness telling you how it *feels* to have the drug administered. It's a breakthrough. The 'subjective' will become the 'objective' through the intervention of the trained observer. I call it 'Historical Psychology.'"

Professor Nesbitt swiped at a piece of lint on his sport coat, "You've got chutzpah, Mr. Bergman, nothing wrong with that; as long as you can produce results. That's what we have to have, results. And then, how to use those results? A very good question—one that should scare the paint right off your porch.

"Having said that, there is precedent for such use of one's life. Every life of course, has value, particularly in Psychology. The question is how do you organize your 'data' to produce something of significance? That is what we seek."

Taking a deep drag off the joint, Bergman gave up the memory: the changing perceptions of pot inebriation, had slowed time to a crawl. Time appeared to expand which is the same as slowing down if you're Time. Slowed—expanded—pot time allowed a visitor to creep closer to the items in our zoological garden, see new arrangements, different colors, sounds and smells, a new way of viewing the whole.

Time itself was not affected. Yesterday was still a crazy out of control bulldozer; today wears a mask and shouts in a strange language, while tomorrow builds his camp out of view and busies himself burning memories. Maybe he was really fucked up, across the river with that crap about 'walls,' and 'focus'; maybe he'd been getting sucked off by Mary Jane so long he didn't give a shit? One or the other. Either or. It didn't matter.

Whatever happened, being stoned could only be a part of it. He knew who he was, even if the guy he was, was the same guy who frequently got high. There was no reason to play the blame game until it were proved that an actual addiction robbed the victim of the use of something he had, like, say, talent.

Berge had that imagination, remember, which could do it all. If you have your cake, find a table and eat it before it dries out.

Then, there was the 'incident' with Chris. Berge knew what he did was stupid to the point of criminality. At the very least it was a malicious trick aimed at one of the weaker of the tribe: Guilty, guilty, guilty. All the more justification to outmaneuver the facts, put distance between himself and the angry truth.

"I had no idea it was gonna crush him like an aluminum can. If it had been anyone else—"

"They woulda beat the shit out of ya," put in Sutter.

"Hmmm," Bergman grunted, "maybe you haven't gotten that far, but the Bible talks about letting go one's anger."

"Screw you!" said Sutter.

"You know, if someone had told me that this would take on

a sexual coloring, I wouldn't have come."

"Asshole!" shouted Jake.

"Well," said Bergman, "if you want to discuss it any further, I have to charge $15 an hour; nothing personal, it's just that as a professional, you listen to a lot of people's complaints and, honestly, most of them are nuts. So I have to charge for services in the realm of communications/sociology just to spare a few moments for myself and the loved ones."

"Fuck you whenever possible," spat Jake.

* * * *

"Hey!" cried Ron detecting someone fidgeting with his door. He sat up in bed. Slowly the door opened and Wayne slipped through. Wayne closed the door gently and stole over to the edge of the bed. Ron was staring, more than a little stoned, at the reflections in his room. He'd lain down after lunch, hoping to speed up digestion, but a strong sea breeze danced frenziedly with the trees outside his window throwing fierce shadows upon the ceiling. A visit from Wayne fit the decor.

"So what can I do you for?" he asked, suppressing his surprise.

"Man, I gotta talk to someone; and you being an ex-marine."

"How'didju know that?" Ron interrupted.

"Hey," said Wayne, assuming a defensive posture with his left hand extended in a three-pronged salute, "shit gets around. This is not a communist-fascist police state yet. That's why I'm here; there's something weird going on."

"Weird? In here?" Ron smiled.

"Look, I don't have much time," said Wayne, grabbing a quick peak over his shoulder, "I shouldn't even be here."

"None of us should be here."

"Just remember this in case, in case of, well, who knows?" Wayne laughed strangely. "They're going to implant devices under our skin," he whispered.

"Who's 'they?'" asked Ron skeptically.

"Don't you know?" replied Wayne.

"Know what? We're here because the government needs–"

"The government?" Wayne mocked. "Who's that?"

"Well, I don't know, exactly." Ron troubled over this, he didn't know his government. They sent him to Viet Nam telling him he had to defeat the enemy of the democratic Republic of Viet Nam. But Viet Nam was in the midst of a civil war where 'republic' and 'democracy' had no meaning. Ron saw women selling themselves for a buck 'U.S.'; wild dogs fighting over a human leg; babies abandoned within hours of birth; theft, bribery, expropriation, assassination, retaliation, terrorism, colonialism, east/west tension, north/south tension, and a thousand cultures leading the parade to the next stage on a float constructed of broken bones and scarred flesh.

He didn't know why the U.S. wanted a slice of Viet Nam, maybe it was the ports, the beaches, off-shore oil, the rumors of gold? Whatever it was, it would have to wait. From the moment he saw the dust, the debris, the people happy to live with a little pot, a little money and little chance, just to be called Vietnamese, he knew the US was defeated. We could kill lots of them, we could destroy their airbases and factories, their homes and highways, but we couldn't make them, us. At the end of the day, they're still 'them,' and Americans weren't ready for the terrible commitment necessary to make the two races one in a space of years. The government—his government—was caught in the middle and was unrecognizable to him.

"I gotta go," said Wayne, and disappeared.

Ron watched him leave; it would have been easy to put a bullet in that big, pineapple-shaped head.

* * * *

They tried prohibition with alcohol but it didn't take. There was a strong desire, too strong for the state to override by bulking up its police force, not in itself a good idea. The desire expressed itself as a 'need' which drew the criminal element—used to working with a thirst for banned commodities. The profit, and the violence, and the prisons, gained enormously. "Just like what's happen'n here, now, with pot." Jimbo paused to let his message percolate. "'Cep't pot should be accepted as the way to ending alcohol abuse."

"Can it really do that?" Chris asked. He felt he would make a good drunk, full of babyish ego and self-loathing, so he didn't drink. The tales he heard—missing keys, wallets, cars—supplied little encouragement. That's what led him to pot, this urge to grow up, to experience things for yourself, especially such things others dare not touch.

"Of course it can cut down your drinking. I'm proof. Get it? I was a drunk. So now I do a doobie instead. It lightens the load. Alcohol depresses, it's rough on the bod; marijuana lifts the drapes: Behold, the Land beyond nod."

"No, wow!" Chris exclaimed. This was just what he'd hoped for, before, ah, 'the incident,' a good drug, one that would wipe away all the bad things about drugs.

"I can't tell you why I was a drunk, but I just couldn't put it down. I closed the bar, I was loud, I was lewd, I forgot things, started fights. Lucky I still had friends by the time I saw I was losing them," Jimbo admitted.

"What happened?"

"Ya gotta hit bottom you know? Well 'bottom' for me happened as I started talking to this really cute girl—that's why we drink isn't it, to talk to pretty girls? When I spilled a bottle of beer on her dress. She was sitting down and I reached for my glass and pushed right through you know, knocking over a bottle that splashed all over her dress."

"That's too bad," Chris said. He saw a tiny woman paddling across a bathtub, rivers of booze pouring over her.

"Listen," Jimbo implored, "she was an angel, an absolute angel! She forgave me for the whole beer bottle thing."

"That's great." Chris pictured a beautiful winged woman with pouty lips and raw cleavage coming towards him irresistibly, like a ship on wheels…

"Yeah, well, as it turns out, there was a limit to her patience. I asked her out to a movie and we got there a week after it'd left town."

"Whooo..." Chris sympathized, "that's too bad." Jimbo's date swung a tennis racquet at Jimbo's deserving semi-bald head.

"Yeah, then I had to borrow $5 bucks for gas."

"I'm sure she was cool with that," Chris offered, excited by the notion of successive failures occurring on other parts of the globe.

"No, not exactly, especially after I locked her coat and the keys in the car."

"You didn't!" Chris laughed. Jimbo's girlfriend filled the gas tank with sugar while spraying the car's finish with Coca-Cola.

"The snow didn't seem to bother her at first."

"You poor guy," said Chris behind a big grin. There were two puncture wounds in Jimbo's neck when they found him.

"Well, only a special type of woman would stick it out after a start like that."

"Very special," said Chris. With a whoosh, this special woman soared toward the light without Jimbo.

"Huh? What's that?"

"Go on," Chris begged. Jimbo's 'special woman' looked like Chris's mother!

"There isn't much more to tell. She told me to call, but I couldn't do it, you know?"

Jimbo's kind never got that 'Hmm…' look in the late night bars they haunted, maybe it was the soiled pants and the twigs in the hair.

"Anyway," Jimbo responded sheepishly, "I was looking for a drug that kinda took off the edge without knocking you off the ledge. Without something, I'd get all bunched up you know what I mean—hyperventilate—when I tried to talk to a girl."

"What happened?" asked Chris, as Jimbo went silent.

"Oh, the booze kicked that door down all right," Jimbo replied.

"Please!" Chris was excited, there weren't many people who had to be begged to talk about themselves.

"Well, it wasn't about women at all as it turns out," Jimbo hesitated, then plunged on. "I useta get together with a coupla buddies just about every night. The first item on the agenda was to get our hands on two cases of beer; one wasn't enough to get each of us that buzz. We didn't have the money all the time, so we got inventive if you know what I mean."

"Un-huh," Chris said encouragingly.

"We found the easiest way to get the required juice was to steal it from the frat parties near campus. Yeah, some plan. We'd cruise the neighborhood looking for people and noise and then push our way in, grab the booze and whoosh.

"Dangerous all right, but it was even worse than that. If we got called on the beer snatch, Joe-Joe pulled his pistol."

"That's pretty crazy," Chris agreed.

"Absolutely insane," said Jimbo. "We'd do anything for that damned 2-case quota."

"Did anyone ever get shot?" Jimbo's round, colorless face had led Chris to underestimate him, he was a man of action.

"One night Joe-Joe pulled the trigger and jerked the gun into the air at the same time hitting this guy's smoke alarm and the damned thing went off scaring the hell out of us! We had no business going out and doing this kinda stuff. It was madness. But see, it was the booze talking as much as anything. Even when we'd get hammered in order to get the girls, for some of us man, it wasn't the girls we were drinking for if you see the picture?"

"And a, what, ah, what kind of a, girls, were these?" Chris asked quietly.

Jimbo laughed. "Oh, these were some babes. We had this one gal, Cami, oh my! She had this, ah, with, ah, well you know."

"Un-huh," Chris blinked.

"But these women were buying pretty big problems, you savvy?" Jimbo stood up and circled. "There isn't anyone who couldn't help his cause by cutting way down on the sauce and, maybe, adding more pot like, you know, if it was necessary."

* * * *

"Today," said Wick in his familiar reedy voice, "you can talk about any subject you want as long as it's one of these three." He handed out brief essays on the nature of *cannabis* to each subject.

**Essay # 1** Scientists believe marijuana's main mind-activating chemical *tetrahydrocannibinol* (THC), binds so tightly with the cerebral cortex—the source of thinking and imagination—that cellular activity is affected. Specialized areas on the membrane surrounding brain cells, called receptors, fit lock-and-key with the THC molecule changing the way the cell processes information leading to the 'high.' *Cannabinoids* so far discovered do not appear to hurt the cell suggesting that THC and some brain cells have a shared history.

**Essay # 2** U.S. involvement in Vietnam, from supporting the French Indo-China empire after WWII, to propping up the corrupt Diem regime, was a complete mistake. Ho Chi Min, leader of the North, is considered the Vietnamese Lincoln. The American-backed South Vietnamese were unpopular holdovers from the French Colonial period. While Americans brought superior weapons, they could not win the hearts and minds of a Vietnamese people who didn't trust the US, knowing we would leave eventually.

**Essay # 3** During marijuana intoxication, consciousness, attention and memory are temporarily suspended. The deliberative processes—our socially constructed sense of time, our functional identities, and automatic verbal labeling—are diluted into a state of pure awareness. Through the enhancement of the senses, 'normal' reality becomes 'associative' reality, the mind accommodating more perceptions in greater detail.

"See," said Jimbo, "that's the story of pot. The brain has sites that fit perfectly with the active ingredient in marijuana. That's not coincidence, that's co-evolution."

"OOOooo," whistled Jake.

"What's your point?" said Berge, attempting to imitate

Shep.

"You've got this, this relationship between man and plant."

"Symbiosis," Shep interjected.

"Is that, 'Plaman' or 'Mant'?" asked Chris.

"Yeah, right," Jimbo acknowledged. "But this natural relationship between people and pot is under attack by the same group that cuts up the earth into chunks and sells it to the highest bidder, turning the world into one vast supermarket."

"Class politics," said Ira matter-of-factly.

"That means you ignore pretty much everything until 'hooligans' burn down the capital," suggested Bergman.

"Precisely," Ira pounced. "Then you spring the trap: government constructs a 'boogeyman' creating instant consensus to cede more power for perceived safety—*Vòila!* Police state!"

"Yeah, my words exactly," Tony chimed in.

"Aren't you one cheery son-of-a-bitch," sighed Thad.

"No happy ending?" guessed Tony.

"The 'enemy' in the War on Drugs," said Ira, "is anyone opposed to consolidation and scarcity—the interests of the ruling class. It's really quite simple."

"What if you're not interested in this war of interests?" asked Ron. "Why are we the enemy?"

"Because the numbers will be on our side someday; that's what scares them," Sutter alleged.

"Yeah, well the pigs don't look scared," scoffed Jake.

"It's not belief so much as conditioning, we're raised in a tradition of all out war against Evil," Ira elaborated.

"So you substitute pot for evil?" Jimbo observed.

"Of course, it's a terrible simplification," concluded Ira, "but that's how the game of wealth is played. You bury all the nuances in simple loyalty to profit."

"I've got it!" hollered Wayne, "get all the big money pro-weeders together, dudes like cookie makers, the potato chip people. Yeah, and Hostess Twinkies, man!" said Wayne, mesmerized.

"The munchie factor," said Tony.

"Well anyway, we pass the hat to these guys with the dough thanks to MJ, and we go out and buy a bunch of eavesdropping equipment, and gas masks and light-weight shields."

"Hey, man," Thaddeus interjected, "you putt'n us on defense from the git-go? I ain't play'n no defense, that's all there is to it."

"No, no, no. Wait!" cried Wayne, "that's so we can wage urban warfare—guerilla warfare—against the oppressor, against them."

"Yeah, I gotcha," said Thad. "That's cool."

"Ok, Col. Lamebrain, call me when you get your army. I'll be in my hooch with the hooch," cried Jake.

# 22

## *The Index of Euphoria*

Normally Wayne didn't do much pot; maybe a puff or two to give him 'the smell'—a second pair of eyes deep in the brain trained to view suspicious activity. What he'd seen so far here in Boston, called to mind the sinister workings of the Army's top-secret Ghost division. The military intervention arm of the Psy-Ops Dept., the Ghost soldiers were especially active versus the Red menace.

Wayne concluded advance elements of the elite 'G' Bananas squadron fresh from mayhem in the lawless southern hemisphere, were conducting this experiment complicit with key Harvard dons. The Ghost hired the world's best chemists to perfect an exotic arsenal of control mechanisms, everything from adrenalin-laced wolf blood to table salt made from fine particles of gold. The Ghost Division first showed its colors during the run-up to World War II when Ghost labs synthesized a potent counter-terrorist cocktail consisting of LSD, cocaine, morphine and turnip extract used experimentally on the Scots, to keep them out of the conflict.

The 'G' Bananas specialized in atrocities, using drugs to break people down until they could be re-programmed as puppets of corporate interests. If the 'G' Bananas could get you high, they could manipulate you into buying jet-skis, doing crossword puzzles or naming your daughter Traci. They wanted baby boomers, and they wanted them so high their testes fused together. Wayne hadn't seen it done, but he had imagined it and that was enough.

Bananas involvement would explain more than a few 'a-nomalies' Wayne had witnessed in the preceding three weeks. The IMP was a fraud; although he'd broken the mystery, anyone could have, all it took was a fall. No way was the IMP legit, it was a plant. But for what? And the open Day-Log; what incompetent would leave out the playbook?! And what about him getting the safe combination, that was easy, man! But what clinched it, what clearly revealed Ghost ownership was that promise of some really neat games. The stuff they did bring sucked, man—the signature joke of leading-edge espionage, thought Wayne.

Like it was supposed to be a marijuana experiment you know, but you didn't hafta smoke; yeah, right! Wayne guessed that the GBananas were taking up perimeter positions outside the facility waiting to track the subjects as they left, probably with homing devices such as an ultra-thin transmitter sewed into his final check (If he demanded cash, then bills marked with weird chemical residue?). Those funny essays we had to read—the whole thing was a cover-up, using stoned imbeciles to rehearse dangerous anti-soviet maneuvers so the real culprits could escape.

'What did I forget?' he quizzed himself while emptying his pockets on the bed. He glanced at the items as they fell: a joint and a half, a cigarette lighter, stopwatch, a large homemade chocolate-chip cookie from Early. He gathered them up and placed them in a box of pilfered goods including a pair of sneakers left too long unattended, a handsome custom pocket-knife swiped as a real life lesson, a neat, 'too beautiful for that peasant,' moss agate clock, various OTC medicines including stool softener, and a pen inscribed 'Congratulations, Harold Nicholson, Doctor of Psychiatry, 1959, from his loving wife Karen.'

Wayne did not retain his trophies from any hope of profit. It was rather a teaching device: when the 'victim' found himself temporarily without the services of a certain object, he was to experience a transcending knowledge that his world faced profound security challenges for which he should prepare himself. But now that Wayne had delivered the lesson, the articles that would trigger this recognition were no longer necessary. In fact, like authentic grave robbing tools held against the day when grave robbing disappeared rendering them rare (and valuable) historic artifacts, they were a definite liability so far as today's ignorant public was concerned.

It would be prudent to get rid of them. Obviously, returning them to their owners would be foolish, restoring trust to those who had to be threatened into abandoning trust in the first place. Wayne, the coyote, the prankster, determined that one of the subjects would inherit his trove of stolen trinkets. He'd drop the stash somewhere where it would stir chaos and confusion thus inhibiting the GBananas design, whatever it was. But he wasn't going to give it all away, he'd keep the several joints he'd palmed, and the stool softener was definitely going to the staff mess.

Before going, Wayne took another peak at the experiment's 'Hit' List, i.e., most pot smoked so far: Shep and Thad, averaging eight joints a day, had a comfortable lead over the rest of the field. They'd be fully under the thumb of GBananas by now. Next, Jake, Jimbo and Bergman at five 'j's per diem; followed by Ron, Tony and Sutter at four. Wayne was ninth on the list at three per day! He couldn't believe it; three joints—and that's only what they knew. GBananas would be on his trail too, measuring him for a green leisure suit, if he wasn't careful. Cover your tracks, get rid of the evidence, blend in, Wayne mused.

Outside Wayne's door, Nicholson worried along the corridor a jumble of concerns.

An ear cocked for the occasional clicker salvo, he searched for that thing, the feeling he'd captured something special, something that would let him plant the flag at an unreachable height. He didn't have it, he should have prepared better, he should have. Being of the counter-culture—literally an army of bad behavior—it occurred to him, they have less trust. Being young, less faith. Imprisoned, and smoking a substance illegal only 50 feet away, it should be expected that this group would become petty violators of the experiment's rules. The question was not 'if?' but 'when?' The bigger question of course, was how this unlawful variable affected the Experiment?

Spotting the infirmary, Nicholson ducked in, surprising Minter and the Badge. "So," shouted Nicholson, making a deliberate attempt to tone down the formal manner he spent so much time practicing. "Guys, I'm looking for Wicks."

"Just missed him," said Badger, one hand balancing his glasses, the other trying to corral his ponytail. "Probably in his car by now."

"Niiaannhh!" Nicholson vented through his teeth. "Look, what can you tell me about this IMP business?"

Beddiker buried his tongue in the corner of his mouth, leaving Minter to address Nicholson. "Yes, we suspect some underreporting," he said. "They've found someway to trick us."

"This is important!" Nicholson insisted. It occurred to him to dig out the smoking totals so far in order to buttress his case. "You've got to get on top of this; we need answers, we need the right answers." Where was that darn list? he wondered, searching each of his two large lab-coat pockets.

"The fact is," spoke Minter, immediately regretting his words, "there is nothing to fear about the clicking... or lack of it."

"I find myself of an entirely different mind," Nicholson argued, "and I believe our friends in the military and in the halls of Congress will agree with me that this is a very serious matter!"

Minter tried to think clearly. "I didn't mean to imply that a problem with the IMP wasn't important, not at all. What I meant to say is that there is no problem with the IMP."

"That we're aware of anyway," Badger added helpfully.

"But the clicking?" said Nicholson, squeezing his starched white coat for some sign of the missing paper.

"The IMP is still being used; there is respect for the totals required. We haven't lost integrity." Minter was distracted by Nicholson's feverish searching.

"Oh, I had the smoking totals but I've apparently misplaced them."

"A week to go, huh? Who's leading the pack?" asked Bedikker.

"Oh, I don't think anyone will be catching Ira, good lord."

"A B-1 bomber couldn't catch Shep, er, Ira," said Bedikker.

"But the numbers?" Nicholson interrupted.

"The numbers are the same," Minter smiled, "it's—"

"It's how they got the numbers," put in Badger.

Nicholson stared silently at Bedikker before returning to interrogate Minter. "What's he saying?" Nicholson asked.

"We think they're doing easy work to get their totals," Dave answered simply.

Nicholson looked stunned. He saw a score of faces he would have to answer to. "Bury it," he mumbled, "bury it."

"Not necessary," Minter countered, "the data is good."

"What are you saying?" Nicholson gasped.

"It's the way the experiment is structured," Minter explained. "There are no bad results."

"As long as you get results," Badge offered.

"Can anyone explain this to me?" Nicholson asked, "and please be brief!" He threw his hands around his head to protect himself from evil.

Custer placed his hands in front of him and intertwined his fingers. "The important thing about marijuana is the high. It's not a big upper like speed or a slow downer like alcohol," he said moving his hands outward, "no colorful hallucinations or four-hour race to nowhere. Just a dependable, short feeling of satisfaction with low risk," he concluded, pulling his hands together once more. "If you want to test that—the high—you have to meet it on its own terms. You have to follow the subjective experience as much as possible; it's the only probable breakthrough in primate research we'll see in our lifetime."

"What are you saying?" said Nicholson, searching for a chair.

"Well," Minter continued, "we replaced the Depressant Index normally used in drug experiments, with the Euphoric Index."

"Oh, God!" choked Nicholson.

Minter went on, stepping carefully while remaining confident that he had explained this to Nicholson and gotten his approval. "In the current context, with subject dehumanization due to setting, linking marijuana smoking and the inevitable rule-breaking in a causal way would not be accurate.

"The key to understanding marijuana's effects lies beyond these obvious links. The key comes from the 'increased sensitivity' that is self-reported by smokers with overwhelming frequency," Minter paused to inhale, he'd practically become inaudible. "We feel," he continued after a meaningful glance at Bedikker, "that this increased sensitivity, if real, would show itself in... in some kind of positive, ah, societal impulse."

"I'm afraid I do not get your meaning, David," Nicholson said coldly.

"Imagine doctor, that you were a heavy drinker. The more you drank, the more depressed you became. Your views grew darker and darker. That's the Depressant Index."

"David, let me remind you that this is Harvard. We rent ourselves out to anyone, well, not just anyone, but to many, many clients. We have an obligation to these institutions."

"Best met by the Euphoric Index," broke in Badger. Nicholson tried to remember where he'd seen this short, hairy person before.

"The Euphoric Index wants to know if you get high, do you also get better?" Minter explained. "If you repeatedly take a euphoric, even a minor one like pot, does your feeling good incline you toward doing good? Do you see the world positively, like a family helping family members instead of a jungle?"

"Hunh?" Nicholson wondered.

"Pot smokers expect to feel good while high," Minter explained. "If you approach them from the morally superior position: 'Stop that! Normal is better.' You lose 'em. These folk don't believe that assertion, for whatever reason, and you can't begin a conversation with them if you begin with that."

"David, I," Nicholson reeled, it was like heat stroke, he thought. "Water," he coughed. Badger took a sample cup to the cooler.

"Moral acts reflect normal values, or so we claim," said

Minter. "We're not surprised to see someone who abuses depressants forfeit moral conduct. Now, let's check euphorics. If you are going to justify chronic ingestion, you have to produce humane impulses. You can't justify a morally demeaning experience."

"I'm still stumped as far as where you're taking my experiment," sighed Nicholson.

"Do normal people sometimes violate the law while smoking marijuana? Yes, by definition, you've made it illegal. Now, the question is: do normal people perform acts of ethical heroism while stoned? What insight have they gained? Does this purported feeling of love for their fellow man translate in some measurable fashion?"

Nicholson was quiet; he did not look well but he was always a basket case at such times. "Just tell me it'll work out," pleaded Nicholson.

"Nuth'n to worry about," Badger broke in.

"It's under control," said Minter reassuringly. "Whether or not we get everything, the data points will lead somewhere. The experiment will have a heart and a soul. I think we'll be able to crystallize all the loose findings into a pivot that might turn public opinion," David smiled.

"You sure?" intoned Nicholson. Custer put out his hand to seal the deal. "Thank you," said Nicholson as he left.

"Gee, think we should have told him about the missing pot?" asked Badge.

"I think he has quite enough on his plate right now," Minter laughed.

"Who da'ya suppose?" Badger asked seriously.

"Well, I don't know, who do you think?" skated Minter.

"Hmmm," Bedikker deliberated, "Berge is crazy enough,

Chris has already freaked out so he's not in the running, Jake has the desire, Wayne has the ability."

"And Thaddeus would sacrifice us voodoo style if Melody told him to," Custer finished.

"That reminds me," Badger responded, "those two are gettn' out of hand, we should do something."

"Catch them in the act, is that what you want?" asked Minter.

"Well, ok, maybe we're better off stay'n out of it," Badge claimed.

"Yeah," Minter agreed. On several scores—the clickers, some of the tests, the disappearing pot—it would appear the kind-hearted but slow staff had fallen for the smoker's shenanigans. But Minter knew he was on solid, if new, ground. A good deal of bait had been spread about, he only needed a single bite.

"Hey, where in the devil is Melody? It's 11:30!" said Bedikker, irritated. "And wha' the hell d'ya mean by 'voodoo style'?"

* * * *

"Ok," said Wick, upon concluding the essential nose count, "today's discussion (pause)... Oh, satellite, I can't find it."

"Is this it?" asked Tony, picking up the stray paper and rubbing it against his thigh before passing it to Wick.

"Oh, yes, yes," said Wick, reading the sheet inches from his face, eyeglasses raised to hairline. "Suppose you found a wallet with lots of cash in it, over $1,000."

"Keep it," Sutter interjected.

"Not so fast," Wick intervened.

"Oh shit," objected Sutter.

"Also in the wallet is a complete identification of the owner.

It so happens that the owner has been accused of embezzlement, tax evasion and drug peddling (though not marijuana). The well-publicized case has not yet gone to trial. The question is would you: A) return cash immediately; B) Keep the cash; C) Return a part of the cash; or D) Return wallet but no cash?"

"Oh, no, not another wallet stuffed with cash moral dilemma?" commented Thaddeus.

"Yeah," said Tony, "they gett'n us ready for life on the outside."

"I just found a wallet this morning," ventured Chris. "Turns out it was mine, a good thing too as I was getting short on cash."

"Do we all have to agree whichisimpossiblewithBerge?" asked Sutter.

"Actually," declared Wick, "these questions you do yourself."

"Yipeeeee!" shouted Tony.

"Then we score your responses and discuss outcomes," Wick continued.

"Oh, no, hey. You promised," Jake whined, rolling his eyes and winking at Sutter.

"Yeah, man, no discussion, I heard it," said Sutter solemnly.

"I didn't promise no discussion, did I?" Wick replied, flustered.

"Absolutely," Sutter insisted.

"But that wouldn't make sense; this is discussion period," asserted Wick.

"But you promised," Jake cooed.

"Anybody else?" appealed Wick.

"I don't know," said Berge. "What do you think Professor Stern?" he asked, turning to Ira, "do we have a bona fide oral contract here, to wit: no discussion?"

Ira twisted his hands together slowly. "I must admit, I recall nothing which could be construed as an offer from management to suspend the customary mass babble that passes in these environs for discussion, a hem."

"Perhaps it was a lesser type of promise," coached Bergman, "the Promised Land type of promise?"

"Hey!" shouted Tony, "some other time, huh? Let's get to the discussion."

Wick watched as the subjects filled out the questionnaires. It was Minter's idea: a simple force test with only two authentic responses, to separate those with morals from those without. The different scenarios allowed a little face saving for the dishonest, 'Sure, I took his money but he had it coming.'

But as he correlated the responses, Wick's attitude changed. The vote was five to return cash (a); three to keep cash (b); one to take part of the cash (c); and one to send back the empty wallet (d).

"This is terrible," he said, "a 50% response to doing the right thing?" said Wick, puzzled.

"Berge, again," Jake sighed.

"Who else?" Sutter agreed.

"But only five of you returned the money," Wick challenged. "It should be a lot more."

"More, less, less, more, more or less. What's it going to be?" asked Thad.

"Hey," cried Tony, "the wallet was lost in Las Vegas, and what's lost in Vegas..."

"Is spent on a high-priced hooker," offered Jimbo.

"Is skimmed by the mob," chirped Berge.

"Buys cement shoes for a swim in Lake Mead," countered

Jake.

"Folks, if you don't mind," Wick called, "I'm going to ask each of you how you voted."

"No!" screamed Tony.

Everyone is tempted, everyone gives in to something, reasoned Wick. The question was, did marijuana assist good behavior or bad? He pointed to Jake.

"It's true, I admit it," Jake burst, "I did it, I entered Berge's twisted mind and voted to give that shithead back his money because what goes around, comes around."

Wick pointed to Wayne. "Yeah, I voted to give back the money, too. But I can't tell you why. It's classified," explained Wayne.

"Next, Thaddeus?"

"I too, took it upon myself to uphold the high moral standards of this mutha-fuck'n country of random violence and racial hatred. Oh, yeah, he got it back alright, he got the gun."

"Yeah, he got it in the back," wheezed Shep.

When Wick finished his tally, it was 10–0 for returning the money. Well, a bit unorthodox he thought, but it's all data.

# 23

# *'So Tiny a Sin, So Grand a Result'*

Wick was more than a little disturbed by the latest 'Exercises.' He wasted no time in bringing it to Minter's attention. His supposed 'second,' was wasting their time with inconsequential blather—the latest being a 'question' concerning the 1894 marijuana tome by the British Indian Hemp Drugs Commission. The report, some seven volumes, exonerated pot from serious consequences, saving it from prohibition throughout the British Raj.

The official policy for 'bhang,' 'ganja' and 'charas' (in advancing order of potency) advocated by the Commission was 'discouragement' via zoning, taxes, and licensing. It was a permissive policy and was never in favor for Britain herself, only for the 'colonies.'

When he found Minter, he waved the Exercises in his face. "I can't do this, it's propaganda, that's what it is."

Minter scratched his head. "It's a well-recognized study."

"They didn't use subjects."

"400 doctors testified."

"In a scheme to tap local revenue to support a colonial regime!"

"The Committee met 40 times in 30 cities, they sought the best available evidence."

"Britain at the time was the largest trafficker in narcotics in the whole world!"

"That was opium."

"What's the difference?"

"You know better than that." Minter paused; Wick had apparently met with Nicholson. "The time to play it safe is past."

"This is dangerous."

"Not as dangerous as ignoring reality."

"But there's so much at stake."

"For you personally?"

Wick turned away, "This is insane," he said, "no one will follow us."

"Exactly, Jon."

"Oh, no!" sighed Wick.

"The data has been coming in for hundreds of years; always the same. You think with repetition, they'll get it? No, Jon, it won't happen. Your blood counts, your pulse rates, your approved psych inventories don't mean a thing."

"You're crazy. If Nicholson gets wind of this."

"Jon, the only facts that matter are those not easily gotten by conventional means. We know what these subjects are going to do in lab. We've got to find out what they might do, and might not do, outside lab."

"That's impossible."

"No, it isn't."

"You've got to lie."

"No. Simulate."

"David—"

"Jon, you've got a 15-year-old daughter, right? Well, you tell me, what's more important, how she acts Wednesday sitting at the table with you, or what happens on Saturday night, when the bottle's being passed?"

"You can't just keep telling them pot is ok."

"I'm quoting from the major investigations that are part of the public record."

"It's not good policy."

"Policy should follow science, Jon."

"You're impossible."

"If we treat them as criminals and imbeciles, that's what they'll become and that data will be meaningless. Maybe that's what you want?"

Wick shot him a fearful, desperate look and fled down the hall.

* * * *

*A gift of himself to mankind from the god Shiva, bhang, or 'Sky-flier,' is the nectar which sweetens an otherwise dreary world. He who drinks bhang wisely escapes the bonds of matter-blinded self. With mind cleared and brain stimulated to thought, the consumer of bhang centers their thoughts on the Eternal. Devotees take the hand of their mighty guardian bhang until they become one with the deity and are received by the divine spirit of nature into the great ocean of Being.*
- ***On The Religion Of Hemp***

* * * *

In the 19th century, opium, not the relatively unknown *cannabis*, had entrenched itself in British society as an indispensable painkiller and general all-around mood alterer. The opium cartel in India—the British East India Company—virtually wrote British colonial policy. When China, alarmed at the incapacitating effects of opium addiction among its population, attempted to stop the illegal trade from India, it was attacked by the British Navy and forced to cede the port of Hong Kong.

The Brits justified the trade in addictive opium with the claim that hemp was more dangerous. This pattern of exonerating opium's effects with the specter of *ganja's* greater threat, eventually led to the British Parliament demanding an investigation into hemp drugs. In 1894, the British Indian Hemp Drug Commission (IHDC) began its investigation, releasing its report three years later.

The Commission planned to overcome their admitted ignorance of the state of hemp affairs 'in-country' with a massive fact-finding effort. The IHDC assembled 1,400 witnesses from the ranks of medicine, religion and the civil service accounting for 3,000 pages of testimony creating 'a substantial foundation of well ascertained facts.'

From this very bureaucratic accumulation, the IHDC determined that the central question it faced—Should the production of hemp drugs be prohibited?—required more than the mere fact that *bhang, ganja* and *charas* are intoxicants. That justification could not be found; 80% of Commission members opposed prohibition.

The Commission ruled instead, that 'under all circumstances' reviewed, their unhesitating verdict, based on the weight of the evidence was 'almost entirely' against total prohibition in respect to any of the hemp drugs. 'Total prohibition' of the manufacture, sale or use of the hemp drugs is 'neither necessary nor expedient in consideration of their ascertained effects, their prevalence and the habit of their use.'

The Commission, in fact, reflected the view of an earlier set of Anglo bureaucrats who investigated no fewer than 10 local intoxicants (including *bhang, ganja* and *charas*) in 1798, concluding: 'With respect to the drugs specified, they are not for the most part represented as producing any very violent or dangerous effects of intoxication except when taken to excess... Most of these articles (including hemp drugs) appear to be useful either in medicine or otherwise (and) we do not recommend that the sale of any of them be altogether prohibited.' (Indeed, Britain licensed the production and distribution of hemp drugs in India beginning in 1793 and drew half its colonial revenue from taxes on this and other popular consumer drugs.)

Satisfied that in their normal use, hemp drugs did not produce insanity and violence (the insanity allegation was based on 'untrustworthy' information), the IHDC took a pragmatic stance. Prohibition would necessitate 'a large preventive establishment,' would be strongly resented as an interference in India's cultural life (*ganja's* medicinal powers were noted in text dating to 1400 BC), might lead to the use of more dangerous drugs, and could hardly be justified if alcohol, felt by a large number to do more harm than *bhang,* were left alone while hemp was repressed. And finally, marijuana was a legitimate personal adaptation to a static society which offered those of lower caste little reasonable hope of a better life.

The Commission advocated a policy of control and restriction, aimed at restraining 'excessive use' of *cannabis* by imposing as high a rate of duty as can be levied without inducing an increase in smuggling. Once the restrictions on cultivation were in place, either through licensing or taxation, sufficient to prevent its use by all save the most dedicated of consumers, then 'there should be as little interference as possible on the part of Government with hemp's distribution.' (Chapter XVI, paragraphs 638, 654 and 678).

*The England that called the hemp question in far off India, was, from our perspective, a sinister environment. A time when the King was assumed to be 'not only incapable of doing wrong, but even of thinking wrong,' (Blackstone, 1769). Prisoners, including debtors, wore chains, and paid for heat and rations or suffered slow starvation; sanitation was a gravity-fed open sewer; doctors moved from handling corpses to examining pregnant women; children worked 10 hours a day; and London choked under the sickening pall of a million daily fires.*

*But London at least, allowed for open speech which produced an era of reform epitomized by the 1894 Indian Hemp Drugs Commission. Jeremy Bentham (1748–1832) expounded the philosophic doctrine of Utilitarianism, which switched the conversation from royal perks to the business of government in promoting 'the greatest happiness for the greatest number.' Bentham trusted to reason to turn the Enlightenment into an age of reform. He answered the conservatives with the simple statement: 'whatever now is established, once was innovation.'*

*A student of Bentham was John Stuart Mill (1806–1873), whose reputed IQ of 200 is the highest ever recorded. Little J.S. Mill was taught Greek at age 3 in an attempt to jump-start British society by producing a genius critique of the old regime. It was a success of sorts, despite a nervous breakdown from too much study, Mill helped create the template for the public-minded citizen of the future.*

*Mill felt that middle-class conformism, unlimited population growth and emphasis on economic expansion would doom the environment and lessen individual liberties to the point of virtual slavery.*

*It was to Mill, that the writers of the IHDC turned for inspiration. Mill headed native relations for the British East Indian Company for much of his career. His fears of the coercive power of government upon the individual led to a 'relaxed' British colonial rule in India—a rarely used model of foreign self-restraint.*

*Mill believed that government could only intrude on the life of the individual as necessary for the defense of society as a whole. Government had the right to offer advice and information to guide personal action, but could only prohibit behaviors clearly dangerous to someone else. Those actions which affect only our persons made up 'that circle around every individual human being which no Government ought to be permitted to overstep.'*

* * * *

**Order the following statements 1, 2, 3, 4, 5, according to how closely they reflect your opinions:**

By the 1890s the British got it right: instead of taxing tea, they'd tax ganja; nor would they seek to 'reform' the natives by imposing their religion and culture upon them.

The British, by their serial fondling of every shoreline they could sic their navy upon, are not to be trusted when 'fact-finding.'

British acceptance of ganja in India contrasts sharply with its prohibition in Britain where it remains the largest cause of arrests.

The British invasion of India is marked by the same evasion, corruption and exploitation that attaches to all colonial regimes.

Marijuana is the perfect drug for slacker Brits.

"Just a clarification your non-pottedness?"

"Yes?" asked Custer, his ripe, crimson mustache twitching.

"Begg'n your pardon and all that," continued Jake, "but the selections while interesting and appropriate, I find difficult to match to the 'statements.'"

"I do believe my esteemed colleague may have given us a nugget worthy of rumination," put in Bergman.

"Oh geez, man, git off my side."

"Yeah, man, you're not cool dude, you're freakn' me out," said Shep.

"But the question remains," Sutter smirked, "are these real

Injuns, or do they come from Indianja?"

"I believe they're rebuilt engines," answered Jake. "Though I'd like us all to consider the question for eons."

"I get it, you're CIA?" spoofed Chris. "Or KGB? UPS? PGA? ADD?"

"Now, we can't really tell you that now can we? Or can we?" said Jimbo. "I've got to check with the misinformation officer."

"I'm feeling an undertow," said Ron, "in the vast ocean of being."

"Hmmph," Badger whined, "you think getting your ya-yas off at the expense of the overweight, beer-drinking, tv-watching American taxpayer is cool? Well, you're dead wrong. This caper is on your tab you hippie fascists, so you better supply full value!

"Of course, I don't need to remind you that there are no wrong answers. Just those that don't make a bit of goddamned sense. But hey, we can deal with that," he purred.

Custer smiled; Badger delivered. But the exercise had gone too smoothly. Unless furnished with some opportunity for rebellion, the subjects coasted. It suddenly struck him that the point of testing pot should not be to describe the perfect environment for the pot smokers, but to attack their comfort zone, place them and their drug of choice *in extremis* and see what happens. These soft-toss statements obviously weren't forcing anyone off their stool, and the essays were perhaps too aligned with pot thinking to be challenging.

"Ok, before you go, we've one more dimension to this exercise," added Minter, pausing to allow the subjects to vent. "I want you," said Minter quickly, "to see if you can, shall we say, peer behind the curtain, to get to a—"

"Higher level?" Jimbo offered.

"Put things in perspective so to speak." Not wanting to be too precise, he fell back on sentence extenders. "Jake, you start off."

"Who in the hell are these damn Brits anyways? Aren't they just Canadians with bad teeth? Didn't we beat their ass a long time ago?" argued Jake.

"Great Britain is supposed to be our friend; we have a similiar language it's said," put in Tony.

"I think they kinda helped us win WW II," added Sutter.

"Are you kidding me?" exploded Ira. "They didn't do shit in WW II. The Russians won the war, the Brits did diddly. Another one of your stupid myths. Don't you people ever read anything but Garfield?"

"Oh, yeah. Garfield. He's cute," nudged Jake.

"Oh, Christ," Ira sighed.

"The Brit's gave us Shakespeare—King Lear, Hamlet, Richard III," crooned Thaddeus, "it would be ungrateful to ask for more."

"Perhaps we should ask the Russians?" Chris offered quietly.

"The Russians?" wondered Jimbo.

"Oh, never mind."

Wayne fidgeted in his chair. "You know, the Roo-skies are pretty ruthless. They mighta won WW2 and all that, but it didn't make them any friendlier, if you know what I mean? Don't get the wrong idea, I think we could whip 'um in a fair fight, the problem is, it probably wouldn't be."

Minter sensed Berge wanted recognition. "Ok, ok. What about you Mr. Bergman, we haven't heard from you yet?" he smiled.

"If you look at the life and times of the IHDC, you see Idealism co-existing with capitalism and weak elected government."

"Are you going somewhere with this?" Jake yawned, "cause if you're not, I've got lots of Garfield books I'd like to look at the pictures in."

"God, you ended your sentence with a preposition!" winced Ira.

"All the better to eat you, grandma," countered Jake.

"Hey, man. That's gross," responded Jimbo. "It doesn't do much for the cause."

"Cause why?" asked Chris.

"Oh," Ron groaned.

"I'm sorry, I can't help it," Chris explained, "it's my pot addiction. Write that down."

Minter dragged a hand slowly across his face. "Anybody want to comment on the subject matter?"

"For sake of argument," Ira barked, "suppose Berge's conditions: commercialism, representative right-of-center government, middle-class consumer culture."

"Hey, who you call'n a what?" joked Thad.

"Let me offer an *amicus curiae* brief on behalf of the plaintiff," Ira continued, his waxy complexion brightening, a frothy spittle lubricating his spewed words. "In their day, major international conglomerates like East India Company planted the flag and government troops followed. Where governments stopped outside trade, attempting to change local habits to resemble those of the colonizers, it didn't work; commerce stalled.

"But idealism could flourish, individual liberties be maintained, and religious freedom respected in a satellite state..."

"Because?" Bergman prodded.

"Ahh... Just a second," Ira asked for more time as he sifted the tumblers in his brain.

"Because Alice had a little lamb while the cow jumped Miss Muffet," offered Jake.

"The real noise is that India had too many psychotic drugs and too few battleships, that's the dirty little story here. Otherwise, there is no colonial India," argued Wayne.

"That's bullshit," said Jimbo. "India's still there, and it's as strong as ever."

"They play cricket," sneered Tony, "cricket in In-d-i-a."

"Because," said Ira, "colonies are monopolies, consumer behavior doesn't have to be as rigidly controlled." He knew he was right even without Berge nodding.

"Dude, it's about race," said Thad weighing in, "the Limeys were overcome in India because it's an exotic land, a land of heat and spices, and dark-skinned people. Whereas, the white races crave table salt, vanilla ice cream, lite beer, filtered cigarettes and macaroni hot dish."

"And green backs, don't forget green backs," said Jake.

"And lynchings," added Tony, "lots of spicy brown gravy in a lynching."

"Oh geez," Thaddeus shuddered, "you creepy, Cro-Magnon racist pig-fucker."

"Hey now, that's some spicy language," laughed Sutter.

"As you were saying Mr. Berge," Minter interrupted.

"That's ok Mr. Experimental guy, my spokesman can share my thoughts with you, albeit in a less amusing way."

"Thanks for the vote of confidence," snapped Shep. "Anyway, what fart face was getting at, is that advanced Capitalism uses government."

"And religion."

"And Science and Medicine too."

"Art, maybe."

"Advanced Capitalism exploits every feature of human activity, bends each facet of culture to the irresistible will for power through profit. And does so not by historical accident but of vital necessity."

"But the war on pot," asked Jimbo listening keenly, "why is that necessary? Everything else—even pornography—is allowed. And porn is pretty addicting."

"Because. May I?" Shep queried.

"By all means."

"Thank you."

"You're welcome."

"Because to ban some item—any item—said to be harmful, gives government credibility and creates the illusion of concern," answered Shep.

"But the ban can be lifted," offered Jimbo hopefully.

"And it will be, when the product's revenue potential trumps the cost of prohibition."

"I couldn't have said it any better," concluded Berge.

"You are absolutely right for a change," agreed Ira.

"What you mean," Wayne insinuated, "is that when pot has addicted enough people, it'll go mainstream, like those subversive Rolling Stones."

"So if we push the drug," mused Jimbo.

"Exactly," concluded Ira, "the market decides. If consumers demand a product, it will be supplied. If demand is in respectable numbers, the product will become respectable."

# 24

## *Workingman's Weed*

The rage piercing Wayne like a spike dissipated into crumpled leaves scratching across the sidewalk. A moment ago, he felt burning anger; suddenly he'd fallen out of the canoe and cooled. First, a chain of fire, then dust. Now, blazing letters, pages of despair. Then retreat, a stealing away into half-heard questions. A failure of discipline! The country abandoned to drugs—a litter of unwanted kittens.

The U S of A was the most powerful country in the world and could whip anybody. But our hands were tied by secret vices, cadres ripe with fraud and incompetence, a low moan of doubt, agendas pregnant with personal ambition: unity of purpose fatally undermined. No wonder our enemies were encouraged!

Of course, there was a lot of fallout because of decisions that led to Viet Nam. Marijuana taught us the government lied; Viet Nam showed it could kill.

Plus, the gnawing suspicion that more could be done to protect the environment. Then there was the general uneasiness of his generation regarding the whole matrix of social and religious beliefs that seemed designed for a smaller, more miserable people. Maybe it was the doubling of the price of a half-gallon of Breyer's ice cream from $.65 to $1.30? Whatever it was, let's face it, the government plain lied about a lot of things. The crack in the mantle of authority struck deeply taking hostage a large chunk of valuable momentum.

He couldn't just give up. So he adopted the name 'Stealth-coate,' fighter for the 'old' U.S., the one before 'victim's' campaigns, 'pro-activeness,' and saving rotting old buildings just because the poor didn't have any other place to go.

Wayne embarked on a personal crusade of harmless terrorism, a kind of shoulder-straightening, by seizing an array of objects from owners he wanted to jolt into a deeper commitment to American muscle and what our country stood for. At some point, he wasn't sure when, simply spying an item of a new or intriguing configuration was enough to trigger a surge of klepto-patriotism.

Wayne fingered the cheap calculator he'd lifted from Bergman's room. He had no use for it but it was enough that Berge did. In a flash of devious brilliance, Wayne transmuted Bergman's sentence from death to 'life imprisonment' palming the honorary token whose value had spared Berge a more egregious fate. The numbered pads seemed much too small for his fingers. Hell, he couldn't get the damned thing started! He took it for the same reason one brown-bags lunch: to relive the event in all its audacity, its triumphal boldness, like a hard-on or a joint.

Theft could bring justice. It had advantages over mortal combat—it was limited and covert.

Under steady bombardment from the pot-inebriated, Wayne saw relations with the other side deteriorate until forced to construct a defensive perimeter bristling with exploding devices. Next to him lay a vast unsettled territory, requiring him to obsess about security, about safety. 'Safety!' Wayne mumbled, shocked by the insight. Safety, and what is that but the Son of Fear... Now what the hell was he going to do with these 20 j's he'd boosted from Jake!

* * * *

'So when I learned that the NEA had funded a version of Shakespeare with the cast on LSD. Well, shit. I called them on it, and they kicked 50 g's to my company…' Melody listened to Thaddeus in a friendly torpor, willing to remain motionless in a bath of baritone emollient. He was going on about bringing 'the Bard' into the streets, and she mused about his giant hands and perfect skin.

"Can you imagine trying to remember your lines on acid?"

Melody shook her head, "I haven't done it. Nor do I feel like apologizing for not having taken a dangerous chemical."

"You haven't dropped? Wow. That's unreal. Not even once?"

"Oh, I had the opportunity," she lied.

"Hey, that's ok," he reassured her. He began to laugh, his warm voice erupting like an undersea volcano. "It's something to think about, not for everyone," he backpedaled.

"Now, I have smoked pot," Melody revealed.

"It's not the same," Thad replied.

"Yes," Melody answered, "I know. But in a lot of ways..."

"Sure, to some extent," he said painstakingly. He had inched closer while they talked, now near enough to feel the temperature difference, warm, moist air from her lungs floating over him like a siren-led advance party before the storm. "But other drugs—even booze—are so much more powerful, that pot's like m-i-l-k," he said thickly.

"I know, but to someone who's not as used to it as you?"

"Yeah, yeah, I suppose."

"Still."

"Of course."

"It's a drug."

"Absolutely." His arm was around her, fingers on her ribs like the keys of a piano. The woman was thin and dark as a spider; he wanted to make love to this pipe-stem insect body.

Melody fought the urge to object, wanting only to surrender so she could be together again, with all her fatigued, splintered to futility parts, intact. His arms were huge, his body round and strong like a bomb. "Please don't take this wrong."

"Hoooo," he whispered, a trail of pot smoke snaking toward her. She sniffed the acrid substance and immediately a fresh, round joint was at her lips. Melody stared into Thad's rich brown eyes, and inhaled.

She knew she was stoned when she felt Thad's hands lock on her waist, slowly drawing her towards his powerful chest, a voice of chocolate truffles, and a throbbing sense of adventure. With tiny arms covered by long, thin strands of reddish hair, Melody clung to Thad, her mouth seeking his.

"Ehhh," he sighed enveloping her.

"For Science!" she said quietly.

"What?" Thaddeus asked languidly, his eyes closed.

"Mmmm!" she responded.

* * * *

Sutter saw his friend's blonde ponytail and sidled over, "Go'nna do anything special for last day?"

Jake spun around, weaving sandy hair and blue cornflower eyes. "Huh?"

"The last supper—you know—of pot?"

"Oh, shit man! You're right," Jake admitted, "the last goddamned grass-travaganza of our tour."

"Should we party, get everybody together?" offered Sutter.

"Ehhhh. I don't know. Everybody means Berge. I ain't

ready for that; besides, we got plenty a' pot," answered Jake. He slipped quietly into his room and, after checking to see if they were being followed, lifted his mattress.

"What the hell are you doing?" laughed Sutter.

"The pot you jerk off, the fuck'n pot!" Jake flipped the mattress and felt the bed frame carefully. He tossed his pillow, bedding and his dirty clothes sack on the floor and gave each item a visual and tactile examination before piling them in a corner. "Not a fuckn' thing," he mumbled in a strangely quiet and detached voice.

"What are you talking about?" asked Sutter, dumbfounded.

"No frick'n pot, that's what I'm talking about!" hissed Jake.

"You're kidding?" Sutter gasped.

"No, asshole, I'm not," replied Jake fiercely.

Sutter went back through the drill Jake insisted upon since the experiment opened. Jake wouldn't let him snarf the roaches, the butt of the marijuana cigarette, instead he was to exchange them for the long, unsmoked marijuana cigarettes that he neatly removed. Jake must have snatched the equivalent of one a day or about 20 of the perfectly-rolled 100 millimeter joints. And now he was saying they were gone?!

"How could they all be gone?" asked Sutter, astonished.

"Maybe the person who stole them wanted to avoid additional trips?" Jake struck back.

"Have you tried everywhere?" Sutter asked, uncomfortable under Jake's stare.

"Yeah, jackass, I've searched where they were, should have been, aren't!"

"Well, wha' happened?" asked Sutter glumly.

Jake shifted his weight, suddenly the little room was entirely too little. "Wha' d'ya mean? 'Wha' happened?' Someone came in and took them. This ain't Fort Knox."

Sutter ached to have a peek into Jake's duffel, but realized this was impossible. "What should we do?" he asked.

"Ah, gee," Jake scoffed, "I think we should tell Nicholson some prick took the pot we stole!"

"You're not really going to tell him, are ya?" Sutter asked incredulously.

"Geez, just how freaking stoned are you?" Jake stammered. "I'd love to be that high."

"You know, we only got one more day to get our stake healthy," observed Sutter.

"Yeah. We gotta find out who? and we gotta act fast."

"Well, it wasn't Chris or Shep."

"Why not Shep?"

"Because he's too stoney. Besides, he gets all he needs with the clicker."

"Today and tomorrow, but after that?"

"It could be Custer, or the Badge?" Sutter proposed.

"It had to be someone who knew I was holding, someone who was watching when the deal went down," guessed Jake.

"Berge," Sutter filled in. "He's always sneaking around, he's never in his room."

"Never?" replied Jake.

"Say, what if it's not him?"

"Then I'd say the devil has found a new pair of hands. Suppose we take a look at yours?"

* * * *

Custer was wallowing in his role of agent provocateur, thought Thaddeus, trying to get the subjects to admit that although the Canadians seem amenable to decriminalization, their science was weak and their attitude too feel-good to assist the Cause. They were discussing the 'Non-Medical Use of Drugs,' the Interim Report of the Canadian Government Commission of Inquiry, 1970.

"And so, in summation..." The word resounded like a hammer dropped in an empty bathtub. "Let me just say, without experimental subjects and verifiable evidence, our lovable Canadian friends have fallen far short of the gold standard of scientific proof. Their theories are just that; their ideas nothing more than the showy reflection of snow crystals across the flat, frozen tundra.

"To say as our northern neighbors do, that 'non-medical use of drugs is so prevalent in modern society, it would be unrealistic to condemn it in principle,' suggests Canada, once again is going to take a stance that while unsupported, still manages to be a thorn in Uncle Sam's side.

"For instance, this sentence: 'We believe that emphasis must shift from a reliance on suppression (of marijuana) to the wise exercise of freedom of choice.'

"The short-term physical effects of cannabis are 'relatively insignificant.' 'Relatively!?' This is not scientific language. 'Relatively' is exactly what science seeks to avert."

"There are no relatives in Science!" Badger shouted.

Minter overlooked the intrusion. He sat down on the edge of the heavy metal desk. There was no reason to hurry: the respondents were tunneling through the lengthy, turgid document with predictable incomprehension. Minter had done his best to paraphrase the document in 10 pages, installing his own terse, updated slants for the looping institutional prose of the bureaucracy.

"Remember that this Commission was content to rely on

the works, the often faulty works before standardization, of others, not being willing to conduct their own investigation into actual use." Being himself Canadian, from Halifax, very near the rocky, beauty-swept Cape Breton, Minter felt he could pick on his own country's predilection to smugness, particularly when it came to Americans.

"Just a second there," Tony cautioned, his voice dropping. "I wouldn't offend the Canadians if I were you."

"Oh?" Minter replied; Ira and Berge leaned toward Tony.

"Well, I suppose it's no secret."

"None whatsoever!" insisted Berge.

"Canada can be very useful to us."

"Wait!" shouted Ira, "I object on procedural grounds."

"I object on coffee grounds," quipped Jake.

"I object on the Polo Grounds," laughed Jimbo.

"I'm serious," confided Tony. "Canada is our way out."

"I think you're way out," interjected Thaddeus.

"'It would appear to produce a more introspective, self-absorbed mood than alcohol.' Granted any investigation into marijuana is going to face problems of interpretation, but 'more introspective'?"

Jimbo suddenly demanded their attention: "The Texas Tower massacre wouldn't have happened if pot were legal."

"Let's assume you are correct," Shep lobbied.

"Assume makes an 'ass' of 'u' and 'me,'" said Tony.

"Let 'm talk," Ron interjected.

"It's real strange," winced Jimbo, "there's never been a single death attributed exclusively to marijuana."

"Yeah," Tony sang, "smok'n weed, smok'n weed—it's a good deed."

"Exactly, that's the deal," Jimbo explained, "no deaths to

those not smoking weed by those who are! You get it?"

"Let me get this straight," Thad giggled, "smoking saves lives?"

"Yes, yes," insisted Jimbo, "don't you see? Charles Whitman wasn't smoking pot, that's what led to the, the, the Texas Tower disaster. We all know it. Pot puts down violence. You never wanna get in someone's face when you're high."

"'Weed incapacitates; no fight.' We've heard this before," smirked Bergman.

"Lotta stoned killing in Nam; stoned GI killing stoned Cong, and vice versa," Ron said.

"Wow, man," Tony choked. "No kidding!?"

Ron nodded.

Shep ground his teeth, beard fidgeting with dry, flaky chin skin. "Are they getting stoned in order to kill, or defending themselves when they just happened to be stoned?"

"Ya gotta figure stoned killing is an accident, otherwise the whole hippie ideal goes up in smoke, get it?" replied Thad.

"Got it," Shep answered.

"Good."

"God!" groaned Bergman.

"I don't know about them," Ron skidded, "but our guys were getting stoned because they were bored and scared."

Jimbo pounded his fist in frustration, "We've got to get some, some sta-sta-tis-t-t-tics!"

"Huh?" intruded Jake's emblematic smile, "we got one legitimate shit-eating egghead, and one pretend egg-shitting head case already. We don't need no stink'n sta-tis-tics!"

"You're wrong, you're wrong!" declared Jimbo, with grand enthusiasm. "Pot is a tranquilizer—a legitimate antidepressant. That's even more important than being legal."

"Tell that to the 50,000 people sent to prison each year for marijuana-related offenses," interjected Bergman.

"That's what I'm saying, look at the so-called legitimate drugs out there. There's got to be a way of adding up the-the-the cost, and ah, seeing where bhang—pot—stands with the other leading tranquilizers."

"You talked me into it," Thad broke in, "garcon, another legitimate though illegal tranquilizer please."

* * * *

"Read the four statements and mark the one which is most correct. Again, the one that is the most correct. Do not select the one you most agree with! No, I won't read that again, it's right there in your damned sheet. Think about your answer for you may be asked to support it."

#1. The use of psychotropic (psychoactive) drugs seems to be an almost universal phenomenon occurring throughout recorded history in virtually all but the most isolated communities. *Cannabis* is the least potent of the psychedelic drugs. It is regarded by many as the 'drug of peace.' At best, it offers reduced fatigue, enhanced perception and a general sense of well-being. At worst, it triggers temporary anxiety, minor depression and nausea. No mental or physical deterioration occurs as a result of *cannabis* use. The Commission recommends that simple cannabis possession be punishable by a fine of $100.

#2. Pot is being used to front an aggressive agenda of far-left politics. Based on contempt for organized religion and long-standing capitalist tradition, *pot*itics offers sexual promiscuity, a loosening of social obligations, and indulgence in a wide variety of so-called 'mind-expanding' drugs supporting an income redistributing, pan-global atheistic hedonism.

#3. People make too much of the use of pot. Quite simply, *cannabis* helps to reduce the tension which results from the stresses of modern life. Pot produces euphoria. This 'instant rest' (an escape from intolerable tension) is most notable in individuals without the necessary ego development to deal with the complex demands of today's world. Such maladjusted individuals are temporarily 'normalized' by tranquilizing drugs. The Commission can find no evidence that such practice involving *cannabis* is morally, psychologically or physiologically harmful.

#4. Again and again, we are reminded of the dangers of 'excessive' use of the stronger preparations of *cannabis*. Remaining in a constant state of marijuana intoxication must be regarded as 'excessive' even if physical damage accumulates at a slower rate relative to other non-medical drug abuse. Whether it's loss of initiative, failure to define and achieve goals, or a chronically evasive lifestyle, too much pot can neutralize one's potential life contributions.

# 25

## *The Limits of Diplomacy*

"Hey slugs," shouted Badger to those lounging around the tv, "get your 'a's up to HQ, we're going to play a little volleyball!" He spun the volleyball and tossed it in the air hoping to balance it on his finger. Instead, the ball jumped out of his hand and raced nosily along the late afternoon blue stone floors.

"And this means you too, grandma," said Badger, pointing at Ira.

"No excuses. You're in the line-up! All you guys, volleyball, hit it—a game of skill and agility!"

Jake harrumphed, "Not the way I play it."

"C'mon," said Sutter excitedly.

"Are you kiddn' me?" Jake yelled. "I invented volleyball!"

"You? I thought I did," rejoined Sutter.

"Well, not volleyball itself," said Jake, "but nude, co-ed volleyball, yes, this was my invention.

"Hey, dude!" Jake interrupted himself upon spotting Thad, "You gotta be on our team. We're going to have a great team, you, me, Sutter here."

"Get Ron too," added Sutter.

"Yeah, we'll get Ron. And maybe Wayne too," Jake went on.

"He's crazy," Thad objected.

"It's a crazy game," Jake responded, "besides he's 6 foot 3 inches."

Jake had set his team when Tony popped into view.

"Hey Jake, I gotta be on your team," said Tony, pursuing.

Jake shook his head, "No can do, we've got five."

"C'mon," Tony moaned.

"Hey, cheer up, you got Berge," Sutter taunted.

Tony checked up. "Berge? He's psychotic. But that's good. We'll beat the shit out of you."

"Or die trying," laughed Jake.

"You sonofabitch," said Tony.

When they reached the grass quadrangle with its newly erected net, Bergman pondered the set up. "No, no, this won't do," he said approaching Badger.

"What's your beef?" asked Badger.

"Oh, c'mon, give me a break," Bergman sighed. "Look at this shit," he elaborated, pointing at Jake's team assembled and jumping at the net. "He's fielding an all-gorilla lineup."

"Who you call'n a monkey?" questioned Thaddeus.

"Oh, excuse us," Berge interjected, "an all great ape team!"

"That's better," Thad relented.

"Hey, wait, I'm a greater ape, too," issued Ira, "I should be on that side."

"No one's gonna ape your hygiene," howled Sutter.

"Besides, you're spastic. C'mon, let's go. Stop monkeying around," shouted Jake.

"But you're not lacking in sagacity," added Chris.

"Thanks kid," laughed Shep, "now, let's kill those racists."

"Well, from here to Armageddon, which should occur soon, you're a digger," Berge instructed Shep. "Just step back here and get between the ball and the ground." Berge dropped to his knees to underline the importance of getting down so as to cup the hands below the ball in the inevitable event of a smash.

"Can you use me?" Chris asked.

"Darn right," Berge answered. "We'll use anybody who can lift his arms. You are a setter," he offered, demonstrating the posture and responsibilities of front-line duty.

"So can we get going?' Badger asked wearily.

"Ah, screw it," Berge sneered. "We're going to cream you rigid institutional types," he said dismissively. He grabbed Jimbo. "Ok, bear, time to wreck havoc.

"They say a whiff of carrion can drive one out of their mind. If that's true, I want you here, next to Ira."

"You know if I were stoned—or even if you were stoned and I wasn't but planned to be—we wouldn't be here right now," Jimbo reported, arms rotating in anticipation.

"Pot can only take you so far man," Tony interjected, "then you gotta grab your nut sack and suck it up."

Chris's jaw dropped; he walked over to Tony and took his hand. "I just want to say I am moved."

Tony nodded. "You should be," he said, "but they don't want you or any of us."

"What the hell is a 'digger'?" Shep wailed.

"That's when you dig your own grave, man," chipped in Thad from the other side of the net.

"Hey, stop your whining. Be an American," said Jake.

"To advocate hard work for others while you're a trust-fund baby, to respect money no matter how it's gained, to revere loyalty to class above competency, to suppress principle for profit—to be fat, stupid, mean and out of touch but able to scratch out a pay check that puts you at the top of the world. Now that's American," countered Berge.

"That's excessive, you leftist weakling!" Ron shot back. He aimed his imposing physique at Bergman.

"C'mon, children," said Tony, preparing to serve, "mixing politics with sport!"

Minter's mustachioed mouth swung skeptically from side to side as the teams congealed around the net that he and Bedikker had erected in the mix of gravel, sand, and pulverized earth.

The hard ground resisted with increasing resolve as they dug into the rocky substrate, so that the net poles sagged, dragging the net to a level sure to draw whatever testosterone bubbled in the vicinity. "So this is what you want?" Minter asked, looking to Jake and Tony. They nodded. "Suit yourself," Minter replied. He paused in front of Berge. "Oh, another thing about pot. It makes you suicidal."

"That's just theory," rebutted Bergman.

"Not after today," exited Minter.

"Rally for serve!" cried Tony, stroking the ball across the net toward Thad who bent it back toward Shep with a two-handed spike.

Gamely, Shep put up his hands and pushed at the ball. Unfortunately, his palms were spread apart, too far apart to impede the ball which struck him directly in the face. "Ouch!" Ira screamed, slumping to the ground. He sat on his ass, stunned, struggling to adjust his glasses, more askew than usual, while keeping an eye out for blood from a nose that felt like a pumpkin dropped off the back of a speeding truck.

"Our serve!" Sutter cried out, pumping his fist in the air. "We're going to nail you guys."

"Wait! Wait just a second," cautioned Berge, impounding the ball. "That's not a legit rally." He knelt beside Shep. "The brain, even your brain, can't stop a bullet," he whispered. "And use your hands; it's ok in this context."

"Piss off!" said Shep, rising to his feet. "You didn't tell me they'd be using artillery," he muttered.

"Gimmee! Give us the damned ball!" barked Jake.

"Just a damned minute," Berge obstructed.

"You're gonna lose anyway," replied Sutter.

"Well, why even play then, we'll just quit."

"Giv'm the ball," put in Jimbo. "I wanna play."

"Ok," Berge sighed, tossing the ball over the net to Jake.

"Ready?" shouted Jake striking the volleyball expertly, driving it on a merciless arc to Jimbo who blocked it awkwardly, the ball puffing into the air dangerously close to the net. Berge launched himself for a set but failed to hit the ball squarely, instead it dove. Tony got to it but could only keep the ball in play, watching helplessly as it climbed toward the top of the net. He and Berge put their hands up defensively, turning their faces to avoid injury.

Ron and Sutter rose simultaneously, extended their arms as if loading a gun and crashed their fists into the round, white sphere approximately the size of a man's head with powerful impact. The volleyball shot across the net clipping Tony's elbows as he stretched to block it, then ricocheted off Berge's jaw. "Yo!" yelled Sutter.

"One to zipa-dee-do-dah," cried Jake.

The next point, Ira swung at the serve and missed, Chris punching the skittering orb into Tony's hip. Ira chased the ball out of bounds kicking and swinging but falling short of actual contact. Jimbo helped retrieve it. "What would you do if you could get a hold of it?" he asked.

"You'll see," said Shep threateningly, he lunged at the ball but Jimbo pitched it back to Jake.

"Two, Zip-ola," intoned Jake. He coiled to serve again but added spin to his normal momentum slowing the ball as it approached the net. Berge saw his chance, intercepting the ball with an accurate blow instantly redirecting it toward Sutter's temple. Sutter ducked, but the ball caught the back of his ear delivering a stinging pain. "You asshole!" he seethed.

"Language reflects thought," Berge taunted.

Jake ignored him and made to serve. But Berge called out, "Score?" Jake stopped. Sutter shook his head. "Score?" Berge repeated.

Jake lifted the ball, "Two, one," he shouted. "And that's your last one," he exhaled, slapping the ball with the heel of his hand causing it to corkscrew like a firebomb past the net minders on a collision course with Ira. Shep turned his back and bent over, the ball striking him loudly on the ribs. "I'm ok, I'm ok," he responded, while sprawled on the ground. He made a move to get the ball but again Chris hustled it away.

"The score," Jake announced, "is three to one. That's three-one-ola. Or three-one." He served for the final time, fast and low, a ball both Tony and Berge stretched to block. As Berge prepared to spring, Thad edged solidly into the net pinning him to the ground. Tony jumped toward the ball, but Wayne, extending over the net, tomahawked it, sending the ball twisting like a missile into Chris's feet.

"Jeez!" shouted Tony, massaging his shoulder where Wayne's fist ended its arc, "that's not volleyball, that's trench warfare!"

"Heh, heh," Jake laughed. "Wayne's our ICBM."

"Yeah," Thad chuckled. "We're 'new—clear' now. Don't you go mess'n with our warhead."

"ICBM. You've either left scat on the floor, or you're searching for the first letters of imbecile," said Berge. "And what, incidentally, became of the rules?"

"Rules are for losers," Sutter claimed.

"Huh?" Berge challenged.

"Four to one," Jake replied.

"Just seems to me," mused Berge fussing to straighten the net, "that they put this here for a reason."

"Wayne?" Jake inquired, "back me up on this, isn't that the Discourage Flying Rabbits initiative?"

"Something told me if anybody'd have it figured out," Berge responded tossing the ball to Chris for serve, "it'd be you." Both teams dug in expectantly but when nothing happened, all eyes converged on Chris. He held the ball at his waist, a quizzical expression stranded on his features.

"Hit it," Jimbo encouraged.

"Over the net if possible," Tony instructed.

"Give me the damned thing!" demanded Shep. "I'll take care of it."

Berge stepped up. "You ever played before?" he asked. Chris shook his head 'No.' "Well," resumed Bergman weighing a telepathic message, "you don't really care to get this, do you?" Chris smiled in relief. Berge took the ball and handed it to Jimbo. "Hey," he shouted to Chris. "You can't leave."

"Stick around, we need you," implored Jimbo.

"Yeah," agreed Tony, "you can block." Chris paused, slowly he crept back onto the court.

"Good," said Berge. He motioned to Tony and they conferred.

"Hurry up, serve!" Jake shouted. But Berge leaned in for yet another secret whisper. "Dammit!" Jake snarled. The powerlessness infuriated; he lengthened his breathing.

Berge walked the ball to Jimbo and they talked briefly, more with hand signals than words. "Time out! Time out!" Jake seethed. "What the hell you doing over there!" he yelled. Tony threw up his hands; Berge gave him a 'T'. 'God, I hate that guy!' Jake mumbled. "Go ahead," he allowed. A bead of sweat formed over his forehead dripping caustic fluid into his eyes, not unlike that other time, that other place of maximum frustration and panic.

Jimbo lifted the ball and delivered a high arching serve to Wayne. Instead of feeding to the front row warriors, Wayne slammed a flat return over the net where Tony stopped it and left a floating set up for Berge. Bergman leaped and pounded the ball with his fist driving it straight into Jake.

"Ok buddy," said Jake bitterly. "Here it comes," he said thinly, locking eyes with Bergman. "Ok everybody—61. Got it? 61, remember?" He smiled at Wayne, "61, right? Translated that means set me up, not them." Wayne nodded. The serve again rose over the net, a fish flying toward Wayne. He softened his return, propelling the ball to Sutter on the edge of the net. Sutter set the ball to Jake within reach of a strike from Bergman. Berge bent to intercept; opposite him Ron and Jake rotated. As he committed to the block and flung himself forward, Ron and Jake converged.

Ron struck first, trapping Berge's arms in the plastic mesh of the net. Bergman fell forward helplessly when Jake crashed into him, steering his torso toward the rocky ground as if it were a tackling dummy. He rolled, an insect entangled in heavy strands of web. Jake pounced, grabbing a handful of Berge's t-shirt and hair. Sitting on top of him, Jake lifted Berge's head and tried to slam it into the ground.

Berge writhed in order to throw Jake off, but Jake had good leverage and with both hands free, pushed Berge's head toward the earth. Just as Berge's melon should have impacted, he began to rise…

Slowly at first, then at an increasing rate, Bergman and Jake too, rose into the air. "Wha' the—?" Jake coughed, releasing Bergman as his feet set to leave the ground. He turned into Thad's sullen eyes. "Hey! What 'cha doing?"

"'Bout to ask you the same," answered Thaddeus in a voice from the well.

"But the sonofabitch deserves it," Jake squealed, still pinioned in Thad's powerful arms. "Look what he did to Chris."

"Chris seems ok to me," Thaddeus replied. "Besides, that's between the two of them. What's your angle?" he asked.

"This is for Chris," Sutter hissed.

"Chris?" Tony repeated, "he's on our side! Hey, Chris c'mere. Hey, team, this one is for Chris! Go Chris!" shouted Tony. He looked at Sutter. "Now, let's leave the homicide for dinner, huh?"

# 26

## *It's Not As If...*

Jimbo slid his pants on and belted them mechanically, there was little time to lose, the expedition left at 7 o'clock. Everyone planned to meet for a joint in the Wreck Room. Jimbo admired the coup pulled off by Jake—Sutter, too—but mostly Jake.

Initially, the word insisted they could not smoke before going to the movie. Nicholson felt he had risked enough by even allowing them outside the ward, itself a severe abridgment to the rules of the experiment. He vehemently refused their demand they be stoned when they went out.

Nicholson insisted it was impossible because his neck was already out too far and that news he loosed 10 'hippie types' stoned at government expense into the community might result in the end of his usefulness.

But Jake, brassy as always, demanded a vote. So much for Nicholson's prestige. Hell, it was the last night of dope availability; Nicholson should have realized he wasn't the sentimental choice. Jimbo grabbed his beret and squeezed it rakishly over the side of his head, tonight the Theater of Excitement was casting, all roles accepted.

Sutter met him in the hall, "Hey, man, that looks good on you," he laughed, pointing to the beret. "Is it real leather?"

"Genuine second hand too," Jimbo enthused.

"Wow," said Sutter, "but wait til you see Jake, the two of you would make a fine pair."

"Where is he?"

"He and Shep are going to see if they can smoke 10 joints before leaving. How spacey is that?"

"I don't know," Jimbo wondered, "I thought once you're stoned, you're stoned as you're going to get. Something about few 'receptors' in the brain that recognize marijuana and they can carry only so much chemical so you can only get so high. I don't think you can back-end it like a battery.

"Of course, 10 joints. That's got to be like a Rail SuperPass or something, huh?"

Sutter nodded happily and Jimbo could see the neon intensity of the lights of the city as if stretched out on the surface of a wave racing down the sidewalk toward him. He would be on that path with Sutter and Jake but it was going to take a l-o-o-o-o-o-n g time to arrive. The pace of events was suddenly ('suddenly'?) slowing to the movement of caterpillar-sized legs.

Jimbo studied Sutter, someone he didn't know much about, because only superficial confidences were exchanged during the Experiment, confirming but never revealing. The narrow brown eyes and the crooked tooth stood out. But Sutter and Jake belonged. In the soil of marijuana imprisonment, they grew the tallest.

Sutter was fascinated by the standard of 10 joints. Often he thought the typical marijuana high did not go far enough. He wanted to go deeper, wanted to be pulled along to regions he couldn't conceive of otherwise, regions which gave him pictures, answers, a map for his life. 'You know,' he thought, 'I do love to get out there.'

Are you committed to Mary Jane?

Yes.

Would you die for her?

I don't know. Would it be quick?

"How we going?" asked Jimbo.

"Custer has a VW bus," replied Sutter.

"Won't that be just a tad small?" wondered Jimbo.

"Oh yeah, man, we'll have to sit on each other's lap!" said Sutter.

"Jeez!" sputtered Jimbo upon spotting Jake.

Shep too, emerged from his cocoon of greasy black pants and stained white tee to stare at the apparition paused in the doorway of the dayroom, "Now that's brazen!" he drawled, lapsing back into snooze mode.

Jake straddled the threshold in a white, silk-like pirate shirt with full sleeves and open throat. Leather boots sheathed his steps and blue jeans softened by repeated beatings accentuated his lean physique. Over his shoulders hung a cowhide vest; and in his hand was an umbrella with a bright yellow scarf wound around it.

"It's going to be a trippy night," said Tony, high-fiving Jake.

Driving the streets of Mattapan on the way to Cambridge, the gusty darkness was punctuated by a promenade of blinking lights; chill winds played with the broad streets like monkey bars. Here and there civilians crept through the maze, while the bug van bombed along nervously, its passengers mind-stripped, absorbing only the perplexing beauty of the city at night.

"Funny," Wayne began, "this whole city could be just flattened in a few seconds by the right-sized storm."

"Oh, geez," cried Tony, "I'm not going to have to employ my first aid skills, am I?"

"No, but keep the restraints handy," laughed Thaddeus.

"A storm?" puzzled Berge.

"Mother Nature," Wayne chuckled softly.

"My Mother Nature?!" Sutter mocked.

"She tests you. You've got to confront her. If you hide in the city, she'll track you down; you have to live in the woods on her terms."

"I'm looking for two little German kids—Hansel and Gretel. You haven't seen them have you?" whispered Jake.

"If you don't stand up to her thunder, the torrential downpours, the bastard mosquitoes, learn her ways, the lessons you need to survive, you're dead."

"An impressive resume to be sure, but normally, we don't employ a village idiot," Berge chimed in. "I know that sounds cruel, but look at it from our point of view."

"Don't call us," said Shep, "we'll call you crazy."

"No, Wayne's onto something," ventured Chris.

"Something's onto him, I'd say," countered Tony.

"He's searching for the Meaning of Life," offered Jimbo.

"There ain't none," said Tony dismissively.

"How can you say there's no meaning to life?" Shep quizzed.

"No offense your intellectualship," replied Tony, "but what is the meaning of life. Something handy, like t-shirt sized?"

Shep winced. "Well, it's complicated…"

"Wait, wait, I've got it!" Chris broke in excitedly. "It just came to me: the Meaning of Life!"

"See," said Berge, "he's not a real genius, he just plays one in his mind."

"This is so hot!" Chris beamed. "I've been looking for this forever. I've done it. I found the Meaning of Life!"

"Life don't mean snot," said Tony. "Man is just an advanced form of mineral."

"There is a Meaning to Life; I just discovered it," Chris insisted.

"A what?" Shep asked Tony.

"A mineral," he answered.

"Hey!" cried Chris.

"Ok, sorry, the Meaning of Life."

"I, ah—" Chris began. "It's, ah—" He paused heavily.

"Yes?" Ira prompted.

"Darn!" whispered Chris. "Darn, darn, dammit!" He wore the look of defeat. "I forgot…"

"You forgot the Meaning of Life?" said Shep incredulously.

"Cheer up," coaxed Jake, "we're just minutes away from real, buttered theater popcorn!"

"Yeah, man," added Sutter, "I'm dying for some Dots too, even though they stick to your teeth."

"Hey, that's the best part," winked Jake.

The van dipped into Massachusetts Avenue and slowed, hoping to flush a parking space. "Shit!" Jake, sitting in the passenger seat next to Custer, shouted. "Look at that goddamned line." Across the street a lengthy cordon gyrated like pigeons in front of the box office.

"Those muthurs were tipped off!" exclaimed Wayne.

"We have a problem here, Houston," observed Thaddeus.

"I can't believe we'd miss the movie," Sutter vented.

"What movie?" said Tony.

Clambering from the van, Ron confronted the marquee. "Hell, I thought this was going to be a war flick? Or at least porn?"

"Cool it," urged Jake. "DM's pulled some strings; we get in for the second show. Ya got a half hour. Be back here at 8:30 sharp!"

The concrete swelled beneath Ron's feet, while the air

swirled with a hundred million illusions. With nothing to do and nowhere to go, Ron was intoxicated with the fluid-like texture of being. While his body occupied tiny coordinates of space, his mind spun and soared, flying to each new sound, every creamy glowing light, on a path of discovery inflated by his own delight.

In the beginning phase after smoking, Ron tightened, alert to a dangerous exposure, conscious that there was no reason at all he couldn't be kidnapped this instant from the very street corner where he stood, taken into a dark woods, and beaten to a pulp—even murdered—for no particular reason. He might as well be a clod of dirt. The anxiety was real, but mainly physiological he thought, the result of rapid heartbeat and a bit of nausea.

Soon, he levitated through this brief alienation from himself, replacing it with a bright flashlight turned on to just about everything. He knew things were the same, but they seemed different, as if he'd put on powerful glasses that suddenly opened up a different world. There was an organic honesty to the warming thing within. His senses were working overtime, breaking down a mountain of data into a recipe for increased enjoyment. He felt one again with existence, clean and refreshed.

Like a major change in weather, a strong wind enveloped him, pushing away the dark tension clouds that roosted over his day, when so much that had to get done could go so far wrong.

* * * *

Bergman stole a glance at the woman in front of him in line: 50–60 years, 5 foot 3 inches, 120 pounds, bats right, throws left, thinks straight. Imagining her bones to be rather flexible, he fashioned her skeleton until it fit, almost exactly, the mouth of a Nile crocodile. In the midst of his reverie, she turned on him, "What do you do?" she asked pointedly.

"You mean, like, for fun, or a living?"

"If that's what you want to call it," she barked.

"I see, well, the truth of the matter is that I am conducting a completely random survey."

"Why?"

"Well, we do so many surveys that are particular to a subject, that we feel the public would want us to do an entirely random survey just to balance it out."

"Oh, yes, I've heard of you."

"You have? A completely random survey?"

"Oh, yes—Random—I remember it very well."

"And do you remember how you came out on the Random Scale that is?"

"I think I passed, but I'm not sure."

"Don't worry mam, 89% of our respondents couldn't remember either."

* * * *

"Say," questioned Tony, "Jake tell you why he picked this flick?"

Sutter leaned close, "His girl lives in Cambridge."

"You're kiddn' me?"

"Hell, no. You know Jake; always an angle. He probably won't even sit down."

Tony nodded appreciatively. A guy with those kind of cohunes deserved respect.

Outside in the parking lot, Jake saw a familiar silhouette coming towards him. He opened his arms and embraced her, absorbing her thick lips. He put his hands on her buttocks and guided her crotch toward his. One hand snaked down to the delicious curve of her full, youthful bosom. "Oh, Kristi!" he moaned. The pot and her scent were driving him over the top. "Oh, here—" he said, placing half a joint in her mouth, "you're going to like it." He let her take a draw as he grazed her cheek with his nose. "Oh, Kristi!"

Tony lit a cigarette and found a sign pole he could lean on in order to survey the street in all directions. He found himself estimating the income of the assemblage of autos that drifted along the curb. Inner suburban types, confused whiners on a junket to view real people in motion, hoping to get caught up in a riptide of coquetry and petty ambition. He stood in his own grant of inebriation, when a dog stopped to defecate on the brick boulevard. "Say," Tony intervened, "you didn't clean up," as the 30-something pulled the animal's leash.

"Why should I?" the clean-shaven one said indignantly.

"Cuz it's against the law not to pick up for your, er, ah, pet," answered Tony, an edge like a newly-honed blade hanging in his voice.

The larger man linked to the smaller dog, stared at Tony coldly. "The dog pooped; I didn't. I'm not picking it up," the man replied truculently.

"What!?" Tony cried out, his attention stolen by an item he'd just spotted down the street. "You what?" he laughed. "That's funny! Hey, get the fuck outta here, you prick!"

He turned to starboard, pulling into view the lump under the lamp at the end of the block some 75 yards away. The tall, gaunt figure could be Ichabod—Wayne! It was him—long hair dangling over his ears—shifting erratically from leg to leg, talking to a cop.

Tony nonchalantly glanced toward Wayne and the policeman only to discover that they were larger and therefore closer than he had first pictured them. In fact, they were coming his way.

Tony kept his head averted as the cop approached. He expected to see a suspicious officer, two Tonys wide, wearing the mask of authority.

"I am told by this man that you possess marijuana, is that correct?" asked the cop. Tony was impressed by his height, and the gray, steely voice.

"Go on Tony," broke in Wayne, "tell him about the experiment. Tell 'm it's all legal. There's not a thing he can do about it."

Tony imploded, "You gotta be kiddn' me!" he wheezed. "Wow!"

"What's so funny?" officer 'Watson' asked.

"Well, it's just that this is the only time I ain't hold'n, no kidd'n.'"

Wayne tossed his arms about wildly. "Hey!" he shouted, "we're legally stoned!"

"Why don't I take you two jerks down to the station?" said the cop, poised on the edge.

"I know this man," said Tony. "I have guardianship." Turning to Wayne he whispered, "Suicide is supposed to be a solo act!"

"Hunh?" questioned the cop.

"I'm certified, officer; it's my job to take care of this big ninny."

"Well then, do it!"

Wayne once again swung into the policeman's face: "The government is paying us to smoke dope, smoke dope, smoke dope!" he chanted.

"May I use a choke hold, officer?" asked Tony, advancing toward Wayne.

"I don't think..."

"Yeah! Stoned at taxpayer expense!" hollered Wayne, dancing away from Tony.

"Hey, you, copper!" aimed Tony, "give me your goddamned gun! C'mon, dammit, give me your weapon, I wanna shoot the sonovabitch!"

"What are you talking about?" said the officer, back-pedaling.

"C'mon, while the bastard's still within range!"

"Coupla damn queers," said Watson, after the retreating figures.

# 27

## *The Great Unawakening*

Badger absently reviewed the latest test data. "I don't have to collate all this crap, do I? It's almost the last goddamned day."

"Exactly," replied Minter. "It's 'almost' the last god-damned day; we can't write the report without it," he warned.

"It's just repetitious bullshit."

Minter let it go. He was coming down from the cocktail of adrenaline and pride that had carried them through the first weeks of the experiment. The idea, the planning, funding, start-up. You kept your hands in your pockets with fingers crossed. Then the avalanche of data as the tests start up, followed closely by a period of intense analysis, brainstorming, reading, consultations, communications, lectures and advisories.

In a month they'd present their report, there'd be press inquiries, a public interest radio interview or two; they'd be called 'Communists' for suggesting that pot wasn't lethal, and then it'd be over in a few weeks, another academic tome on a subject as slippery as a Teflon skating rink: legalize and get more stoners; criminalize and get more violence.

If you take a cautious approach, advocating more long-term study, then you're stalling to line your pockets: Give it to us now, your verdict. 'Aye or nay,' and it better be the latter. Opposition to the topic from the Timid Generation—believers because time moved too quickly to be trusted—pushed marijuana legalization over the horizon. A lack of morality had attached itself to the drug. To the 'premier' generation, the image of the drug was that it made one silly, i.e., stupid. This was intolerable to age cohorts steeped in the mythology of wartime heroics and the Lord's guiding hand in all things American.

But the kids who smoke it today will become fathers who are perhaps less afraid of pot than were their fathers. It may take 50 years, but pot would eventually outnumber and out-maneuver the kids with one bad experience, religious reluctance, or who had just never got around to it. In the end, the drug would survive even its most ardent enemies until it was common as chicken soup and as unassailable as Christmas. It would be laughed at, laughed up and the last laugh for this harmless euphoric.

Oh, it will be studied and restudied, but the result will be the same: acceptance. It simply can't bear the weight of paranoia that should fall on far more dangerous substances such as meth amphetamine, heroin, tobacco and alcohol.

Sure, they'll find a way to detect it and you'll be prosecuted if you're caught behind the wheel stoned. But you're safe at the beach, the park and of course, your own home. Eventually, they'll tax the hell out of it to pay for highways, policemen and presidential libraries, but you'll have it and we sincerely hope it doesn't have you.

"Hey. Perk up," whispered Badger. "This could be our rat now. He's buzzed the place three times."

Minter froze. There was a piece missing. Only one piece in the infinite skeins of information collected on this sample group of enzymes. A very important piece of the picture, however perhaps the most important, had remained out there in the dark. But it circled the light, was it trying to come in?

"Ssshhsh!" Badger hissed at the loud scrape of Custer's chair. Neither of them looked up when one of the residents put his arm on the door jamb. According to the protocols, the resident had to speak first; Badger pulled a chart over his face rather than give away his excitement.

"Excuse me?"

Custer composed himself. "Good evening, Berge. What can we do for you?"

"Well," said Bergman, "my toilet's full of shit. I was hoping you could get your plunger, you know, and clean it out?"

"Yeah, let me plunge you right in the—"

"So, Mr. Bergman."

"Galen."

"Ok, Galen," Custer repeated. "Have you dropped in for a profound, emotional good-bye?"

"Something like that," Bergman admitted. "No fool'n, you guys are ok."

"We did so want to go with the beatings," taunted Badger.

"I'm glad you didn't," Bergman acknowledged, "the sight of you in leather—that would be torture!"

"Ah, shut up," replied Badger.

"Good. I'm so glad we could go out the way we came in—despising each other," said Berge.

"Wait. We don't despise you," laughed Custer.

"Who said any thing about you?" replied Bergman.

"Now, seriously," Minter cornered him, "was it 'ok' or would you do some things differently?"

"No," said Bergman thoughtfully, "it kinda went the way I thought an experiment with free drugs would go."

"C'mon, be straight with us; you guys are never straight with us!"

"I hope you don't mean that," Bergman stammered. "I tried, I really did 'guys,' I tried to be straight with you," he said, breaking up.

Custer grinned too; the protocols were adamant about this next point. "So what did you come here for, our phone numbers?" To hell with the protocols.

"No, no, not really. I'll probably see you the next time there's a need for doping dangerous psychotics with exotic medicines."

"Yous' come over to my house," Badger challenged, "I'll start experimenting right now."

"I'm sure youse will," Berge giggled.

"Get out, get out!" Badger shouted.

Now, this was against protocols. "Berge, Berge. Just a sec," broke in Custer with a withering glance at Badge, "Everything's cool, right?"

"Why you ask'n me? Cuz if your' askn' me copper," said Berge shabby, squint-eyed and belligerent, "then I got nothing to say. You hear me? Nuth'n!"

"I swear you're holdin'. Are you stoned?" Badger asked excitedly. That indeed, would go against the protocols.

"Well, if I was stoned," said Bergman with a wink, "where do you suppose I'd be gettn' the stuff?"

"I don't know," answered Custer, "where?"

"Well, now," said Bergman haughtily, "who, at least nominally, runs this affair? Who might have a safe full of pot in full view? And who might be audacious enough to try to walk away with it?

"So you're saying?" inserted Custer.

"Well," said Berge, taking a step closer to his audience, "if a certain vault full of said drug were maintained without concern for security, would it not inspire someone with a deeper, more protective feeling toward the herb, to want to secure it and treat it with the respect it deserves? Well, go check and see if there's so much as a doobie remaining."

"But it's a combination lock," Badger protested.

"Yes, 24-32-16-40? It's a frigg'n high school lock for crissakes."

"So you're saying you stole some of the test material?" asked Custer according to the protocols.

"Me? Are you kidding?" Bergman questioned. "They wouldn't cut Mother Teresa in on this deal."

"Well, why should we trust you?" asked Custer.

"Well, not cuz I was in on it, because I wasn't, but one hears things. And then there is the basic temperament of those involved..."

Custer leaned back in his chair. "Do you want to share these things you overheard while not plotting to carry them out?"

"Well yes, I think that makes sense."

"Ok, tell me again, how you came to learn of a conspiracy among some of the residents to steal government property?"

Berge got up and looked out into the ward. No one was near the door to the nurse's station. "That's easy," he said lightly, "Wayne told me."

"Wayne told you?" Badger repeated.

"Yeah," Bergman agreed. "Of course, I had my suspicions about that bunch but when you get it from the horse's mouth."

"So what did Wayne tell you?" asked Custer. "Was it something you overheard, or did he tell it to you directly?" The answer was important if you were still following the protocols.

"He just sat down beside me outta the blue, and said 'We're

gonna hit the bank.' I asked him what he meant and he went into that 'wouldn't you like to know' snake routine like he was some kind of natural woodland creature instead of an urban ghetto misfit. Anyway, he let on they were going to grab the ganja, lift the leaf, heist the hay, so to speak."

"Who was?" shouted Badger.

Bergman stared at him. "Must you be so goddamned loud?" he whispered.

"What do you get out of this?" Custer asked.

"Well, sir," sniffed Berge, "I get the satisfaction seldom known to the little guy, of seeing justice done."

"But," Custer objected, "Wayne doesn't seem like a guy that needs pot?"

"It ain't pot he's lookin' for," answered Berge. "So I think I'll be moving on."

"Ok, one last question," Custer begged, "did you do this on your own, or did someone put you up to it?"

"Satan," Berge answered, "he put me up to it."

"That won't work," broke in Badger, "Satan isn't real."

"Are you kidding," Bergman objected, "look what he's done to the Red Sox!"

"It's got to be a person."

"Satan's a person, well, a fallen angel actually," Berge argued.

"No good, not a person for our purposes," groused Badger.

"Oh," said Berge. "Well then, no one I guess."

"So it was your idea?" Custer pressed.

"Well," Bergman shrugged, "it's really two millennia of western culture bearing down on my thin, underdeveloped survival skills to be honest, but you need a person huh?"

"You're getting it," said Badger.

"Then we'll go with the 'Ok, I did it with my little bow and arrow, I killed that lousy goddamned noisy, lice-ridden, sparrow.'"

Badger shook his head, beginning to laugh, "You know, you've got to be the biggest pain-in-the-ass I've ever known!"

"What's that, I'm a bigger pain than your folks who dropped you on your head as a child? Or Aunt Lucy and Uncle Earl—the ones who wallpapered their place in the dark? Who tried to swing but didn't know which way to go? I'm a bigger pain than them?" Bergman trumpeted.

"Get! Get out!" Badger hollered.

As he left, Custer, smiling strangely, shook his hand. Custer and Badger even took the unusual measure of watching him recede down the hall. When Berge disappeared they ducked back into the nurse's quarters. Badger threw his hands up. "Meets every protocol."

Minter quickly notified Dr. Nicholson, in an adjacent annex. "Let's get to the risk/reward index," he urged.

"Some risk involved, especially after the volleyball game."

"And reward?"

"Revenge?" answered Badger.

"No, not altogether," thought Minter, "he tried that. It didn't go so well. I think he now finds the 'me' thing so reprehensible, so dangerous to the validity of the experiment and what it might mean to the acceptance of marijuana, that he's just doing his duty."

"And John Wayne?"

"Hardly a plea for mercy, most likely, a boast."

Nicholson's silvery temples jutted around the corner. "Congratulations," offered Minter.

"So the obnoxious Bergman proves your theory that doing

the right thing isn't affected by pot?" Badger gloated.

"Well, roughly," Nicholson responded. "We simply sought to prove that if pot did not alter one's moral pattern, it couldn't be classed as a dangerous drug. And we needed one of them to commit a voluntary act of self-abnegation."

"Why only one?" said Badger.

"When you have a situation of some risk and very little or negligible gain, there is very low potential for unselfish, or charitable action because leadership won't lead in that direction."

"Plus, what we know about ward situations," said Minter.

"Absolutely," Nicholson commenced, "I recognized the need for an extreme arrangement early on. Typically, drug users see themselves as outlaws. When users of alcohol and harder drugs are quarantined like this, they band tightly together against their perceived 'oppressor.' There is no unselfish act among such groups."

"But this is pot, so I set up the experiment differently, instead of planning around chaos, we planned for it. Instead of one anti-authority leader emerging, the Experiment planned that two would contend."

"Jake was a natural," Minter explained, "although a conservative personality, his endorsement of marijuana was so strong he was perceived as a leader of impeccable antiestablishment credentials."

"Yeah," said Badger, "he dressed the part, that's for sure. But what about Berge, what's the take on him?"

"Bergman was chosen to participate because he wasn't a 'natural,' yet wanted the part," responded Nicholson. "He possesses intelligence but also a dangerous edge, a real outlaw in that he questions all laws even those made by outlaws."

"Well, if you do overturn the laws on the books, pot's legal, right?" ventured Badger.

"Mmmm. Probably not. You've got to understand that mood-altering drugs pose a threat to the unturned on mind. Pot has few friends in Congress. Remember what they said about Mae West: 'She wasn't real bad, but she was bad enough.' Well, pot is bad enough to scorch anyone who touches it—and that situation won't change for generations."

"Will that day ever come?" asked Badger.

"Oh, absolutely!" Nicholson exulted, "and it's thanks to you..." His hand began to shake. "It's thanks to people like you, who've put this mighty effort together that we... That truth shall prevail. All hail the Experiment."

Badger was stunned; Custer licked his lips nervously. Nicholson exploded, "That's a joke! I got carried away, sorry. The point is, the results are great, they're out of this world, I'm grateful.

"We have the chance to significantly affect the debate on an issue that may make an enormous difference in how our country operates. Maybe some day the guilt of the perpetrator will depend not upon on a set of archaic laws, but on the actual intent of the accused, whose penalty we can assess and administer on the spot, a nanosecond after the infraction. But I digress..."

# 28

# *A Threat to the Dominant Social Order*

"Ok, ok," Nicholson calmed the group, "we'll answer that question at the appropriate moment. First, these are the facts. Nearly half of those who have smoked *cannabis,* what you call marijuana—about 100 million in the U.S.—eventually tire of its pleasurable but routine effects, and put it down forever. These are the 'experimental users.' For some reason, we don't study this population.

"'Intermittent use' constitutes 20% of long-term (six-months plus) users. 'Intermittent' means once a week—a social activity that facilitates relaxation and friendliness. This user is likely to be creative, intellectually-oriented, and seeking a sense of well-being created by pot intoxication.

"Now, 'moderate', or daily marijuana use constitutes just 5% of long-term users and they appear to share profile traits with the 'intermittent' group. No research is done on this population.

"The final category—the classic American pothead—people like you are the 'heavy' users who toke up more than once a day. It is commonly believed that only 2% of all who have smoked marijuana wind up as long-term heavy users.

"The heavy user wants 'kicks' in the form of an expansion of awareness and understanding. He is an unconventional thinker—we say 'he' because men prefer pot, women like amphetamine—who hates routine and might be termed restless, moody, and insecure. Curious, sensitive to the needs of others, he fashions his own credo out of the remains of Unquestioned Authority.

"He is emotionally immature, a pleasure seeker, irresponsible and non-conforming, his repeated pursuit of psychedelic-like effects producing social 'impairments' such as erratic job history, itinerant living, withdrawal, and moderate psychological dependence.

"Also, among heavy users, we've had reported with some frequency, a decrease in hostility. We haven't decided yet whether that's to remain an 'impairment,'" Nicholson laughed.

"In the study in which you just participated, we hoped for 'intermittent' users but couldn't find enough. Some of you were 'moderates' when you joined the study, but most of you became heavy users toking up several times a day. With more or less free access, you tripled normal use. This allowed us to monitor heavy daily use over an extended period, a period we refer to in our report as the 21-day Boston Free-Access Study.

"Now, you'll probably be interested to know that in our study, no harmful effects were seen on general bodily functions, motor functions, mental functions, personal or social behavior or work performance. Total sleep time increased; uniform weight gain was observed.

"There was no evidence of physical dependence or signs of withdrawal. Moderate psychological dependence was evident in the heaviest smokers by increased negativity after marijuana access ended."

"Marijuana intoxication did not significantly inhibit the ability of subjects to improve with practice on psychological-motor tasks such as *time estimation, short-term memory, and shooting-gal-*

*lery skill.*

"Oh man, I jus' knew that pot was gonna make me a better killer," exclaimed Thad.

"Neither immediate nor short-term (21-day) high-dose marijuana intoxication decreased motivation to engage in a variety of social and goal-directed behaviors. Over this period of time, work performance of simple tasks remained consistent, as did participation in aspects of the research study, personal and athletic activities.

"Some marijuana smoking appeared to be centered around group social activity and behavior. Other smokers withdrew from social interaction to concentrate on the subjective drug experience.

"Intermittent users especially, decreased their total interaction. However, heavy users increased their interaction above pre-smoking levels during the later parts of the smoking period. The quality of the interaction was more convivial and less task-oriented when marijuana was available to the group.

"Finally, in a risk assessment, daily use led to more conservative decision-making under conditions of risk.

"As proved in our study, even during periods of heaviest marijuana smoking, users maintained a consistently high level of activity, whether reading, writing, involved in sports or communication. None of the Boston subjects exhibited the characteristic lassitude, indifference, carelessness in personal hygiene or lack of productivity of the classic heavy user," Nicholson read.

"Yet, despite superior intelligence, they perform well below their capability in a variety of menial tasks. Within their 'ideological group' they maintain stable careers while they search for new, albeit drug-assisted, awareness. Heavy users generally have parents who engaged in a wide variety of drug intake.

They remain at odds with society, possibly because of a dominant mother and a distant father.

"This heavy user group feel burdened by tradition, whether it's the formal achievement-reward ladder, regular adult-oriented activities, mainstream civic and religious institutions or other components of the contemporary system for social control. They feel a strong identification with other regular marijuana smokers instead, frequently building their self-identity among a peer group of unconventional users.

"All we know with any certainty is that when anger is turned inward instead of directed at family and society, drug use becomes a form of passive self-destructiveness.

"Incidentally, the three heaviest users—by volume of cannabis consumed—" Nicholson commented, "could be considered 'constantly intoxicated.'"

"Whooeeee!" shouted Wayne.

"Please, no writing this down two people or 20% smoked more than seven joints per day."

"We all know who that is!" shouted Wayne.

Shep and Thad raised hands to acknowledge their feat.

"You'd take credit for creation," said Bergman, "if you didn't think it was such a botched job."

"It's only fair to tell you, I'm planning improvements," Thad laughed.

"Hey, ass-mol-es!" belched Badge, "there's more." The subjects gazed in curiosity as Jonathan Wicks stumbled to the temporary podium placed on the monitoring station's bleak gray desk.

"Gentlemen, I'm sorry to inform you that projections indicate that half of you will become life-long cannabis abusers, indulging every two hours during wakefulness. You will combine alcohol most likely with cannabis, entering a pot/alcohol paralysis: aware, comprehending, but immobilized from any effort on behalf of anything. Please," he paused, "don't let this happen to you."

"Actually," broke in Shep, "I was planning just such a stupor—float—would you care to join me?" he asked Thad.

"Normally, yes," replied Thaddeus, "normally, I'd join you in your alcohol/pot-induced float. But I am at this moment with child and..." Thad began to giggle.

Wicks abruptly left the stage; Nicholson returned. "I'll take one question," he offered.

"When are you going to legalize?!" Jimbo hollered.

Nicholson considered. "I'll admit that U.S. policy for the last 50–60 years substituted myth and fear for fact and understanding. And I'll admit that the overwhelming majority of marijuana users today will not become either a threat to public health or to the Constitution."

"Then legalize it, goddammit!" said Jake.

"Yeah right, along with public masturbation," blared Tony.

"Reluctantly, I must refrain from either course," cringed Nicholson.

"Why not?" Wayne demanded.

"It's very simple really," Nicholson replied, "you're a threat to the dominant social order."

"Of which you 're a member," accused Jimbo.

"Yes, it's true, I am."

"So how are we a threat to you," Berge asked, "when we've all been castrated by Mary Jane?"

"Put yourself in my shoes," Nicholson argued. "Any legal policy which institutionalizes availability of the drug carries with it a likely increase in the at-risk population."

"If you're willing to rephrase that," said Tony, "I'm willing to overlook your inflated opinion of my IQ."

"Suppose marijuana were legalized, there'd be an enormous amount of the population that would try it now that it was 'approved.' Even if half these 'experimenters' stopped in a relatively short time, the group of heavy users, if still only 2%, would increase considerably in absolute volume and then what is not a public health problem, may become one..."

"These heavy users are older, right?" urged Ira.

"Yes, yes, they would be," Nicholson agreed.

"Well, I thought you said adult users are not generally viewed as a significant social problem?" Ira argued.

"That is correct," replied Nicholson.

"Then where is the problem?"

"Society should not approve or encourage the recreational use of any drug. It removes all support for individual restraint. It's irresponsible."

"It's not irresponsible to use drugs," Shep responded, "it's irresponsible not to, if you're epileptic, have high blood pressure, bi-polar, psychotic. We use all sort of drugs to moderate the extremes of our condition. This is Human 101."

"Hey, hey man," Jimbo broke in.

"Say what?" Ira asked.

Jimbo splayed his hands, weaving new spaces before their eyes. "You're talking medical here."

"Yeah?" Shep challenged.

"Well, we don't have to take the high road and talk of marijuana as an antianxiety drug," Jimbo fumed. "It's not an anti-anything drug. It makes people happy and maybe they see and feel a little bit more. Don't tell me marijuana is ok because it hasn't killed anyone; it's ok because it spreads joy and let's see the law stop that!" Jimbo took the drug's reputation personally, standing a little straighter, taller.

"Actually," said Ira, "in this context, 'irresponsible' means not living up to your 'most productive' self. And I don't think the good doctor there can say pot smoking is irresponsible."

"You have to look at this: Repeated use results in drug-seeking behavior. Psychological dependence increases with frequency of use. Drugs should be servants, not masters."

"This sounds a tad kinky: 'Herr Doktor, Drug Master!" intoned Berge.

"There should be suitable incentives and disincentives," said Nicholson, "at the disposal of society..."

"Funny how 'high' society gets about this disposal thing," said Berge.

"If you feel bad," offered Jimbo, "wanting to feel better is only natural. So when is it good to feel bad? I mean, it doesn't drive you mad or into the oncoming lane."

"...in order to maintain formal control over the issue without treating the user harshly," continued Nicholson.

"Boy, you got that ol' hambone and you ain't given' up a lick of it!" laughed Thad.

"In all honesty," Nicholson continued, "*cannabis* use must remain under criminal sanction."

"This whole fuck'n experiment didn't teach you nothing," jeered Sutter.

"Hear me out," Nicholson pleaded, "discouraging use, while at the same time," his voice rose to match taunts from the subjects, "reducing the penalty for personal use to a misdemeanor—"

"Why bother?" shouted Ira, "follow the data!"

"Because we made a mistake once with alcohol, declaring a

drug that kills 100,000 people a year in the U.S. alone, to be a personal choice."

"So you're going to deny personal choice to a drug that's killed no one?" asked Jimbo.

"We must prevent growth of marijuana use; we know it would be useless to try and eliminate it. But we must oppose any policy that would increase its availability as society should of any substance that promises an escape from reality," proposed Nicholson.

"I didn't know it was flag day, or I would have worn my swagger stick," interjected Bergman.

"There! There it is!" exclaimed Nicholson, "the reason we don't wish to enlarge the circle of marijuana smokers is you—people like you!"

"Hunh?" replied Bergman.

"No, it's people like you, with your cynicism, your ideological underachieving, your marijuana banner challenging authority, that have linked marijuana with enemies of the United States."

"Your own science says the introduction of a single element such as reefer, would not significantly change the personality structure of the individual," cried Jimbo.

"Geez, that boy's been reading," laughed Jake.

"Yes, I know the science," Nicholson fumed, "but this is a matter of defining a moral imperative. Should the hippie point of view—disrespect for the law, expanding the mind, less attachment to religion, emphasis on the here and now, willingness to change society, experience for the sake of experience—be institutionalized? Because that's what will happen if we decriminalize. We'll be legitimizing the hippie point of view while discrediting the current dominant social order."

"Tax it," said Chris. They all turned to look. "Pay for what damage pot does and use the rest to buy open space so that when future generations get high, they'll have someplace nice to go."

"I'm sorry," Nicholson responded, "to decriminalize now would doom all drug law enforcement, maybe the criminal justice system itself."

"Well, nice of you to go down with the ship, but I want to know where you keep the lifeboats?" Bergman challenged. "You're that old lady who always voted 'No.' When asked why, she said, 'because I can.' You don't have very good reasons for opposing legalization, but dammit if that's going to stop you."

"This is about fear, your fear," said Jimbo, "and now your fear is poisoning your life."

"And if I can't stop you," said Nicholson, pointing at Jimbo in his original weed t- shirt, "then I count on legal inertia to save the day."

"It's like fear of homosexuality," added Berge, "if you can't stop it, then it must be ok, even destined to take control. You've taken the minority opposition stance, you've seen the numbers move against you and now you're waiting to be eaten up."

"And that ain't the last of it," laughed Wayne.

"Hmmm?" muttered Nicholson reflexively.

"Hey dude, you ain't, like—"

"Yeah, well wouldn't he like to know?" effused Wayne.

"Group decision there, Private York," stated Tony.

"Maybe it's time for a vote?" asked Ron.

"A vote? Now?" marveled Sutter.

"Yeah. Why not?" cried Shep.

"Ok," shouted Jake, "All in favor of revealing our dirty little secret, show us your armpits. That about seals it," he said at the show of hands. "Now, who's gonna stoolie?"

"What's going on?" asked Minter.

"Well, folks," Jake began, turning to face the research staff. "Seems like we cheated a bit on the tests."

"How many tests?" said Nicholson numbly.

"How many ya got?" Thaddeus cracked.

Nicholson felt his knees buckle. Minter was able to grab him and find a seat. "Even the IMP?" David asked.

The subjects eyed each other, "Especially the IMP!" they cried in unison.

"You didn't cheat on all of them!?"

"We might have overlooked one or two..." said Jake.

"This has to be kept quiet, of course," whispered Nicholson. Wick and the others nodded in agreement.

"Hey, before you guys get to rounding off the record, just what did all this prove?" asked Berge.

"Hmm," Minter reflected, "well as far as supporting the prosecution of the individual for smoking pot, we can find no compelling reason."